Dynamics and Change in Organizations

Dynamics and Change in Organizations

Studies in Organizational Semiotics

edited by

Henk W.M. Gazendam

Faculty of Management and Organization,
University of Groningen, Groningen, The Netherlands and
Faculty of Business, Public Administration and Technology,
Twente University, Enschede, The Netherlands

René J. Jorna

Faculty of Management and Organization,
University of Groningen, Groningen, The Netherlands

and

Ruben S. Cijsouw

Faculty of Management and Organization,
University of Groningen, Groningen, The Netherlands

KLUWER ACADEMIC PUBLISHERS
DORDRECHT / BOSTON / LONDON

A C.I.P. Catalogue record for this book is available from the Library of Congress.

ISBN 1-4020-1477-5

Published by Kluwer Academic Publishers,
P.O. Box 17, 3300 AA Dordrecht, The Netherlands.

Sold and distributed in North, Central and South America
by Kluwer Academic Publishers,
101 Philip Drive, Norwell, MA 02061, U.S.A.

In all other countries, sold and distributed
by Kluwer Academic Publishers,
P.O. Box 322, 3300 AH Dordrecht, The Netherlands.

Printed on acid-free paper

Printed in the Netherlands.

Contents

Contributors

BARANAUSKAS, M. CECILIA C.
Institute of Computing, State University of Campinas – Unicamp, Av. Albert Einstein, 1251, Caixa Postal 6176, 13083 970 - Campinas, S.P., Brazil, cecilia@ic.unicamp.br

BOUISSAC, PAUL
University of Toronto, Victoria College, 73 Queen's Park Crescent East, Toronto, Ontario, Canada M5S 1K7, bouissa@attglobal.net

BRAF, EWA
Jönköping International Business School, P.O. Box 1026, 551 11 Jönköping, Sweden, ewa.braf@jibs.hj.se

CHARREL, PIERRE-JEAN
Université Toulouse 1 & Institut de Recherche en Informatique de Toulouse, 21 Allée de Brienne, F-31042 Toulouse Cedex, France, charrel@univ-tlse.fr

CHONG, SAMUEL
Accenture Ltd Resources, Kingsley Hall, Manchester M904 AN, United Kingdom, samuel.chong@accenture.citytonic.com

CIJSOUW, RUBEN S.
Faculty of Management and Organization, University of Groningen, PO box 800, 9700 AV, Groningen, The Netherlands, r.s.cijsouw@bdk.rug.nl

DIETZ, JAN L.G.
Faculty of Information Technology and Systems, Delft University of Technology, P.O. Box 5031, 2600 GA Delft, The Netherlands, j.l.g.dietz@its.tudelft.nl

EMMITT, DAVID
Merseyside Police, UK, postal address: 28 Gateacre Rise, Liverpool, L25 5LA, Merseyside, United Kingdom, david.emmitt@tesco.net

GALARRETA, DANIEL
Centre National d'Etudes Spatiales, 18 avenue Edouard Belin, 31401, Toulouse cedex 9, France, galarreta@cnes.fr

GAZENDAM, HENK W.M.
Faculty of Management and Organization, University of Groningen, PO box 800, 9700 AV, Groningen, The Netherlands, h.w.m.gazendam@bdk.rug.nl

GOLDKUHL, GÖRAN
Department of Computer and Information Science, Linköping university, SE-581 83 Linköping, Sweden, ggo@ida.liu.se

JORNA, RENÉ J.
Faculty of Management and Organization, University of Groningen, PO box 800, 9700 AV, Groningen, The Netherlands, r.j.j.m@bdk.rug.nl

KAKUSHO, KOH
Center for Information and Multimedia Studies, Kyoto University, Kyoto 606-8501, Japan, kakusho@mm.media.kyoto-u.ac.jp

KRYSSANOV, VICTOR V.
Japan Science and Technology Corporation, Center for Information and Multimedia Studies, Kyoto University, Kyoto 606-8501, Japan, kryssanov@mm.media.kyoto-u.ac.jp

LIU, KECHENG
Department of Computer Science, The University of Reading, PO Box 225, Whiteknights, Reading, RG6 6AY, United Kingdom, k.liu@reading.ac.uk

MINOH, MICHIHIKO
Center for Information and Multimedia Studies, Kyoto University, Kyoto 606-8501, Japan, minoh@mm.media.kyoto-u.ac.jp

OKABE, MASAYUKI
Japan Science and Technology Corporation, Center for Information and Multimedia Studies, Kyoto University, Kyoto 606-8501, Japan, okabe@mm.media.kyoto-u.ac.jp

RÖSTLINGER, ANNIE
Department of Computer and Information Science, Linköping university, SE-581 83 Linköping, Sweden, aro@ida.liu.se

SALTER, ANDY
School of Computing, Staffordshire University, Beaconside, Stafford, ST18 0DG, United Kingdom, a.m.salter@staffs.ac.uk

SHISHKOV, BORIS
Faculty of Information Technology and Systems, Delft University of Technology, PO Box 5031, Mekelweg 4, 2600 GA Delft, The Netherlands, Shishkov@IS.TWI.TUDelft.nl

XIE, ZHIWU
Department of Computer Science, The University of Reading, PO Box 225, Whiteknights, Reading, RG6 6AY, United Kingdom, z.xie@reading.ac.uk

Editors' Preface

Organizational Semiotics occupies an important niche in the research community of human communication and information systems. It opens up new ways of understanding the functioning of information and information resources in organised behaviour. In recent years, a number of workshops and conferences have provided researchers and practitioners opportunities to discuss their theories, methods and practices and to assess the benefits and potential of this approach. Literature in this field is much in demand but still difficult to find, so we are pleased to offer a third volume in the miniseries of *Studies in Organizational Semiotics*.

This book is based on the papers and discussions of the fifth workshop on Organizational Semiotics held in Delft, June 13-15, 2002, hosted by Groningen University and Delft Technical University in the Netherlands. The topic of this workshop was the dynamics and change in organizations. The chapters in this book reflect recent developments in theory and applications and demonstrate the significance of Organizational Semiotics to information systems, human communication and coordination, organizational analysis and modelling. In particular, it provides a framework that accommodates both the technical and social aspects of information systems. The mini-series presents the frontier of the research in this area and shows how the theory and techniques enhance the quality of work on information systems.

Participants in the workshops exchange and discuss new ideas in this field. Because the contributors come from several different research communities, they tend to examine each other's ideas very critically. They are establishing a discipline for the study of information and communication in the context of organizations, whether or not they make use of information technology. The workshops also serve as important platforms for anyone – educator, researcher, practitioner or student – who is interested in bridging the gulf between the technical and social aspects of information systems as currently studied in organizational contexts. This gulf does not exist in the long-established field of semiotics, which

therefore has the potential to remove many persistent misunderstandings
that are holding us back in both theory and practice.

The editors wish to thank Jessica Bakker for her efforts to correct the
English of the non-native speakers, and Paul Bouissac, Göran Goldkuhl
and Kecheng Liu for their contribution to the revision process.

Henk W. M. Gazendam, René J. Jorna, and Ruben S. Cijsouw

April 2003

The Programme Committee

Peter B. Andersen, Alborg University (Denmark)
Samuel Chong, Staffordshire University (UK)
Rodney Clarke, Wollongong University (Australia) / Staffordshire
    University (UK)
Henk Gazendam, Groningen University & Twente University (The
    Netherlands)
Göran Goldkuhl, Linköping University (Sweden)
René Jorna, University of Groningen (The Netherlands)
Morton Lind, Technical University of Denmark (Denmark)
Kecheng Liu, Staffordshire University (UK) / University of Reading (UK)
Ronald Stamper, University of Twente (The Netherlands)

Introduction

Henk W. M. Gazendam, René J. Jorna and Ruben S. Cijsouw

DYNAMICS AND CHANGE IN ORGANIZATIONS

The topic of this book is the dynamics and change in organizations. An *organization*, as discussed in the workshop, can be characterized as a group of people, a culture, which not only shares rules of language, custom, and habit, but also participates in the social construction of these rules (Baranauskas, this volume). A central topic of discussion has been the concept of norms. Norms can be seen as social constructs that drive, coordinate, and control our actions inside an organization (Baranauskas, this volume). Norm analysis takes a central place in the methods of the Stamper school of organizational semiotics, in this book also characterized as information field based organizational semiotics (Stamper, 1973; Liu, 2000). In the discussion about what it means that an organization changes, what the cause of these changes is, and how we can describe the dynamics of organizations, a variety of answers has been given in the workshop, namely:

1. Problem solving within the context of bounded rationality, and propagation of adaptive patterns of behaviour in evolutionary time.
2. Communication, consisting of the exchange of object signs and norm signs, leading to the perturbation of self-organizing psychic and social systems.
3. Creation and annihilation of social affordances (social constructs) and the norms attached to them.

4. Actions, for instance (1) communicative actions, and (2) the design/ creation / change of information systems and other artefacts.
5. Creation, change, conversion and transfer of knowledge.

Based on these answers, this book has been subdivided into three parts. Evolutionary approaches (corresponding to answer 1) and systems-theoretical approaches (corresponding to answer 2) can be found Part I. Behaviour-oriented approaches can be found in Part II. Part II comprises the information field oriented approach (corresponding to answer 3) and the interaction oriented approach (corresponding to answer 4). Knowledge oriented approaches (corresponding to answer 5) can be found in Part III. Note that these three parts partly correspond to Andersen's (1991) distinction between signs as *systems,* a psychological view of signs as *knowledge*, a sociological view of signs as *behaviour*, and an aesthetic view of signs as *artefacts*.

THE NATURE OF SEMIOTICS

In the workshop, the nature of semiotics was discussed. How does semiotics relate to evolutionary biology and to cognitive psychology? Most discussants shared the view that one goes too far when one sees semiotics as a part of cognitive psychology by saying that 'semiotics is an inquiry into the working of the mind or brain'. Semiotics is certainly no rival to cognitive psychology in explaining the working of the human mind. It would be acceptable to say that semiotics should be based on, or use, the findings of cognitive psychology and evolutionary biology, but semiotics has its own topic. *Psychology* studies mind and behaviour as a system that interacts with the (task) environment (including other actors) and uses and produces signs. The focus is on cognitive architectures performing tasks. *Evolutionary biology* studies animal and plant populations as part of ecological systems (or ecological niches), and their dynamics are based on the transfer and selection of genes and memes. *Semiotics* studies signs or texts or documents or sign-based artefacts or perhaps memes as relatively autonomous and persistent phenomena. These texts, signs, and documents are studied in their relation to their author, their reader, the world they represent, and other texts. There seems to be a triadic system (Peirce would be pleased to hear that) consisting of living creature, ecological system and sign. All three disciplines study this triadic system, but focus on a specific and persistent part of it. Psychology focuses on the living creature as a system having a mind, evolutionary biology focuses on the ecological system as a whole, and semiotics focuses on the sign.

There are three fundamentally different approaches to the elementary unit of communication in semiotics, and all three have now found their way into organizational semiotics. These three approaches are based on the text, the sign and the meme as fundamental units, respectively. The choice of one of these approaches will have consequences for the type of empirical work to be done. *Text-based semiotics* has its empirical foundation in reading and analyzing texts, because texts are seen as relating to other texts. In *sign-based semiotics*, signs relate to the world (as object) and to the human mind (as interpretant). Empirical work will have to be done with regard to the relation of signs to the human (or animal) mind, and to the world referred to, using the results of, for instance, cognitive psychology or physics, but one should not want to rival with cognitive psychology or physics. In *meme-based semiotics*, memes are primarily seen from the viewpoint of transfer and selection. Memes relate to their carriers (living beings) that form populations. The empirical work in meme-based semiotics will focus on the study of the dynamics of populations of memes and of their carriers, and on the mechanisms of transfer and selection. There will be much quantitative and statistical work to do.

Organizational semiotics has found its place based on its practical applications in the field of analyzing and designing organizations, economic transactions and information systems using approaches, frameworks and methods that have been developed as alternatives to mainstream methods. Well-known methods are, for instance, actor interaction analysis, actor task analysis, semantic analysis, and norm analysis. These approaches, frameworks and methods, however, define only part of the area covered by organizational semiotics. Organizational semiotics tries to understand organizations based on the use of signs, texts, documents, sign-based artefacts and communication, thereby using the results of for instance psychology, economics, and information systems science as basic disciplines. One of the aims of organizational semiotics is to show what one is doing when trying to understand, design or change organizations in terms of the use of, for instance, models and metaphors. This is done in order to liberate people from being trapped in the (unconscious) use of a specific metaphor or model type, and to make visible design space.

We will now give an overview of the three parts of the book: (I) evolutionary and systems theoretical approaches, (II) behaviour-oriented approaches, and (III) knowledge-oriented approaches.

EVOLUTIONARY AND SYSTEMS THEORETICAL APPROACHES

Evolutionary and systems-theoretical approaches focus on the dynamics of the social system, for instance society, the web, an organization, or a collection of organizations, as a whole. Evolutionary approaches choose strategies for survival and selection in evolutionary time as basic mechanism, while systems-theoretical approaches focus on state functions and mutual influence of interacting systems.

Evolutionary approaches

In an argument criticizing contemporary grand-design semiotics, **Bouissac** characterizes semiotic behaviour from the point of view of the boundedness of rationality and the natural selection of behaviour through evolutionary time. Semiotic behaviour is seen as a set of adaptive cognitive tools that have survived through evolutionary time because they improve the efficiency of reasoning and communication in terms of time, energy, space, and acquiring codes. This leads to a definition of *bounded semiotics* as a discipline analyzing semiotic behaviour from the viewpoint of fast and frugal heuristics that bypass the step by step analysis of the choice situations with which they are confronted. Some of these fast and frugal heuristics can be characterized as semiotic adaptive shortcuts that enable an efficient sorting out of the relevant information for decision-making. Following the work of Gigerenzer and Selten (2001), four of these semiotic adaptive shortcuts are explained, namely (1) innate releasing mechanisms, (2) imitation or copying, (3) stereotyping, and (4) emotions. This approach to semiotic behaviour enables semiotics to liberate itself from rationalistic schemes of thought that explain the whole gamut of human sign use by a few abstract concepts. Recognizing that people have limited time, knowledge and computational capabilities, requiring the development of semiotic adaptive shortcuts in a process of natural selection through evolutionary time is a precondition for the further development of semiotics in the direction of a science of signs.

Systems-theoretical approaches

In the systems theoretical approach presented by **Kryssanov, Okabe, Kakusho and Minoh**, the universe of discourse is seen as consisting of two types of autopoietic systems: psychic systems and social systems. A psychic system consists of objects. Objects are behaviour patterns or representations in the mind that govern behaviour. A social system consists of norm signs. Norm signs are norms, or social affordances, authorized by the social system and existing as signs. The psychic system expresses its objects by producing object signs; this process is called externalizing. The psychic system evolves by interpreting signs stemming from social systems, giving interpretants a lead to new objects (behaviour patterns). The social system produces norm signs by a process called authorization. The social system evolves by incorporating the object signs produced by the psychic systems. Psychic systems and social systems have a dynamics based on self-organization and mutual perturbation by the exchange of object signs and norm signs.

BEHAVIOUR-ORIENTED APPROACHES

A fundamental viewpoint of behaviour-oriented approaches in organizational semiotics is that there is no knowledge without a knowing actor, and that there is no knowledge without action.

Information field based organizational semiotics

Information field based organizational semiotics (the Stamper school of organizational semiotics) is based on the idea of an information field (Stamper, 1973, 2001; Liu, 2000). Humans are seen as agents. Agents act influenced by the forces that are present in an information field. These forces originate from the norms that are shared in an organization or social community. An information field consists of physical affordances and social affordances, and the norms attached to them. Physical affordances are physical objects, physical spaces, and other physical agents that afford certain behaviour by a species. Physical affordances correspond to behaviour patterns, and are defined in terms of these behaviour patterns. In the Stamper school of organizational semiotics, it is said that affordances *are* behaviour patterns. For instance, a car affords driving by humans and transportation of humans and other species from one place to another. Physical affordances often have norms attached to them based on an associated social affordance. For instance, a car will generally be associated with ownership, and ownership has norms attached to it regarding who is allowed to decide about the use of the car. Social affordances can be seen as social constructs existing as signs that can be created and annihilated by agents having the appropriate authority. Sometimes, these social affordances have the character of contracts between agents. Once they exist, social affordances afford, that is, authorize and stimulate, certain behaviour patterns of the agents concerned. Norms are attached to each affordance type governing the creation, annihilation, and use of particular affordances belonging to that type. A social affordance may be the prerequisite for another social affordance.

Important steps in the analysis of organizations in information field based organizational semiotics are semantic analysis and norm analysis. In semantic analysis, agents and the affordances which they create and use are distinguished at the type level. Agent types, affordance types, and their relationships together form an ontology chart. In norm analysis, the responsibilities of agents with respect to affordances are investigated, and the norms governing the behaviour of these responsible agents are specified. In information system design, the ontology chart can be the basis of an object model, while the norm description can be the basis for a behavioural specification, for instance in the form of use cases.

Baranauskas, Liu, and Chong present a semiotic framework for evaluating websites. They follow Andersen in interpreting the website as a medium, a physical substance in which signs can be manifested, and that is used in communication. Communication means the sharing of elements of behaviour (affordances) by using signs. There exists a correspondence between affordances at the individual level and norms at the social level, because norms are social constructs that drive, coordinate, and control our actions in organizations. In e-commerce, agents (users) communicate with agents (stores, business organizations) by using artefact systems (websites). This communication can be seen as consisting of Peircean triads, for instance the user (interpretant) communicates with the store (object) by using the website (sign). This communication can be further analyzed by using a fractal model of communication. In the fractal model of communication, the basic triad interpretant - sign - object is recursively decomposed into new triads, where the original interpretants, signs and objects can take new roles as interpretants or objects, connected by new signs that emerge in this decomposition. This leads to several perspectives on the role of the website in communication. After having done this, Stamper's semiotic ladder is used to derive criteria for evaluating websites as communication media between users and business organizations.

A method for improving the Rational Unified Process (RUP) method based on organizational semiotics is presented by **Xie, Liu, and Emmitt**. In the RUP method, use case models and object models are made and compared, leading to an iterative process of mutual improvement. The problem is that the RUP method offers no criteria to stop these iterations, so that these can be endless (in theory). Organizational semiotics can be helpful by bringing convergence in these iterations through the use of an adequate level of abstraction of modelling, whereby the iterative process will be brought to an end. The level of abstraction must be strictly kept to the level of affordances, their ontological dependencies, and the norms attached to them. Agent behaviour is analyzed in terms of affordances, which are behaviour patterns. The behaviour of an actor in a specific organizational role with respect to a certain subject can be seen as an affordance. Things and social constructs (for instance, crime) can be seen as corresponding to one or more of these repertoires of behaviour, and thus as corresponding to an affordance or a package of affordances. Affordances can be translated into use cases and/ or classes. The relationship between affordances is analyzed in terms of ontological dependencies. If an affordance has necessary antecedents, it is ontologically dependent on these antecedents. Ontological dependencies can be translated into inheritance relationships as well as aggregation relationships. The behaviour contained in affordances can be specified precisely, and in a flexible way, by specifying the norms attached to that affordance, where the norm format allows for the use of deontic operators.

Salter analyzes how intentions of agents can lead to differences in behaviour. Semantic analysis can be used to determine the agents of which an organization is made up, as well as the affordances, the patterns of behaviour available to these agents. The affordances stemming from this analysis are universal. Particulars are the specific instances of successful individual realizations of affordances. Affordances are ontologically dependent on either one or two antecedents which have to exist before the patterns of behaviour represented by the affordance become available to the agent. In ontology charts, this is represented in the semantic schemas as a right to left relationship, where affordances connected to affordances to their left are ontologically dependent on them.

Each particular exists in time, and, therefore, requires not only particulars of the antecedents on which it is ontologically dependent, but also a start (and possibly a finish) at a certain time, and authorities responsible for that start (and possibly, the finish), and their intention. These authorities also have to exist as particulars. The intention of an authority starting a particular determines which norms (that belong to the package of norms attached to the corresponding universal) are triggered when the particular is started. When different norms are triggered, different processes will follow.

According to **Shiskov, Xie, Liu, and Dietz**, the software community still lacks consistent guidance for use case identification. They present a method for deriving use cases based on norm analysis. It is essential to recognize that norms are not as rigid as logical conditions. Within the actions that are 'permitted' in a certain situation, the choice of the action to be performed by an agent is seldom deterministic. Furthermore, the individual that breaks the work pattern of a group does not have to be punished in any way. Prior to the norm analysis, an ontology chart containing the relevant affordances and their ontological relationships has to be prepared. A complete norm analysis can be done in four steps: (1) responsibility analysis, (2) proto-norm analysis, (3) trigger analysis, and (4) detailed norm specification. Responsibility analysis identifies agents and actions, and assigns responsible agents to each action. Each affordance in the ontology chart generally corresponds to two actions: its starting act and its finishing act. Proto-norm analysis identifies the high level norms attached to the affordances by adding a condition and a deontic operator to each agent - action pair. Trigger analysis elaborates the norm conditions by considering the relationship of the action to be taken with absolute time (calendar time) and with relative time (relationship to other performed actions). Detailed norm specification elaborates norms based on a norm format, and adds norms for exceptions. After this, use cases can be specified. This leads to a detailed use case diagram in which a use case corresponds to one or more norms.

Interaction structure based organizational semiotics

Interaction structure based organizational semiotics has its roots in the language action perspective and focuses on actions and the actors performing these actions. Humans are actors. Human actors can act on behalf of an organization; in this case the human actor is an agent of the organization, and the organization can be seen as an actor.

An organization is (1) an agreement (a communicative fact) between the principals and other parts of the society, and (2) a pattern of everyday actions that is continuously reproduced through communicative acts of its agents. Organizations are constituted and maintained through communication. Information systems are organizational sign artefacts with action capabilities. Information systems can also act as agents of an organization. Information systems are established through design actions.

These design actions having a regulative force are of a communicative nature.

Actions can be part of a structured interaction between actors, for instance, a business interaction. Such an interaction has a default structure consisting of generic phases based on social convention. Actability is a property of something which enables and/ or contributes to the performance of the action.

In interaction-based organizational semiotics, the analysis of organizations and the related design of information systems typically focus on the charting of actions and language actions (communicative actions) between actors within organizations, and between organizations conceived as actors. This charting of actions generally leads to interaction diagrams. Frameworks that offer basic concepts and typical patterns of interaction are used to sharpen observation and to standardize modelling.

Goldkuhl and Röstlinger investigate three theories inspired by the language action perspective: the theory of practice, the business action theory, and the information systems actability theory. The common theoretical thread in these theories is reconstructed and articulated, and called socio-instrumental pragmatism. The basic concept of socio-instrumental pragmatism is action, a purposeful and meaningful behaviour of a human being. Other main constructs are the action's performer (actor or agent), action objects as preconditions and results of actions, patterns of actions, and relations between actors. Actions can be communicative actions. There are two fundamental types of action: intervening acts aiming at external change and receiving or interpreting acts aiming at internal change. Actions of actors are governed by assignments, norms and judgments, and are facilitated by knowledge and artefacts. Organizations are constituted and established through communicative acts of the principals behind the organization and by legal authorities. Organizations as patterns of everyday action have to be continuously reproduced through the communicative acts of the organization's agents.

KNOWLEDGE-ORIENTED APPROACHES

Knowledge-oriented approaches to organizational semiotics consider knowledge as representations or sign structures in the human mind, enabling adequate behaviour of the human actor. Newell and Simon's (1972) symbol system hypqthesis of cognition has been a very important step in the development of knowledge-oriented approaches in semiotics. In the ecological environment or semiotic Umwelt of the actor, actor-made signs express intentions, help remembering and enable communication. These signs can be seen as knowledge moving between actors, and are sometimes called information to distinguish them from knowledge in the actor mind. A further distinction is made between tacit or sensory knowledge and coded or codified knowledge. Tacit or sensory knowledge is knowledge that is optimally organized in the actor's mind for the purpose of perception and action, and remains sometimes tacit, that is, not expressed as signs in the semiotic Umwelt. Coded knowledge is knowledge that is expressed in signs in the semiotic Umwelt. Coded knowledge adds a communicative dimension to tacit knowledge. This communicative dimension consists of language representations that have a knowledge organization and representation according to conventions of communication. Theoretical knowledge adds a theoretical dimension to coded knowledge. This theoretical dimension consists of conceptual representations that have a knowledge organization and representation that is optimal for reasoning, especially theoretical or formal reasoning. Knowledge is created and changed by learning. Learning can occur by practical experience, imitation or communication using signs. In learning processes, knowledge transfer and knowledge conversion can occur. Knowledge conversion is the change of knowledge from one type to another, for instance, the change between tacit knowledge, coded knowledge, and theoretical knowledge. Since the work of Boisot (1995) and Nonaka and Takeuchi (1995), knowledge conversion is an important perspective for studying the dynamics of organizations. Typical methods of knowledge-oriented organizational semiotics are task analysis, analysis and characterization of organizational knowledge, and developing simulation models of organizations based on social constructs such as tasks, norms and contracts.

Braf criticizes Stamper's view that all knowledge consists of norms and attitudes. There are other kinds of knowledge than regulative knowledge. Knowledge is something known by a subjective holder. Books and databases do not contain knowledge as such; they contain representations of knowledge (information). Norms are units of knowledge of a governing nature. Knowledge can consist of norms, categorizations, explanations, and narratives. Knowledge is a prerequisite for the establishment of norms. Norms act as a value standard for actions and for action results. Action norms help determine what to do and how; quality norms help determine how to evaluate the action and the action result. Norms can exist as intrasubjective knowledge (individual thought), intersubjective knowledge (shared thought), and in the form of information in the semiotic Umwelt, that is, expressed as oral signs, written signs or artefact functionality. Norms can be established through habitualization in a group of actors (for instance, work practices emerging in a work group), or through a process of creation by actors legitimized to do so followed by a process of transfer to those concerned (for instance, the definition of laws defined by the government, followed by transfer to the citizens). Norms are socially agreed rules affecting and, to a large extent, directing the actions within an organization. In order to understand organizations, we have to consider the norms influencing the work practice of the actors, and pay attention to possible norm conflicts.

Gazendam analyzes knowledge in terms of its organization in models. He focuses on models we use for understanding organizations and for designing information systems which belong to the theoretical knowledge type. It is explained how models can be considered from a semiotic point of view, how people use models, how the coherence and boundaries of a model are established, and which role models play in organizations. From a semiotic point of view, a model is a coherent sign structure, consisting of a network of a diversity of signs, and used by an actor for understanding or constructing a system of application. People use models because they are coherent, cognitively manageable units of knowledge organized by the use of semiotic adaptive shortcuts and sign layers. Through their efficient organization, these knowledge units enable the development of flexible and adequate habits of action. Based on their use, models perform processes of self-organization, thus adding new sign layers or dimensions to the representation, namely iconic representations, language representations, and conceptual representations. Models change and find their boundaries based on a dynamics of coherence. The coherence mechanism works by a mutual adjustment of the model elements, and of model elements and elements in the system of application. The coherence mechanism should be seen as an alternative for foundational reasoning and fits well into an open, constructivist world view. An organization can be seen as a multi-actor system based on habits of action aimed at cooperation and coordination of work. These habits of action are supported by organizational knowledge in the form of shared artefacts, shared stories, shared institutions, shared designs and shared plans. Shared institutions, shared designs and shared plans are shared normative models that make up for the difference between the organization or social system as a whole and 'the sum of' the individual actors. They act as the glue that keeps the system together. Norms as isolated elements cannot account for coherent normative behaviour. They have to be integrated in the models that an actor has of other actors and about himself. An important characteristic of norms is that they are reciprocal. Shared normative models are created by actors and, in turn, influence actor behaviour by forming habits, thus creating a cycle of selection and reinforcement, where some models and norms are reinforced and other models and norms disappear.

Cijsouw and Jorna characterize organizational knowledge in terms of its position in a (metaphorical) knowledge space. A knowledge space can be constructed using the distinction of sensory knowledge, coded knowledge and theoretical knowledge. Sensory knowledge ranges from rough to detailed, coded knowledge ranges from weakly to strongly coded, and theoretical knowledge ranges from concrete to abstract. The knowledge space can be used for characterizing the knowledge in an organization, while change of knowledge as well as knowledge conversion can be depicted as trajectories that an organization follows in this knowledge space. For analyzing knowledge transfer between organizations, it helps to depict the positions of these organizations in the knowledge space. Shared knowledge can be seen as a means for coordination in organizations, and therefore it is interesting to investigate

Mintzberg's (1979) organization types and their corresponding coordination mechanisms from the point of view of their positions in the knowledge space.

In the contributions of **Galaretta** and **Charrel**, the construction of knowledge based on viewpoints is explained. Knowledge about something that has to be constructed (in a technical universe) has to be attained by a process of discourse. In this process, actors take viewpoints based on their specialist knowledge and organizational role. Based on these viewpoints, views are expressed. A view is an utterance selected from the representations a viewpoint has of the technical universe. In a process of negotiation, views are exchanged. If, in these negotiations, views remain logically or semantically incompatible, they remain merely information. If the views that are produced after a process of negotiation are compatible, the viewpoints can be seen as correlated, and the views produced can be seen as knowledge. A viewpoint can be seen as a meeting place of an object (the thing that has to be constructed), an actor, and a context (defined by the specialist knowledge and organizational role). If we connect viewpoints to the views in terms of statements (expressions) and meanings attached to them, views and viewpoints can be analyzed and correlated.

CONCLUSION

Organizational semiotics is not a field that is characterized by hazy notions. Organizational semiotics has well-articulated theories and well-developed methods for analyzing human behaviour in organizations as a prerequisite for organizational change and information system design. This book shows that by using those methods and theories some progress has been made in the formulation and integration of theories, in the articulation of methods, and in the accumulation of practical experiences.

REFERENCES

Andersen, P. B. (1991). A semiotic approach to construction and assessment of computer systems. In H. E. Nissen, H. K. Klein, & R. Hirschheim (Eds.), *Information systems research: Contemporary approaches and emergent traditions* (pp. 465-514). Amsterdam: North-Holland.

Boisot, M. H. (1995). *Information space: A framework for learning in organizations, institutions and culture.* London: Routledge

Gigerenzer, G., & Selten, R. (Eds.). (2001). *Bounded rationality: The adaptive toolbox.* Cambridge, MA: The MIT Press.

Liu, K. (2000). *Semiotics in information systems engineering.* Cambridge, England: Cambridge University Press.

Mintzberg, H. (1979). *The structuring of organizations.* Englewood Cliffs: Prentice-Hall.

Nonaka, I. & Takeuchi, H. (1995). *The knowledge-creating company: How Japanese companies create the dynamics of innovation.* New York: Oxford University Press.

Stamper, R. K. (1973). *Information in business and administrative systems.* New York: Wiley.

Stamper, R. K. (2001). Organisational semiotics: Informatics without the computer? In K. Liu, R. J. Clarke, P. Bøgh Andersen, & R. K. Stamper (Eds.), *Information, organisation and technology: Studies in organisational semiotics* (pp. 115-171). Boston, MA: Kluwer Academic Publishers.

Part I

Evolutionary and systems theoretical approaches

Chapter 1

Bounded Semiotics: From Utopian to Evolutionary Models of Communication

Paul Bouissac

ABSTRACT

In this chapter a frontal attack on classical semiotic approaches is formulated. Contemporary semiotics can be defined as a speculative and descriptive discourse based on a tradition of argumentation and intuitive evidence. It relies only indirectly on experimentation through the occasional use of meta-analysis to support its arguments. This semiotic endeavor is called "semiotics as utopia". Part of this approach is its fundamental trust in ultimate or optimal rationality. In this chapter a plea is given for rethinking rationality along evolutionary lines. This seems to be a relatively recent epistemological endeavor. Herbert Simon coined the term "bounded rationality" in the mid-1950s. This notion of bounded rationality is used to formulate what I call "bounded semiotics". This should be concerned with the adaptive shortcuts, which evolved with respect to efficient (that is, fast and accurate) sorting out of relevant information and adaptive decision-making, rather than with the complex logical architectures, which purport to theorize (i.e., make intelligibly visible) an assumed universal semiotic competence. Examples of shortcuts are a) innate releasing mechanisms, b) imitation or copying, c) stereotyping and d) emotions. The notion of "boundedness" can also be applied to organizational theory, resulting in what I like to call "bounded organizations".

1. THE MAGIC OF SEMIOTICS

The purpose of this essay is to argue that the models and methods offered by the various schools comprising contemporary semiotics are inadequate for understanding organizations, explaining their processes and solving their problems. It will endeavour to characterize today's semiotics, question its epistemological validity and outline an alternative view, which appears better suited to the study of organizations.

Contemporary semiotics can be defined as a speculative and descriptive discourse based on a tradition of argumentation and intuitive evidence. It relies only indirectly on experimentation through the occasional use of meta-analysis to support its arguments. Typical of this approach was, for example, the reliance of Roman Jakobson on aphasiology data (e.g., 1956; 1971:229-259) to provide an empirical flavor to his systematic elaboration of the metaphorical and metonymic axis of language, or Thomas Sebeok's ethological illustrations of sign typologies (e.g., 1976; 2001:105-114). Most of the time, however, semiotic discourse offers in its debates standard examples borrowed from the tradition of the doctrine of signs found in Greek and Latin authors such as smoke signals and clouds (e.g., Deely, 2001: 688-733) or from the natural phenomenology of every day's experience construed as thought experiments which are adduced as a source of supposedly "hard evidence" (e.g., Eco, 1976: passim). Semiotic research in general consists of developing lines of argument derived from authoritative sources or endlessly refining qualitative models (e.g., Sebeok and Danesi, 2000). Its mode of inquiry is mostly exegetic, hermeneutic and intuitive. In its more data-oriented versions, called sometimes "applied semiotics", semiotic research engages in descriptions mediated by the models provided by a composite tradition formed by the successive accretion of notions coming from Judeo-Christian theology, western medieval and classical philosophy, phenomenology, empirical and pathological psychology, cybernetics, telecommunication and information technology. It is usually recognized that the models and terminologies upon which semiotic discourse is based lack consistency, but afford the means of interesting descriptive and interpretative strategies for an indefinite set of cultural and natural objects (e.g., Danesi and Perron, 1999).

It is rare that semioticians claim for their works scientific validity by making explicit their methods and procedures so as to facilitate the replicability of their results. More frequently, they take for granted some general notions and express themselves either in the form of abstract speculations in the apodictic mode inspired by metaphysics and logic, or indulge in the essay genre, while acknowledging eclecticism as their heuristic method of choice in the service of intellectual hedonism. Some writers, however, claim doctrinal purity and coherence with reference to an axiomatic or exemplary discourse from which they derive their own speculations and descriptions. This was, for instance, the case of Algirdas J. Greimas (e.g., Greimas & Courtés, 1979) who, under the aegis of Saussure's legacy, constructed a semio-linguistic method of textual analysis extrapolated from Louis Hjelmslev's axiomatic system (1961). But these works are usually mere teasers towards some future achievements indefinitely postponed to better epistemological days.

The notion of "sign" or "signs system", which is at the core of semiotic discourse, remains highly problematic. The "sign" can be characterized at best as a notion by default, that is, it appears that there is no other way to account for phenomenological experience than to assume the action of such functional agencies. Through a magic trick, signs are pulled from a "black box": an operative mediation must be assumed to occur, about which it is impossible to know anything definite. Of course, the notion of "sign" or "system of signs" can be given some speculative (intensional) descriptions or can be defined (extensionally) as an open-ended collection of "typical" objects and behaviours. Once abstract features and dimensions have been specified, categories can be easily constructed and conceptually manipulated, thus generating a coherent narrative through which the interactive flow of the life world can be shown to be approximately translatable into the vocabulary of a sign theory. But claiming that signs are agencies, which account for observed behaviours without providing the explanations which would make controlled experimentations possible is not too different from assigning the causes of events to specialized deities like it is being practiced in polytheistic cultures. These systems tend to explain failures as coming from the ill-will of invisible agencies, or the lack of proper rituals and sacrifices. Divine intentions are hard to decipher even with the help of various mantic techniques. In the past, theophanic cosmologies forced individuals and societies to navigate through a world of dangers very costly to neutralize because of their fundamental irrationality. Entrusting a doctrine of signs with the capacity of solving real-life problems, rather than confining these speculations to textbook thought-experiments, is perhaps eventually as costly and unproductive as sacrificing resources to moody deities. All semiotic spin-doctors know that, whatever is being said or done, most problems, like many diseases, run their natural course toward a state of equilibrium. Nevertheless, semioticians confidently articulate their diagnostics through the rhetoric of rationality and scientificity, with an unproven presumption of predictability.

2. SEMIOTICS AS UTOPIA

Modern semiotics was ushered by the Enlightenment (Dascal, 1987; Bouissac, 1998). Since then, an exclusive reliance on rationality is at the core of the semiotic discourse, whose purpose is to explain how information flows from organisms to organisms and how meaning permeates the world. Modern semiotics is fundamentally optimist both in the epistemological sense, as far as its agenda implies the rationality of the processes it describes, and in the pragmatic sense, to the extent that the problems it identifies are considered to be solvable by rational methods of thinking. Occasional dysfunctions can be understood as resulting from deceptions and, ultimately, as caused by a lack of knowledge that is remediable. Reminding C. S. Peirce's "first rule of reason" ("Do not block the way of inquiry") (1898) is here in order. Trusting genuine reason, as opposed to "sham reasoning", which he identified with businessmen and theologians, opens the way to truth (Brunning and Forster, 1997: 240-261). Likewise the Saussurean legacy, if not F. de Saussure himself who is far more ambiguous in his notes than his editors-disciples were, assumes the ultimate intelligibility of all semiological systems, which are based on logical relations that rigorous reasoning can be trusted to uncover.

As a result of these historical roots in the Age of Enlightenment, the virtual world of signs or sign systems described by modern semiotics in all its variegated forms has many of the characteristics of utopian discourse.

First, it is absolutely *comprehensive*. Nothing is left out of its virtual relevance. In its bio- or cosmo-semiotic versions (e.g., Hoffmeyer, 1996; Sebeok, 2001), all interactions are conceptually recast as sign actions which are coextensive with the universe whose theoretical descriptions potentially exhausts all possible events. In its semio-linguistic versions (e.g., Greimas, 1987), all meaning is necessarily articulated by discourse, which saturates the universe of sense, from philosophy to physics, from history to logic, and, naturally, including in principle the bio-semiotic and semio-linguistic discourses themselves.

Secondly, semiotic discourse represents phenomenological experience as *homogeneous*. The complexity and resistance of the life world is presumed to be amenable to a close set of fundamental elements and relations which make it possible to virtually reconstruct not only the human mind but also its natural environment, either in the mode of communication or in the mode of signification.

Thirdly, semiotic discourse claims to be the universal key to *intelligibility* thanks to the discovery and mastery of some general algorithms from which both biological events and texts can be shown to be generated. This intelligibility is intuitive.

Fourthly, semiotic discourse is *unbounded* in the sense that it downplays to a minimal level any constraints, which are not of a logical nature. Factors such as the energetic and political costs of signs, the capacity of communication channels, the computational liability of artificial or natural decision-making, and the speed limit of information transfer are conceived as mere contextual variables of idealized semiotic processes.

Finally, semiotic discourse is *anthropocentric* in its more or less explicit celebration of human language as a supreme ontological or evolutionary achievement. Not only does semiotic discourse assume the rationality of the processes it endeavours to describe but it also presumes that human rationality is adequate to discover and understand these processes.

Semiotics has produced to date many formulae and diagrams, which purport to embody conceptual models of communication or signification. Let us mention Saussure's diagrams and equations, Peircean triangles, Hjelmslev's schemas, Greimas's squares and algorithms, Jakobson's and Lotman's orthogonal models, to name only the most successful ones, which have been abundantly reproduced in the semiotic literature with various modifications. The epistemological and ontological status of these graphic representations is often ambiguous as it is not always clear whether they are used as mere heuristic tools or are considered to visualize an ultimate truth regarding the processes upon which they are mapped. What is certain is that they populate the theoretical imagination of semioticians and determine their research strategies. The metaphysical roots and historical depth of these drawings, which make a metaphorical use of the notions of levels, vectors and symmetries, are rife with tacit assumptions. However, they are treated by most as rational evidence of a phenomenological or axiomatic nature, and used to process and order experience toward intelligibility or pragmatic efficiency.

However, the problem is whether these models actually lead to productive methods, which make it possible to acquire new, rather than tautological, knowledge and improve the human capacity to control and predict the vital complex processes of the biological and social life world.

There is no doubt that any of the semiotic models or diagrams of the sort listed above has proven its capacity to generate discourse either as theoretical explications and controversies or as interpretive mapping of natural and cultural objects. The issue is whether they have demonstratively been shown to provide the means for solving actual problems either theoretical or practical. Success stories remain ambiguous because semiotic approaches have made extensive use of the special knowledge accumulated by scientific disciplines such as, for instance, empirical psychology (e.g., human face information processing) or computer science (e.g., development of semantic algorithms). Many results have been thus co-opted and opportunistically exploited by semiotics. The potential afforded by semiotics for integrating various sources of knowledge is not negligible and represents a precious cognitive commodity as long as coherent meta-analytical methods are developed. But mere selective reviews of scientific literature for the purpose of identifying data that can illustrate theoretical speculations is a futile exercise whose sole purpose is often to lend an empirical flavor to semiotic discourse. Argumentations, empirical research methods and meta-analyses are genuine ways of discovering new knowledge, not convenient strategies for unfolding the textual potential of tautological propositions.

3. BOUNDED RATIONALITY

Grand-design semiotics offers all-encompassing systems, which claim to reveal a universal code, which underlies the apparent heterogeneity of the world of experience. It ultimately rests upon a taken-for-granted rationality, conceived as a human faculty, which allows sound inferencing and decision-making as long as its judgments are not clouded by irrational emotions. Rationality is supposed to warrant the access to truth, given sufficient time and discipline. Reason, however, is a historical notion whose ontological status and epistemological significance depends on a variety of beliefs, a fact that can cast radical suspicion on rationality itself, but, more legitimately, can lead to an evolutionary ecological contextualization of human cognition.

Rethinking rationality along evolutionary lines seems to be a relatively recent epistemological endeavour. Herbert Simon coined the term "bounded rationality" in the mid-1950s (Simon, 1956; 1960) in the restricted context of economics. The notion remains productive in this latter domain in which theoreticians of economic behaviour are confronted to the fact that while individuals intend to be rational in their contractual transactions, they cannot be truly so because of the limits of the quantity of information their psychological resources can access and process (Klos, 2000). This notion has also been exploited in sociology. In 1999, the notion of "bounded rationality" was the focus of the 84th Dalhem Workshop, now published under the editorship of Gerd Gigerenzer and Reinhard Selten (2001). This multidisciplinary volume addresses the issue of the actual, shortcut strategies humans have evolved to reach adaptive decisions, as opposed to the virtual, idealized notion of universal reason whose normative logic would require exhaustive examinations of the data and time-consuming cognitive procedures. This applies far beyond mere economic behaviour to encompass all sorts of decision-making such as, for instance, mate selection, trust and suspicion, interpretation and the like[1].

Rationality, like cognition in general (Dukas, 1998), is constrained by the ecological context in which it has evolved. "Bounded" refers to the limits of the computational capacities of the human brain, the time and energy constraints of its processes, and the cultural and historical conditioning of the norms it follows. This approach claims that humans have evolved "fast and frugal" strategies that bypass the step-by-step analysis of the choice situations to which they are confronted. This "heuristics" makes extensive use, for instance, of stereotyping, imitation and emotions, which provide a set of ready-made, fast-track answers (a sort of "cognitive adaptive toolbox") to physical, social and intellectual challenges. While these strategies for quick estimation, comparison or categorization do not necessarily lead to optimal choices, they are nevertheless cost-efficient responses which have proved to be statistically adaptive, hence their natural selection through evolutionary time.

---

[1] *Bounded Rationality* (2001) is divided into four parts, each comprising three to four position papers and being concluded by a "group report". The first part introduces and defines the main concepts, which are aimed at "rethinking" rationality in terms of evolutionism. The second part explores simple and robust heuristic strategies, and tries to determine why they are effective in the environment in which they have evolved. The third part focuses on the role played by emotions and social processes in decision-making, both on the individual and collective levels. The fourth part is concerned with the role of culture in bounded rationality and examines how the cultural transmission of norms allows individuals to rely on simple behavioural algorithms that greatly cut the cost of search, experimentation and data processing and storage. The contributing authors represent an array of disciplines including economics, cognitive science, evolutionary biology and anthropology.

Obviously, this range of reflections is relevant to semiotics, since signals, signs, symbols can be considered from this point of view as "irrational" shortcuts to decision-making. What was once called "instincts" by opposition to "reason" in philosophical and psychological dualistic discourse now remerges in the debates triggered by evidence relating genome to behaviour in evolutionary perspective.

The constraints involved include for instance the limits of perceptual patterns of identification, the respective capacities of the several memory systems located in the brain, and the specificity of various domains of relevance such as determined by the needs of the organism and the affordances of its environment.

Dominant semiotic models are markedly at odds with the new approach outlined above. As the products of the philosophy of the Enlightenment, they are rationally based, with variations dependent on the kind of psychology to which they relate, implicitly or explicitly. In spite of early interests of some psychologists like Romanes (1882) and Morgan (1890) who discussed aspects of animal cognition as evolved traits, or the pervasive influence of Darwin's thought on James (1890) and Baldwin (1902) as documented by Richards (1987) and Wozniak (1998), the discipline of semiotics developed eventually along different lines. First, behaviourism restricted the scope of psychology to observable empirical variables, then the shift toward cognitive psychology kept the focus on the social and individual dimensions of the human mind and endeavoured to describe them irrespectively of how these cognitive capacities had evolved from earlier forms in specific environments. The general lack of interest of mainstream psychologists for information processing and their ecological and evolutionary constraints, opened an epistemological space which semiotics attempted to fill while mostly remaining biased by the dominant psychological and psycholinguistic paradigms (Bouissac, 1998). As a consequence, some psychological models such as Charles Morris's selective use of Peircean semiotic notions or Karl Bühler's linguistic communication arc have been very influential in distracting semiotics away from ecological and evolutionary considerations. These models, in their semiotically updated forms, are still at the core of the inquiry into signs and communication. Roland Posner (1997), for instance, perpetuates the Morris's tradition in the conception, organization and presentation of his monumental handbook. All semiotic transactions are conceived as taking place in a sort of rational "ether" in which both senders and receivers of messages are assumed to share the same code, or at least benefit from a sufficient overlap between their individual knowledge of the code. The notion of code is sufficiently ambiguous to accommodate a range of interpretations and ontologies such as those discussed in Umberto Eco's tentative "summa semiotica" (1976). Each act of communication is assigned a theory-dependent description in the form of algorithms or diagrams, which map on space the cognitive or physiological processes, which unfold in time. Identifying individual acts of communication requires the artificial isolation of a segment of behaviour. This is a procedure that is easier to achieve with thought experiments than with actual interactions in which it is generally difficult to keep track of what is going on without the help of very sensitive recording devices.

An issue which is rarely, if ever, raised is the comparative assessment of the actual time it takes for an interactive instance to occur and the time which would be required for the step by step semiotic models of communication to be implemented through neuronal circuitry. A consideration of the energy cost involved is also conveniently ignored, as well as the adaptive liability potentially involved in information sharing. Furthermore, how the neurons and neuronal architectures necessary for information processing have emerged through natural selection under particular environmental and social constraints and, therefore, what is the specificity of the sort of problems they are designed to solve, are questions which are generally not addressed in the semiotic discourse. Semiotic models assume that such considerations are irrelevant. They also assume that the codes are already available in the cognitive resource of the interactants and do not factorize the cost of acquiring such codes and keeping abreast of their constant modifications and transformations. Furthermore, they ignore the fact that decoding messages is not a virtual event but involves decision-making and that all behaviours have consequences for the social or physical survival of the individuals concerned. Communication cannot be modelled as the mere exchange of information in the form of signals or sentences, but it always performs vital moves on the chessboard of life.

4. THE NOTION OF BOUNDED SEMIOTICS

It is doubtful that a semiotic competence of the sort described by the dominant disembodied semiotic models could have evolved as an adaptive general capacity. Time is too short, resources are too scarce and the stakes are too high for any organism, including humans, to play by the rule of the utopian semiotics of communication. Processing information, and processing it correctly in the right time, is too vital for being dependent on too costly operations. The management of information is necessarily "bounded" by evolutionary constraints. "Bounded semiotics" should be concerned with the adaptive shortcuts, which evolved with respect to efficient (that is, fast and accurate) sorting out of relevant information and adaptive decision-making, rather than with the complex logical architectures, which purport to theorize (i.e., make intelligibly visible) an assumed universal semiotic competence (Maranda, 2001).

It has now become evident that complex outcomes do not necessarily require complex algorithms in order to account for their structural and dynamic features. The blind behaviours (i.e., behaviours which are not guided by long-range, design-oriented goals) of multiple autonomous agents adequately and economically explain phenomena, which appear extraordinarily complex at certain levels of perception or cognition both in the natural and the social sciences. What some are now controversially dubbing "a new kind of science" (Wolfram, 2002) sets a research agenda which is undoubtedly very important for semiotic inquiry[2]. Evolutionary semiotics, or the study of "the evolution of grounded communication" (Steels, 2002), opens novel perspectives, which could at long last take semiotics on the path of empirical research and lead to a range of counterintuitive discoveries and effective applications.

Four of the semiotic adaptive shortcuts which can be potentially interesting with respect to a rethinking of the "science of signs" and its applications are already the object of intense current scientific attention, but other will not fail to emerge in the near future. They are: (i) *innate releasing mechanisms*, (ii) *imitation* or *copying*, (iii) *stereotyping* and (iv) *emotions*. But before turning to a brief review of these "adaptive tools", it is important to underline that the term "shortcut" should not be understood here as a strategy devised by organisms with the purpose of saving time and energy. It does not imply a rational choice among available means of reaching particular goals. It simply appears to be so with respect to the idealized and normalized logical operations and schematized communication processes of the rational utopia constructed by the speculations of semiotic discourse.

(i) *Innate releasing mechanisms*. This first category of behaviours has been abundantly documented by philosophers under the name of instincts, and then empirically demonstrated by ethologists. While the latter have

---

[2] If we consider that the complexity of the phenomenological world is in the eye of the beholder rather than assume that the processes, which generate it, must be still more complex, a new approach to scientific inquiry is indeed possible as Stephen Wolfram (2002) suggests. Instead of looking for daunting mathematical equations or the principles of grand architectures almost impossible to fathom, we should look for "simpler" programs, such as cellular automata whose interactions can produce very complex patterns and structures. For instance, the honeycomb with its characteristic hexagonal wax cells has been the object of philosophical speculations regarding the origin of this complex architecture. Mathematicians are still discussing the algorithms, which must be assumed, and marvel at the bees' instinct which "knows" how to elegantly optimize their 3D storage space. However, if a number of agents are genetically endowed with identical biologic clocks which time the pace of their movements and if they space themselves at a constant distance from each other (as many animals do) before starting to build the wax cells, pushing the material as far as they can in all directions, the end result will necessarily be hexagonal cells as in many other physical processes which produce such regular tesselations (Kelso, 1995: 6-8 and plate 1). In the same manner, the apparently sophisticated decision-making process through which a swarm selects a new home requires only from each individual bee a surprisingly simple skill (Seeley, 2001). The semiotic community of researchers has been brought up in a conceptual environment, which assumes a high, almost intractable level of complexity of its object of study and is still under the spell of the intellectual acrobatics of structuralism (Maranda, 2001). Its theological roots and its dependence on the fiction of classical rationality has made it immune, so to speak to Darwinian thinking. A movement like biosemiotics, whose main reference is Jakob von Uexkull, appears to take for granted a Leibnizian view of nature permeated with signs, which ensure an optimal harmony. From this point of view, semiotics as a science consists of discovering the underlying structure of this universal functionality.

engaged in detailed discussions and controversies which eventually have brought human behaviour into focus (e.g., Eibl-Eibesfeldt, 1984), semioticians have tended to treat this kind of phenomena as unproblematic under the heading of *signalling*. This played a significant part in the ideological construction of an assumed gap between animals and humans. However, during the last few decades, intensive research spanning a vast array of domains from molecular biology to the genomic basis of behaviour have expanded the relevance of signalling to human complex behaviour and have blurred the Cartesian line of control which persists under the name of "anthroposemiotics".

For instance, the scientific investigation of human facial displays and their underlying muscular and neural substrates (e.g., Young, 1998 and its review by Westbury, 2001) have yielded many results which cast a new light on face-to-face interactions and their social impact through mass-media communication. The evolution of trust, for instance, as a strategy which bypasses the lengthy scrutiny of past records and provides statistically adaptive ways of making decisions, relies for a significant part on visual information gathered from the face. Cues on age, status, mood, intention, and reliability combine to trigger immediate responses of trusting behaviour. The fact that these cues can be analyzed through comparison as separate signals and manipulated through make-up and deceptive performance cannot explain the ways in which they have evolved. Trusting a face (and a voice) as a path toward making snap decisions is obviously not an optimal solution since charisma and rhetoric often overrides discursive contrary information. But reaching a fast decision may be indeed more adaptive than looking for all the facts by oneself when time is crucially of the essence. Even only slightly more adaptive behaviours pay off and make the difference between life and death for a statistically significant number of reproductive individuals. The risk involved is a part of the cost of a semiotic behaviour, which is not optimal but may be successful in a statistically significant number of cases.

(ii) *Imitating, copying, or conforming to* others' behaviour is receiving increasing attention both from developmental psychologists (e.g., Meltzoff, 1996), evolutionary ethologists (e.g., Dugatkin, 2001) and cultural anthropologists (e.g., Sperber, 1996). Imitation was of course an important focus of interest at the beginning of the 20th century (see Wyrwicka, 1996), but this interest was displaced by communication models, and semiotics has paid only scant attention to mimetic phenomena, as if they were unproblematic. The *meme* hypothesis (e.g., Blackmore, 1999; Aunger, 2002) and the discovery of so-called mirror neurons (Stamenov & Gallese, 2002) have forced a reconsideration of the evolutionary significance of this behavioural process (Meltzoff & Prinz, 2002). While both developments remain controversial and require further research, they have far-reaching consequences for an overdue rethinking of semiotics. Copying behaviour is particularly interesting because it is selective, that is, it is both domain-specific and model-specific. It is a cheap shortcut, which overcomes limitations of knowledge and computational capability and enables individuals to gain a competitive advantage as undetected plagiarism often demonstrates. But the most interesting issue is of course to specify who copies what from whom.

To address these processes with all-purpose communication models is obviously inadequate. On the one hand, imitation is akin to a physical event like the spreading of a wave; on the other hand, the status of the source, or model, is relevant. Vertical and horizontal imitation processes have distinctive characteristics, which are not yet fully understood. It is known that in a group high-ranking individuals serve as models. It has also been consistently observed that innovative behaviour originates in low-ranking individuals (Laland, 2001). Conformism and novelty are precisely the two forces which drive evolution through natural selection. Both manipulate information within a socio-ecological context, which is subject to the Baldwin effect: each move modifies the state of play and introduces new selective constraints. Organizational semiotics cannot overlook this evolutionary dynamics in its attempts to rationalize and optimize management and economic transactions. It must rethink the notion of rationality upon which its theoretical and methodological semiotic principles rest.

(iii) *Stereotyping* in the form of profiling or standard narratives has the interesting property of packaging a large quantity of information and appropriate instructions about how to deal with this information in relatively small units, which are sorts of mental models, easy to recognize and to manipulate. Reaching decisions through relying on a few stereotypes or anecdotes which can be mentally quickly compared is more effective than using a predicate calculus of formal logic. Reasoning most of the time consists of engaging in the former rather than in the latter. Standard narratives also economically encapsulate solutions by reducing the complexity of multi-linear events to some simplified uni-linear formulas, which domesticate information, so to speak.

(iv) *Emotions* are both biological states of the brain and patterned social events. Their traditional categorization in psychology reflects earlier philosophical speculations, which assume a fundamental resemblance (natural, instinctive, irrational, somewhat like the *seven sins* of reason) underlying their phenomenological differences. This deep ontology of emotions has interfered with their scientific investigation. Emotions are still the focus of intense controversies, some reducing them to facial expressions which act as social signals (Fridlund, 1994), some other emphasizing their biological primality while a few others point to their rationality and functionality (de Sousa, 1980). Neurological research has shown that some "emotions" such as, for instance, fear and disgust are supported by distinct neuronal architecture and circuitry which automatically produce facial signalling highly relevant to the transfer of information among a group of con-specifics. Emotions cannot be treated simply as the mark of animality on the human psyche as opposed to ideal rationality, but must be considered as a set of separately evolved adaptive strategies with their own neuro-chemical make up. Emotions, like shame and pride, indeed influence decision-making in many ways including the weighting of cost-benefit assessments (Fessler, 2001). Emotions are shortcuts to the definition of events and other individuals, and represent often expedient solutions to problems which otherwise would be intractable such as the optimization of mate selection. The issue of the evolutionary significance of emotions has been tackled, among others, by Ledoux (1996) and Hinton (1999) and is an important component of the current inquiry in bounded rationality as it should be, obviously, in bounded semiotics[3].

Fundamentally, semiotics is an inquiry into the working of the brain. This is true in more than one sense: not only does it investigate the ways in which information is transformed into meaning and action but it also tries to understand and explain the production of theoretical discourses, such as semiotics itself, and their consequences.

First, the evolutionary approach, which is encapsulated in the notion of bounded rationality, may lead to consider semiotic behaviour as dependent on a set of adaptive cognitive tools, produced by the tinkering typical of natural selection (Dawkins, 1986). This approach is markedly distinct from the assumption that semiotic research is the quest for some grand and optimal rational architecture whose laws generate complex algorithms to be discovered. Rather than abstract relations that unify within an elusive virtual representation the whole gamut of humans' and other organisms' treatment of information, signs and their constructs could be more productively considered as the accumulation of evolved adaptive solutions not only to the problems of a variable environment but also to the problems created by these evolved solutions themselves as they become a part of the environment. For instance, the sharing of information may be adaptive among related con specifics but this advantage is the source of new problems if vital information leaks beyond its adaptive boundaries. All shortcuts have a cost and semiotic behaviour conceived from an evolutionary point of view should not be expected to be fully consistent and cost-effective as the result of a rational design could be expected to be. Perhaps such a Darwinian turn is the precondition for beginning to implement Saussure's and Peirce's dream of a science of signs.

Secondly, the question of the possibility of semiotics, evolutionary or otherwise, cannot be avoided. All scientific inquiries have their limits. They often lead to intractable complexity that the human brain is not

---

[3] The abundant literature on emotions ranging from the legacy of Descartes's "passions" to Darwin's offers a rich debate from which emerge various theories of consciousness and of the self. These efforts progressively connect the neurosciences with the cognitive and social sciences. A review of this literature is not in order here, but published and on-going works by Ronald de Sousa, Keith Oatley, Paul Ekman, Joseph Ledoux, and Antonio Damasio among others, indicate promising lines of inquiry.

equipped to conceptualize (Barrow, 1998). The themes of infinite regress, elusive horizon, daunting task, incompleteness, aporia, and the like are prominent in the semiotic discourse. Greimas once wrote that, theoretically, we should use a nonsensical language in order to be able to say something sensical about meaning. This paradox reveals the deep epistemological anxiety, which drove some semioticians to various forms of intellectual nihilism, such as postmodernism and psychoanalysis. Perhaps they were the victims of a utopian notion of rationality and threw away the baby with the water of the bath. Perhaps the notion of bounded semiotics offers a better opportunity to the advancement of human knowledge within a more modest agenda, both ontologically and theoretically.

5. THE NOTION OF BOUNDED ORGANIZATIONS: SOME METHODOLOGICAL CONSEQUENCES

As synergic and structured groups, designed to achieve specific goals, organizations can be considered as micro-cultures. However, these micro-cultures tend to be perceived and to perceive themselves through their individual members as organisms. Various metaphors determine the self-representation they project towards the social environment from which they derive their variable resources. Darwinian evolutionism has provided from its inception a rich stock of images, which permeate organizational discourse. The extrapolation from biological to social evolution is mostly due to Herbert Spencer (1820-1903) who coined the phrase "survival of the fittest", the *motto* of social Darwinism. This ideological stand, which reinterprets Darwin's theory of evolution in terms of social conflicts, was amplified in America by economic philosophers such as William Sumner (1840-1910) who construed economic Darwinism as the natural principle of progress through the elimination of the weakest competitors. More than a century later, this biological metaphor continues to shape the corporate ethos as witnessed by a recent advertisement promoting a "one-year MBA for executives", offered by the School of Management of a major Canadian University: "Species have always had to adapt in order to survive [...] Take giraffes, for instance. As feeding competition on the ground intensified, the giraffe's neck extended, enabling it to reach the highest treetops where food was most abundant. Such a simple solution, really. [...] Most species evolve over centuries [sic]. We propose one year". (*Globe and Mail*, September 25, 2002: A21)

While offering self-serving images of superior biological value to corporate leaders in order to secure their high registration fees, the evolutionist discourse also promotes a view of organizations as organic entities struggling for survival in a Darwinian world where predators are construed as the winners of the game. Notwithstanding its shortsightness and its definitely undarwinian version of evolutionism and ecology, this ideological fantasy received some epistemological credibility in organizational science through the work of cultural evolutionist Donald Campbell whose writings since the 1960s (e.g., Campbell, 1960; 1969; 1981) are celebrated as seminal by contemporary organizational evolutionists (e.g., Baum and Singh, 1994). It is fair to point out that Campbell's approach is much more complex and balanced than the crude advertisement quoted above. The following statement opens avenues of research which implicitly suggest a crucial role for methods inspired by the notion of "bounded semiotics" which was introduced above: "The use of evolutionary theory in management science should not be limited to cultural evolutionary analogues focused on the selective survival of firms. It should also pay attention to the human nature produced by biological evolution, especially by the genetic competition among the cooperators so conspicuously absent in the ultra-social insects and the naked mole rats. This mixture of cultural level of group selection and biological individual selection means that firm-level adaptations will be under continual undermining pressures from individual and face-to-face group preferences." (Campbell, 1994: 38)

Nevertheless, the dominant paradigm in evolutionist theories of the firm, or organizations in general, tends to foreground a model of natural selection encapsulated in the mantra: "variation, innovation, selection, retention, adaptation" which is applied to organizations as if they were organisms. Actually, the underlying organicist metaphor suggests a conception of cognitive dynamic process for the firm (see, for instance, Choo's *The Knowing Organization*, 1998), which owes more to Piaget's developmental psychology with his notions of assimilation and accommodation, than to Darwin's natural selection, which implies the sexual reproduction of the organisms. Although corporate mergers are often billed as marriages of reason, nobody could seriously stretch the metaphor to the point of contending that organizations reproduce sexually. At most, it could be claimed that they engage at times in some kind of cloning.

It should be obvious that the evolutionary models of the kind which have been sketched above are analytical tools as abstract and inadequate as any of the semiotic models which were outlined in the first two sections of this chapter. Not only the term evolution itself, but also all the technical concepts which are used in the discourse of evolutionary biology are ambiguous. They are indeed all borrowed from common language and redefined as theoretical terms. They are therefore prone to semantic fuzziness and can shift across epistemological contexts. Adaptation, for instance, slides on a semantic axis going from referring to deliberate changes in design which take into account new situational factors to meaning the chance fit between random variations and unpredictable states of the environment. Adaptation in the evolutionary sense is a relative notion, which is time- and context-dependent, not an absolute optimization. There have been four mass extinctions in the past 450 million years of earth's history during which up to 90% of living organisms, which were all perfectly adapted since they had been reproducing for millions of years, were wiped out by catastrophic variations.

The way in which organizations and corporate micro-cultures represent themselves is certainly an interesting topic of research. Virtual realities can function as motivators or regulators of actions. Memetics (e.g., Blackmore, 1999; Aunger, 2002) may offer useful insights into the modus operandi of these algorithms and their impact on behaviours. But organizations are not only "bounded" from the top, so to speak, but more fundamentally, by the evolutionary make-up of their members. Any top-down approach, let it be a self-serving Darwinian or Spencerian narrative, or an all-purpose cascade of Peircean diagrams, will necessarily miss the most relevant which cannot be the ones dreamed by unbounded rationality and the philosophy of communication it has generated. Communication itself is a strictly "bounded" evolved behaviour rife with risks, which can be as much a liability as an advantage (Bouissac, 1993).

An increasingly prevalent view is that human sociality is an evolved form of survival which is constrained by conflicting forces which have been variously negotiated and theorized by cultures but which cannot be totally domesticated. This sociality is sustained by a robust wired-in signalling endowment, which provides the backbone for domain-specific semiotic behaviours, that is, adaptive behaviour in a range of prototypical situations constrained by selective pattern sensitivity and chronobiological rhythms rather than by logical calculi and explicit reasoning. While learning may play some decisive role in regulating interactive social processes, it cannot offset the gene-based behavioural endowment. Whatever the virtual image that is constructed by an organization in the form of a logo, a rhetorical theme, an organigram or a flowchart, the group is made up of individuals competing for material and symbolic resources, who may or may not fully cooperate within sub-groups and within the organization as a whole. The production patterns which emerge from the behaviour of these autonomous agents are always only in the eyes of the beholders. It is doubtful that these dynamic patterns have a system of their own, let alone an organic status. At best they can be sporadically distributed as mental representations among group members. However, this view might not hold completely in the case of strictly-family small businesses or exclusive castes in which individuals are genetically related. This may indeed mitigate, but not suppress, the evolutionary forces, which drives biological agents. Family feuds are indeed rather common occurrences.

It is in this sense that organization can be said to be "bounded". The strong claim made here is that it is not possible to understand organizations and to address effectively their problems if the micro-level of interactions among actual agents is overlooked and if virtual images and abstract models and roles are fore-grounded. Naturally, the latter approach is far easier to handle and has already generated a huge but mostly inconclusive literature illustrated by anecdotal evidence. The debate between the champions of microanalysis and those who contend that macro-phenomena form the appropriate level of understanding has divided organization science for many decades. Even the population ecology perspective (e.g., Harman and Freeman, 1977) tends to skip micro-level processes where idiosyncratic skill and memory reside, and decisions are made (e.g., Burgelman and Mittman, 1994). Developing a method of organizational inquiry based on evolutionary, rather than utopian semiotics remains the challenge of the day.

6. CONCLUSION

But is not this agenda itself an epistemological utopia for the very reason that its premises are correct? As it stands now, it appears obvious that organizational research is by and large based on abstract models and case studies. Typically, researchers endeavour to map the former into the latter and infer from this some theoretical propositions and general principles of management (e.g., Nonaka and Takeuchi, 1995; Choo, 1998). The initial models are dependent on a variety of epistemological traditions, from behaviourist psychology or social Darwinism to philosophical semiotics or information theory. The processing of documents made available by the organizations provides the case studies themselves or those which happen to be in the public domain for other reasons. Researchers are bounded by two main conditions: first, in a live organization there will always be sources of relevant information which are off limit for investigators; secondly, it is impossible to conduct organizational experiments in order to gain knowledge by trial and error. Simulation will be always constrained by the incompleteness deriving from the first condition. The first condition could be overcome in principle in the cases when an organization has come under criminal investigation or is totally out of business but, then, researchers must engage in some sort of uneasy archaeology or autopsy in order to reconstruct a puzzle in which, in any case, some important pieces are very likely to remain inaccessible for legal or political reasons.

   Some exponents of evolutionary economic theory (e.g., Winter, 1994) have called attention to still another, perhaps more fundamental constraint: the discrepancy that exists between the virtual representation of an organization in its flowcharts and the actual networks of tacit knowledge competencies and loyalties distributed among its members, which are fundamentally inaccessible to investigation. It is well known that working by the rules is often more disruptive than going on strike because the latter usually leaves in place sufficient resources for ad hoc local decisions while the former can immobilize an organization under its own bureaucratic weight. Naturally, multilevel administrative structures are always the end-results of efforts made towards the rationalization of organizational processes. Assuming heuristically a fundamental irrationality, or at least a logic which is at odds with the dominant rational paradigm, might be eventually the only way of coming to terms with the complexity of organizational inquiry.

The critical perspectives, which have been developed in this chapter, are not meant to propose a ready-made alternative to the theories and methods, which currently prevail in organizational semiotics. Above all, they do not claim to be endowed with a superior immediate problem-solving capacity, which could provide corporate organizations with some kind of more efficient consultancy. However, this approach may usher in a few productive directions of research in the long term and offer a few caveats.

First of all, it suggests that probably too much weight is given to case studies in the theoretical elaborations of organizational semiotics. These case studies are not raw data. They are narratives most of the time produced in close cooperation with the corporate culture itself in the terms in which organizational self-meaning is constructed. They are not the result of socio-historical inquiries, which would have had access to complete archives, unconstrained memories and all contextual parameters. Nevertheless, these case studies often serve as a basis for generalizations and models for thought-experiments.

Secondly, it seems that only rarely do inquirers tackle the real temporal depth of the organizations they study, but instead focus on functional processes which are circumscribed by a synchrony of limited thickness. It could reasonably be assumed that a much wider time scope could reveal more significant dynamic morphologies. But can a discipline like organizational semiotics afford such an epistemological distance given the fact that its most pressing justification is most of the time to help solve short-term or medium-term corporate problems while remaining within the boundaries of client-management relation and commercial civility? The scientific understanding of a phenomenon usually requires its translation into a more abstract vocabulary and eventually into formal equations which do not necessarily ensure the immediate possibility of controlling this phenomenon. Effective research must find ways of overcoming the predicaments of case studies and the opacity of the protective layers of managerial secrecy.

Assuming that these two related obstacles can be cleared, a step towards implementing a research agenda based on the premises of bounded semiotics could be to engage in comparative organizational semiotics, looking for instance into the types of organizations which sustain the viability of groups in social species, such as primates, rather than eu-social species which are often used as utopian metaphors in organizational discourse, although the comparison is of little biological relevance. Many primate species have been thoroughly researched from the point of view of group structure dynamics and effective leadership, and with respect to the ability of these groups to solve problems arising from their environment and their own inner tensions and conflicts over long period of time. Many of these longitudinal research endeavours have been summarized in books rich in insights (e.g., de Waal, 1982; Kummer, 1995; Sapolsky, 2001), but the actual scientific literature upon which these accounts are grounded provides the actual data and the methods through which they were obtained. The objection that a troupe of baboons and a human organization are two totally different objects is valid only to a limited extent. They are both bound by a similar goal that is to survive and prosper in a hostile environment under some form of evolutionary constraints. They constantly have to make decisions and they are confronted with inner tensions which must be resolved if these tensions are not to cause the group to implode or dissipate.

The primate behavioural heritage of *Homo sapiens sapiens* cannot be ignored, still less eradicated, but must be negotiated in any cultural institution. Whatever functional or technical roles humans are assigned within an artefactual group cannot automatically cancel out the natural dynamic of group formation and evolution. This is a dimension which has not escaped the attention of one of the main promoters of evolutionary interpretations of organizational dynamics. In a chapter tale-tellingly entitled "How individual and face-to-face-group selection undermine firm selection in organizational evolution", Donald Campbell (1994: 23-38) engages in some comparative exercises with other species but, symptomatically almost exclusively focuses on ultra-social or eu-social species against which he tends to negatively position human anarchical individualism.

Human organizations of whatever scale are usually dreamed, or virtually represented, as eu-social constructions in which all altruistically cooperate toward unique goal following specified mandates and job descriptions. Dysfunctionality is assessed with respect to this fantasy and considered as deviance. But a deep understanding of organizations of any kinds, and perhaps all sensible managements of their dynamics, must come to grips with the fact that each individual has his/her own agenda, elective network based on personal histories, socio-biological priorities and corresponding temporal frames.

It ensues that an analytical method which exclusively takes into consideration flow charts, chains of command, standardized information sharing, distributed responsibility, process monitoring and quality control, while characterizing each transfer of information as communication through standardized, disembodied signs, cannot address some of the most essential factors and parameters of organizational processes. The assumption of rational altruism which grounds cooperation on self-interest behaviour, and which is implied in such models, necessarily biases their abstract representation toward a utopian fantasy. It is typical in works published under the aegis of organizational semiotics that references are made almost exclusively to the literature produced within its own academic culture. While it is a tenet of professionalism to demonstrate one's knowledge of the field, and to pay at least formal homage to the main authors who have shaped it, it can easily lead to epistemological introversion and preclude any significant advances. Abundant relevant resources are available beyond the disciplinary fences. An advantage of semiotics is its facilitation of interfacing and integrating knowledge. Research in comparative ethology (e.g., Chagnon & Irons, 1979), evolutionary biology and psychology (e.g., Barkow et al., 1992) notably in issues relating to human altruism (e.g., Fehr & Rockenbach, 2003), could bring novel perspectives and deeper understanding of organizational dynamics and its theoretical representations.

In conclusion, organizational semiotics has developed an academic culture in close cooperation with its object of study. Its main agenda appears to be primarily the improved management of organizational processes toward increased efficiency (productivity, innovation, expansion, profitability) through the semiotic rationalization of these processes. It uses communication models inspired by behavioural semiotics, which tend to reduce actors to their organizational role and assume their rational cooperation in the transfer of information through passive signs. An approach based on the premises of bounded semiotics would take into consideration the socio-biological dynamics of organizations as groups in which each agent has necessarily a double agenda: enhancing its own fitness and implementing an organizational function. Under what conditions the two can coincide, or at least overlap, would then be an important problem to solve with respect to the ultimate goal stated above. Perhaps exploitations and frauds are not mere deviances or dysfunctions, but emerge from conflicting agendas which abstract semiotic models cannot adequately describe, neither control. Furthermore, bounded semiotics would not assume the inertia of signs as tools, as mere packaging of information (following the various models of sign categorizations offered by the current literature), but would focus on their power to structure and control behaviour along the lines opened by memetics. This approach would construct a richer, more complex object grounded in evolutionary biology within which socio-economic transactions and the institutions which support them are necessarily embedded.

REFERENCES

Allott, R. (2000). *The Natural Origin of Language: The Structural Inter-Relation of Language, Visual Perception and Action*. Knebworth UK: Able Publishing.

Aunger, R. (2002). *The electric meme: A new theory of how we think*. New York: Free Press.

Baldwin, J. M. (1902). *Development and Evolution*. New York: MacMillan.

Barkow, J., Cosmides, L. & Tooby, J. (1992) (Eds.). *The Adapted Mind: Evolutionary Psychology and the Generation of Culture*. New York/Oxford: Oxford University Press.

Barrow, J. (1998). *Impossibility: The Limits of Science and the Science of Limits*. London: Vintage.

Baum, J. & Singh. J. (1994). *Evolutionary Dynamics of Organizations*. New York: Oxford University Press.

Blackmore, S. (1999). *The Meme Machine*. Oxford: Oxford University Press.

Bouissac, P. (1998). Converging Parallels: Semiotics and Psychology in Evolutionary Perspective. *Theory and Psychology, 8, 6* (pp. 731-753).

Bouissac, P. (1993). Ecology of Semiotic Space: Competition, Exploitation, and the Evolution of Arbitrary Signs. *The American Journal of Semiotics, 10; 3-4*, (pp. 143-163).

Brunning, J. & Foster, P. (1997) (Eds.). *The Rule of Reason*. Toronto: University of Toronto Press.

Burgelman, R. & Mittman, B. (1994). An Intra-organizational Ecological Perspective on Managerial Risk Behavior, Performance, and Survival: Individual, Organizational and Environmental Effects. In Baum & Singh, 1994 (pp. 53-75).

Campbell, D. (1960). Blind Variation and Selective Retention in Creative Thought and in other Knowledge Processes. *Psychological Review 67*, pp. 380-400.

Campbell, D. (1969). Variation and Selective Retention in Socio-cultural Evolution". *General Systems, 16*, pp. 69-85.

Campbell, D. (1981). Levels of Organization, Selection and Information Storage in biological and Social Evolution. *The Behavioral and Brain Sciences, 4*, pp. 236-237.

Campbell, D. (1994). How Individual and Face-to-Face-Group Selection Undermine Firm Selection in Organizational Evolution. In Baum & Singh 1994 (pp. 23-38).

Chagnon, N. & Irons, W. (1997) (Eds.). *Evolutionary Biology and Human Social Behavior*. Belmont CA: Duxbury Press.

Choo, S. W. (1998). *The Knowing Organization*. New York: Oxford University Press.

Damasio, A. (2003). *Looking for Spinoza: Joy, Sorrow and the Feeling Brain*. New York: Harcourt.

Danesi, M. & Perron, P. (1999). *Analyzing Cultures: An Introduction & Handbook*. Bloomington: Indiana University Press.

Dascal, M. (1987). *Leibniz: Language, Signs and Thought*. Amsterdam: Benjamins.

Dawkins, R. (1986). *The Blind Watchmaker*. London: Longman.

Deely, John (2001) *Four Ages of Understanding*. Toronto: University of Toronto Press.

De Sousa, R. (1980). The rationality of emotions. In A. O. Rorty (Ed.). *Explaining Emotions*. Berkeley: University of Berkeley Press.

Dror, I. & Stevenage, S. (2000) (Eds.). *Facial Information Processing*. Special issue of *Pragmatics & Cognition*, 8,1.

Dugatkin, L. (2001). *The Imitation Factor: Evolution beyond the Gene*. New York: The Free Press.

Dukas, R. (1998) (Ed.). *Cognitive Ecology: The Evolutionary Ecology of Information Processing and Decision Making*. Chicago: Chicago University Press.

Eco, U. (1976). *A Theory of Semiotics*. Bloomington: Indiana University Press.

Eibl-Eibesfeldt, I. (1984). *Die Biologie des menslichen Verhaltens*. Münich: Piper.

Engler, R. (1990) (Ed.). Ferdinand de Saussure. Cours de lingistique générale. Edition critique. Tome 2. Appendice. Notes de F. De Saussure. Wiesbaden: Otto Harrassowitz.

Enquist, M. & Arak, A. (1998). Neural Representation and the Evolution of Signal Form. In Dukas, R. (Ed.) (pp. 21-87).

Fehr, E. & Rockenbach B. (2003). Detrimental Effects of Sanctions on Human, Altruism. *Nature, Vol 422* (pp. 137-140).

Fessler, D. (2001). Emotions and Cost-benefit Assessment: The Role of Shame and Self-esteem in Risk Taking. In Gigerenzer & Selten, 2001 (pp. 191-214).

Fridlund, A. (1994). *Human Facial Expression: An Evolutionary View*. New York: Academic Press.

Gigerenzer, G. & Selten, R. (2001) (Eds.). *Bounded Rationality: The Adaptive Toolbox*. Dalhem Workshop Reports. Cambridge MA: The MIT Press.

Golembiewski, R. (1990). *Ironies in Organizational Development*. New Brunswick NJ: Transaction Publishers.

Greimas, A. J. (1987). *On Meaning*. Minneapolis: Minnesota University Press.

Greimas, A. J. & Courtés, J. (1982). *Semiotics and Language*. Bloomington: Indiana University Press.

Hannan, M.T. & Freeman, J.H. (1977). Population Ecology of Organizations. *American Journal of Sociology 83)* (pp. 929-983).

Hjelmslev, L. (1961). *Prolegomena to a Theory of Language*. Madison: University of Wisconsin Press.

Hinton, A. (1999) (Ed.). *Beyond Nature or Nurture: Biocultural Approach to the Emotions*. New York: Cambridge University Press.

Hoffmeyer, J. (1996). *Signs of Meaning in the Universe*. Bloomington: Indiana University Press.

Jakobson, R. (1971). *Selected Writings*. The Hague: Mouton.

Jakobson, R. (1980). *The Framework of Language*. Ann Arbor: Michigan Studies in the Humanities.

Jakobson, R. & Halle, M. (1956). *Fundamentals of Language*. The Hague: Mouton.

James, W. (1890). *The Principles of Psychology*. New York: Dover Publications.

Kelso, J. A. S. (1995). *Dynamic Patterns: the Self-Organization of Brain and Behavior*. Cambridge, MA: MIT Press.

Klos, T.B. (2000). *Agent-based Computational Transaction Cost Economics*. Capelle aan de IJssel: Labyrint Publication.

Kummer, H. (1995). *The Quest of the Sacred Baboon: A Scientist's Journey*. Translated by Ann Biederman-Thorson. Princeton: Princeton University Press.

Laland, K. (2001). Imitation, Social Learning, and Preparedness as Mechanisms of Bounded Rationality. In Gigerenzer & Selten, 2001 (pp. 233-248).

Lane, C. & Bachman R. (1998) (Eds.). *Trust Within and Between Organizations*. New York: Oxford University Press.

Ledoux, J. (1996). *The Emotional Brain*. New York: Simon & Schuster.

Lorenz, K. (1965). *Evolution and Modification of Behavior*. Chicago: University of Chicago Press.

Maranda, P. (2001) (Ed.). *The Double Twist: From Ethnography to Morphodynamics*. Toronto: University of Toronto Press.

Meltzoff, A. N. (1996). The Human Infant as Imitative Generalist: A 20-year Progress Report on Infant Imitation with Implications for Comparative Psychology. In Heyes, C.M. & Calef jr. B.G. (Eds.) *Social Learning in Animals: The Roots of Culture*. New York: Academic Press.

Meltzoff, A. & Prinz, W. (2002)(Eds.). *The Imitative Mind: Development, Evolution and Brain Bases*. Cambridge: Cambridge University Press.

Morgan, L.C. (1890). *Animal Life and Intelligence*. Boston: Ginn.

Nonaka, I. & Takeuchi, H. (1995). *The Knowledge Creating Company: How Japanese Companies Create The Dynamics of Innovation*. New York: Oxford University Press.

Peirce, C. S. [1892] (1992). The First Rule of Logic. In Ketner, K.L. & Putnam H. (Eds.). *Reasoning and the Logic of Things*. Cambridge: Harvard University Press.

Peterson, I. (1999). The Honeycomb Conjecture: Proving Mathematically that the Honeybee Constructors are on the Right Track. *Science News, 156, 4* (July 24, 1999) (p. 60.)

Posner, R., et al. (1997)(Eds.). *Semiotik/Semiotics, HSK 13.1*. Berlin: Mouton de Gruyter.

Richards, R.J. (1987). *Darwin and the Emergence of Evolutionary Theories of Mind and Behavior*. Chicago: University of Chicago Press

Romanes, G. (1882). *Animal Intelligence*. London: Kegan Paul.

Sapolsky, R. (2001). *A Primate's Memoir*. New York: Simon and Schuster.

Sebeok, T. A. (1976). *Contributions to the Doctrine of Signs*. Lisse: Peter de Ridder Press.

Sebeok, T. A. (2001). *Global Semiotics*. Bloomington: Indiana University Press.

Sebeok, T. A. & Danesi, M. (2000). *The Forms of Meaning: Modeling System Theory and Semiotic Analysis*. Berlin: Mouton de Gruyter.

Seeley, T. (2001). Decision Making in Superorganisms: How Collective Wisdom Emerges from the Poorly Informed Masses". In Gigerenzer & Selten, 2001 (pp. 249-261).

Simon, H. A. (1956). Rational Choice and the Structure of Environment. *Psychology Review, 63* (pp. 129-138)

Simon, H.A. (1960). *The New Science of Management Decision*. New York: Harper & Row.

Sperber, D. (1996). *Explaining Culture: A Naturalistic Approach*. Oxford: Blackwell.
Stamenov, M. & Gallese, V. (2002). *Mirror Neurons and the Evolution of Brain and Language*. Amsterdam / Philadelphia: John Benjamins
Steels, L. (2002) (Ed). The Evolution of Grounded Communication. Special issue of *Evolution of Communication 4, 1*.
Waal, F. de (1982). *Chimpanzee Politics*. New York: Harper and Row.
Westbury, C. (2002). Symbols in your Face. *The Semiotic Review of Books 12,1* (pp. 4-8).
Winter, S. (1994). *Organizing for Continuous Improvement: Evolutionary Theory Meets the Quality Revolution*. In Baum & Singh 1994 (pp. 90-108).
Wolfram, S. (2002). *A New Kind of Science*. Wolfram Media.
Wozniak, R. (1998). Thought and Things: James Mark Baldwin and the Biosocial Origins of Mind. In R.W. Rieber & K.D. Salzinger (Eds.) *Psychology: Theoretical-Historical Perspectives*. Washington DC: American Psychological Association (pp. 429-453).
Wyrwicka, W. (1996). *Imitation in Human and Animal Behavior*. New Brunswick/London: Transaction Publishers.
Young, A. (1998). *Face and Mind*. Oxford: Oxford University Press.

Chapter 2

A theory of communication for user interface design

Victor V. Kryssanov, Masayuki Okabe, Koh Kakusho and Michihiko Minoh

ABSTRACT

This chapter investigates the phenomenon of communication, and proposes a theory for the design and analysis of user interfaces of distributed information systems. It is argued that the explanation of communication offered by the classical theories is not adequate to fully account for computer-mediated communication. Therefore, a new model of communication is proposed to compensate for the theoretical shortcomings found. The process of communication is represented by a partial sequence of semiosis processes defined recurrently, as emerging from the interaction of at least one psychic system with one or more social systems. The psychic and social systems are characterized as self-organizing systems and their dynamics are described. We have conducted a pilot study on the basis of which we draw conclusions.

INTRODUCTION

As the networked technologies, connecting a vast number of information resources, become more and more powerful, the task of providing users with adequate means for accessing these resources – the task of user interface design – becomes, somewhat contrary to common expectations, increasingly difficult, and its complexity quickly exceeds the comfortable level of empirical and "common-sense" decision procedures. Many attempts have been made to formulate a scientific theory or, at least, a credible theoretical framework that would provide systematic guidelines for the design of a user interface, which, in the case of distributed systems, often determines the design of the whole information system. It may be said that a theory is satisfactory as far as it allows for comprehensive analysis and prediction of certain phenomena or else guarantees a pragmatic application. In the case of user interface design, the phenomena in focus are usually information transmission phenomena, and it is therefore natural that presently, a large group of the user interface design theories strive for utilization of an information theory (e.g. Shannon-Weaver Information Theory) by borrowing its conceptual apparatus and applying its analytical procedures to better design user interfaces (de Souza, 1993). Another large and alternative group of design theories gathers methodological generalizations, which pay little attention to understanding the processes underlying the transfer of information but, instead, endeavour to methodologically generalize and extend the best-known engineering practice to new design cases (e.g. Beaudouin-Lafon, 2000). While this classification of theories may appear too cursory and simplistic, it should suffice to justify the fact that most of the currently available approaches to user interface design can hardly be considered satisfactory. Indeed, information resources are by and large created by people and for people, and their user interfaces are, first of all, to ensure communication between people. As long as there is no brain scanning device that shows explicitly what is the information sent and received through communication, the "transmission-inclined" theories will fail to provide for a sufficiently precise analysis of the communication process and user interfaces coordinating it. On the other hand, by substituting a theory with a methodology – no matter how general or universal – one never touches the theory *per se* but is forced to continuously adapt methodological procedures to a potentially infinite number of communication situations and develop "meta-methodologies" (sometimes called "ontologies") to systematize these situations that, for most practical cases, result in unmanageably complicated design models.

It is likely that any theory of user interface design has to be based on a theory of communication. The difficulties with the development of such a theory arise from the necessity to concurrently address two seemingly incompatible aspects of computer-mediated communication: communication as a physical – technological, measurable, and quite predictable – process, and as a mental – in effect experiential, partially unconscious, and emergent – phenomenon. A communication theory has thus to locate itself somewhere between two threats of category error: the error of models identifying communication as a mere physical act, and epiphenomenalism – theories struggling to remove any physical grounding (particularly causality) when describing communication. In seeking to avoid the evident dangers, scientists investigating communication and, lately, information systems and the user interface, have embraced philosophies, specifically semiotics, that steer clear of the absolutization of either the physical or mental by distinguishing and explicitly defining connections between these two at the very conceptual level. Relevant questions, however, come up: whether the mental can be dealt with in the same way as the physical (i.e. can it be measured and predicted) and if so, is a communication theory to be a distinct scientific discipline and not an empirically derived unstable compromise between technology and the humanities – psychology, sociology or art.

Thus, we investigate these questions. User interface design theories are divided according to a transmission/interpretation distinction, and the weak and strong points of each group are examined. Next, we attempt to formulate definitions and propositions on an axiomatic basis, which could allow us to uniformly describe the mental and physical phenomena of communication with a precision sufficient for practical application, either through user interface design or analysis. In so doing, we proceed from the assumption that although it may be difficult to unequivocally define user interface design as a single discipline, it will always involve some autonomous behaviour (e.g. human-computer and human-human interactions) constituting a communication language, as well as environments – physical and social – imposing constraints (principal and potential) on this language. The latter determines our choice of autopoiesis theory and sociology as the source of conceptual ideas; semiotics is used as a general philosophy to effectively organize all the different concepts within one coherent theory, and quantum physics provides major inspiration as to how interpretation would "work." In a sense, this chapter opposes the mainstream in contemporary user interface design studies, as it does not offer or advocate particular technological solutions, but rather establishes a theoretical basis that aims to find and validate appropriate techniques, without *a priori* commitment to a specific methodology or technology. We therefore apply the developed principles to design and analyse an adaptive user interface for distributed information systems.

COMMUNICATION MODELS IN USER INTERFACE DESIGN

When it comes to user interface design, there are two basic approaches to modelling communication: through the process of message transmission, and the process of the development of meaning. The modelling of the transmission of messages goes back to Shannon and Weaver's Mathematical Theory of Communication and its conveyor-tube model first proposed over 50 years ago for solving the technical problem of reducing physical noise in communication channels (Shannon & Weaver, 1963). In the last few decades, this model has significantly been improved upon and adapted to a variety of domains, interface design inclusive, so that nowadays it is widely considered as a general model for communication studies. In spite of the changes made, however, the basic concept of communication as transmission of messages remains the core of the approach. In whatever terms a transmission-focussed model is defined – probabilistic, software development-related, or even semiotic, it postulates that:

- there is an active source of information – the sender – that produces and "encodes" a message;
- the message is sent through a channel to the target that receives and "decodes" the message;
- the sender's and the receiver's information may differ, owing to the physically noisy channel and/or semantic alterations caused by the encoding and decoding;
- besides the sender and receiver, there is a third party – an observer (which may be identical to either of the communicating parties) that intervenes in the process by determining the correctness of the information transmitted.

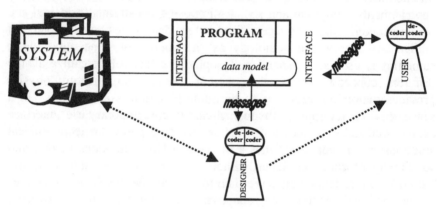

Figure 1. User interface as the transmission of messages

Figure 1 gives a generalized representation of the transmission-focussed communication models used in user interface design. According to the model, the interface is composed of messages allowing for and explaining the control and operation of the system (which can, for instance, be a program or a physical mechanism). The messages can be about the system domain, the computational domain, or about user-computer possible interactions. Both the user and the system can send and receive information, and a computational data model implemented in the computer program plays the rôle of an observer, determining the "correct" (i.e. "understandable") messages and interactions. This data model reflects the designer's understanding of the controlled system's structure and functioning encoded and sent to the user through the interface.

The work by Joseph A. Goguen (Goguen, 1999), although it addresses many other issues not immediately related to our study, gives a well-elaborated and sophisticated example of the application of a transmission-focussed communication model for user interface design. The model is defined in semiotic terms, and it employs the novel technique called "algebraic semiotics" that suggests a formal interpretation of de

Saussure's Semiology (see de Saussure, 1974). A user interface is characterized in terms of a "semiotic morphism" that is mapping (translation, re-representation, etc.) from a sign system representing the controlled system (as conceived by the designer) to a sign system representing the user interface, where a sign system is defined as a loose algebraic theory with some extra-structure. It is argued that determining formal properties of the corresponding semiotic morphism can help one estimate the user interface functionality and quality. In particular, it is advocated that in user interface design, morphisms preserving structure should have a higher priority as they are (ethnomethodologically) more important and "better" than morphisms preserving content. The chapter describes the application of the proposed model to designing user interfaces of a distributed collaborative system, and it reports the experiences with regard to using the interfaces. It, however, remains obscure why the developed interface should be "good" (apart from being "good" in the formal sense, i.e. logically consistent) and for whom it would be good.

The author justifies the developed model through studies of ethnography, social science, and linguistics which find and evaluate characteristics of communication (seen as the movement of signs) that are average or common for a certain community, e.g. a group of system users. The appeal to semiotics, however, appears weak: the chapter does not explain but, rather, makes it difficult to see, if and how anything but the terminology of this discipline can help the designer cope with the complexity of communication caused by numerous socially converging but still subjective and never uniform meaning-making processes. Furthermore, by utilizing the proposed approach "as is", one can tell little if anything about the personal and social dynamics of communication. Another example of reinterpretation of the conveyor-tube conceptual model in semiotic terms is the work by C.S. de Souza (de Souza, 1993).

Communication models of the second – interpretation-focussed – class are usually associated with the Peircean conception of a semiotic triad (Peirce, 1998) connecting a sign with its object by meaning, which may or may not be another sign, that is the conceived sense made of the first sign. In user interface design, the application of such a model (frequently simply called semiotic model) is concerned with the generating and exchange of meaning, when the divergence of meaning is not a failure but a natural attribute of communication. In a semiotic model, communication is dealt with as the development and re-interpretation of signs that are representations of the physical world. A semiotic model of communication postulates that:

- there are no senders and receivers – they are replaced by interpretants, i.e. by those which proceed semantically from the processes of interpretation;

- not a message but meaning emerges, which is externalised, and (re)determined through interactions between a carrier (e.g. gesture, text, picture, sound, and the like) and the culture;
- decisive notions, like "correct" and "incorrect," are subject to both individual (i.e. experiential) interpretation and socio-cultural convergence.

Figure 2 depicts a semiotic model of communication applied in user interface design. The model suggests that the interface is composed of signs, which are to represent "meaning" created by psychic or/and some physical systems. These systems externalise meaning by producing signifieds (generally seen as behaviour; in other words – objects), which may activate the "generation" of signifiers (i.e. signs standing for something) through interaction with the social system. The interface is a realization of the social system, while signs are individually interpreted but still have socially and culturally induced meaning. There can be more than one social system, but no communication is possible beyond a social system. All the systems involved have internal dynamics affecting their output: signifieds/objects in the case of psychic and physical systems, and signifiers/signs in the case of social systems.

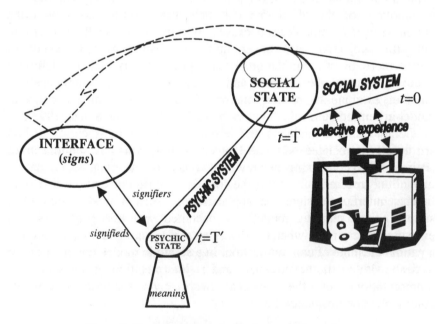

Figure 2. User interface as the development of meaning

Peter B. Andersen sketched the range and applicability of the semiotic (i.e. interpretation-focussed) models for human-computer interaction (Andersen, 2000). It was argued that whenever computation and interpretation have an effect on each other, they can and should be analysed semiotically, and that not only straight human-computer interaction, but also any storage and retrieval of data are communicative processes. Building on the knowledge of older and traditional semiotic disciplines, such as literature and art, the author elaborated two theses: *a)* the interface should not just be "user-friendly" but should also correspond to and expose what really goes on behind the interface, – i.e. it should reveal the actual semantics of the physical world; and *b)* apart from being interpretable (at least potentially), the interface should be verbalizable in terms of the user's work-language that may be seen as a realization of the corresponding social system. To illustrate the theses, an example of user interface design is provided in the chapter. It is shown that projecting features from verbal communication onto the user interface can enhance the communicability of a multimedia computer system. The developed interface is expected to be "good" because it can effectively and correctly be understood within a social group. Furthermore, the language in focus determines the social group for which the interface is intended. A serious obstacle preventing the interpretation-based approach from a broad application, however, is that it is hard to use on a formal, and thus computational, basis. This, at least partially, results from the rather confusing array of contemporary semiotic theories, which build on different and yet intricate conceptualisations while describing the same phenomena. (Other related examples of the use of semiotics in user interface design can be found in Schmidt-Isler, 2000, and Condon, 2000.)

Being quite aware of the risk of confusing the reader with the terminology, we nevertheless deliberately presented two examples, where the semiotic terms were used to formulate the principles for designing user interfaces. Our motivation is that most naturally, communication is indeed a semiotic phenomenon, and the two perspectives (one focussed on the transmission, and another on interpretation) correspond to two distinct but overlapping parts of semiotics named by Umberto Eco as Theory of Sign Production and Theory of Codes, respectively (Eco, 1976). In fact, semiotics offers a common basis for discussing, analysing, and designing user interfaces. In a more general vision, the two different approaches to modelling communication can be related to studying two aspects of interpretation of the same element of the interface or, in other words, two different systems of "semiotic coordinates," as an object which is interpreted (e.g. a sign in Goguen's sign system, which is, in itself, a system of interpretance) and as an object of interpretation (e.g. meaning in Andersen's terms) that may be seen just as an ordered pair of objects interpreted with two systems of interpretance accommodating syntax for one element of the pair, and semantics – for the other (Sonesson, 2002).

It is now understood that each of the design approaches surveyed in this section has serious limitations in modelling human communication. The use of the semiotic terminology alone does not make a statistical conveyer-tube framework capable of dealing with the complexity and subjectivism of communication, neither does a semiotic analysis "automatically" make the task of interface design more understandable or more easily formalizable. The separate treatments of the different aspects of interpretation eventually led the authors of these, as well as many other models of communication, to the study of information (re)representation with little attention to the issues of communication motivation, dynamics, and success that, for most practical cases, made analysing and designing user interfaces (along with information systems behind them) ad hoc, ambiguous, and/or unreasonably complicated. Therefore, new approaches to modelling communication need to be found, which could compensate for the drawbacks of the classical theories.

TOWARDS QUANTITATIVE SEMIOTICS

In this section, we will describe a new model of human-computer and human-human interaction derived from a general definition of communication made in terms of autopoiesis theory. The model is to overcome the limitations of both the transmission-focussed and the interpretation-focussed classical approaches.

Grounding

Autopoiesis is a theory of the organization of complex systems, such as living organisms (Maturana & Varela, 1980). An autopoietic system is a form of self-organization: it consists of a network of processes, which recursively produces and reproduces its own components and boundary, thus ensuring the survival of the system as a whole, and which has a particular (physical) embodiment or structure. The principal property of an autopoietic system is its autonomy in respect to the environment; the inner state of the system at any time is determined solely by its structure and previous state. Environmental perturbations can only be a potential cause for the changing of the system state, and the system cannot be controlled from the outside. Hence, all observed behaviour – the output – of an autopoietic system is a result of its inner state and history. Through behaviour, the system can interact with the environment that may cause it to change its structure. If this changing does not break autopoiesis (e.g. by destroying the whole), the system is defined as structurally coupled with the environment. An important case is when the environment has structural dynamics (e.g. is in itself a self-organizing system) so that the (coupled) system and the environment may then mutually trigger their inner states so that the system undergoes self-adaptation. The self-adaptation processes of several autopoietic systems embedded in the same environment may become coupled, recursively acting through their own states. All the possible changes of states of such systems, which do not terminate this coupling, establish a consensual domain. Behaviour in a consensual domain is mutually orienting. Perhaps most fundamentally, *communication is the (observed) behavioural coordination developed from the interactions between autopoietic systems in the consensual domain* (Di Paolo, 1998).

Terminology and conceptual framework

Adopting the terminology coined by Niklas Luhmann (Luhmann, 1995) (though not his theory itself), we will assume that all the psychic, or any other systems involved into communication are higher order autopoietic systems acting in the consensual domain. Each of these systems "belongs" to at least one self-organizing social system seen as a realization of the consensual domain. We will also assume that the psychic system is composed of interpretants (meanings) and is observationally equivalent to, or is interpreted as, the totality of subjectively, or experientially, effective behaviour called *objects*. The social system is composed of *signs* and is equivalent to the totality of socially valid behaviour that maintains the social system as a whole. (The reader with a semiotic background should be warned that our treatment of the semiotic triad *object-sign-interpretant*, although it does not generally contradict the concept of infinite semiosis (see Peirce, 1998), goes beyond the canonical Peircean definition by elaborating on the ideas originally formulated in Andersen, 2002.)

We will consider communication as a usually finite, partial time-sequence of interdependent – through signs seen as behaviour and in the sense of the behavioural coordination revealed as (contextual) relations between the signs – semiosis processes $C=\{S_1,S_2,...,S_K\}$, where $S_t=\{Object_t,Sign_t,Interpretant_t\}$ is a single semiosis process specified through its manifestation as an interpreted sign, and t is a discrete time-mark.

The dynamics of a self-organizing system can generally be described as follows:

$$\begin{cases} \mathbf{x}(t+1) = f(\mathbf{x}(t),\ y(t)), \\ y(t+1) = g(y(t),\ \mathbf{x}(t+1)), \end{cases} \tag{1}$$

where $y(t)$ is the state of the system at time t, $\mathbf{x}(t)$ is the vector of states of the system parts, which constitute its structure, and f and g are some operators specifying the behaviour of the system parts and the system as a whole, respectively. The dynamics of the communication process can then be described by the following equations:

$$\begin{cases} \mathbf{Objects}_{t+1} = \text{Externalising}(\mathbf{Objects}_t, PsychicState_t), \\ PsychicState_{t+1} = \text{Interpreting}(PsychicState_t, \mathbf{Signs}_{t+1}), \end{cases} \tag{2.1}$$

and

$$\begin{cases} \mathbf{Signs}_{t+1} = \text{Authorizing}(\mathbf{Signs}_t, SocialState_t), \\ SocialState_{t+1} = \text{Evolving}(SocialState_t, \mathbf{Objects}_{t+1}), \end{cases} \tag{2.2}$$

where "**Objects**" is a state vector representing the behaviour, i.e. psychic states as (self)observed, which are subjectively effective, and "**Signs**" is a state vector representing the socially valid behaviour.

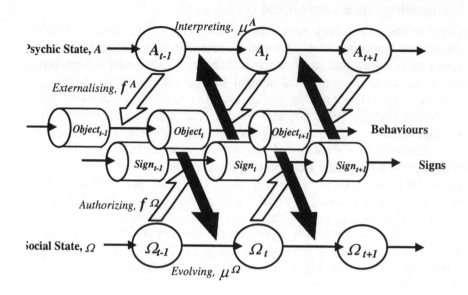

Figure 3. Semiosis of Communication

"Externalising" and "Interpreting" are operators that represent the uttering and the understanding processes, respectively; likewise, "Authorizing" and "Evolving" represent the corresponding (implied) processes of social dynamics. In these formulas, neither "social" nor "personal" time is given explicitly, but by the effect they have on the semiosis processes.

The pair of the simultaneous equations (2.1-2.2) allows us to conceptually characterize communication as a complex semiosis process (also see Figure 3). It should be noted that the number of equations of the form (2.1) and (2.2) necessary to define a particular communication depends on the number of psychic and social systems involved. It is also noteworthy that for all the systems, the state at time t does not necessarily differ from the state at time $t+1$, and for a psychic system engaged in communication, it is not necessary to produce *Objects* to receive *Signs*.

To refine and formalize the proposed conceptual framework, i.e. appropriate for computer treatment, the apparatus of algebraic semiotics can be used (Goguen, 1999). For the purposes of this chapter, it suffices to consider a sign system Ξ as a logical theory that consists of sets of signs (that are not the same as *Signs*, and that are usually understood as symbols), which have sorts arranged in a partial hierarchy, together with some operators, relations, and axioms. We will call a semiotic morphism $f:\Xi\rightarrow\Xi'$ a mapping (translation) from a sign system Ξ to a sign system Ξ'. This mapping is composed of partial functions defined on the sign system elements, and it preserves some of the structure of the first system (although not important for the presented study, formal details of the definitions can be found in Goguen, 1999).

Let us introduce the notion of a basic semiotic component as follows:

$$\mu_{t+1} : f_t[\Xi_t] \xrightarrow{\quad P_{t+1} \quad} \Xi_{t+1}, \qquad (3)$$

where f_t is a (composition of) semiotic morphism(s) that specifies the dynamics of signs in Ξ_t, and μ_{t+1} is a *"probabilistic" semiotic morphism* that represents a set of L_{t+1} possible translations (i.e. semiotic morphisms) from Ξ_t to Ξ_{t+1} with probabilities $P_{t+1} = \{p_1, p_2, ..., p_{L_{t+1}}\}$, one for each translation.

Axiomatic basis and essential derivations

Inspired by the conceptual compatibility of semiotics and quantum physics (see Nadin, 2000), we will now introduce an axiomatic basis for a semiotic theory of communication as follows.

Axiom I. Each psychic system can be represented by a sign system Ξ. The state of the psychic system – the psychic state – is fully described by a set of related signs in Ξ. ◆

Definition 1. Two states of the psychic system, α and β, are called orthogonal, written $\alpha \perp \beta$, if α implies the negation of β, or vice versa. ◆

Definition 2. For a subset of states $A \subset \Xi$, its orthogonal complement is $A^{\perp} = \{\alpha \in A \,|\, \forall \alpha' \in A^{\perp} : \alpha \perp \alpha'\}$. ◆

Definition 3. $A \subset \Xi$ is orthogonally closed if $A = A^{\perp\perp}$. ◆

Definition 4. We will call *Object* an orthogonally closed set of psychic states with a single *Interpretant* understood as a distinction. ◆

An interpretant is hence a psychic state but also the result of interpretation.

Axiom II. Immediately after the interpretation of an *Object* standing for some psychic states γ, which resulted in α, the psychic system is represented by α, i.e. the original states γ are translated to the *Interpretant* α by the interpretation. ◆

Similarly with a quantum system, the psychic system is *normally in multiple states simultaneously,* and it cannot be uniquely interpreted: at every single moment, more than just one interpretation of the psychic system state can be made. This is postulated with the following *context principle*:

Proposition I. For every two distinct psychic states $\alpha \neq \beta \subset \Xi$, there exists a context state $\alpha \cup \beta = \gamma \subset \Xi$ such that $\forall \delta \subset \Xi$, if $\delta \perp \alpha$ and $\delta \perp \beta$, then $\delta \perp \gamma$. ◆

Axiom III. Each interpreted psychic state can be represented in a unique way by a probabilistic semiotic morphism μ with $P = \{p_1, p_2, ..., p_L\}$ on Ξ. The probabilities of the morphism correspond to the possible interpretation results. ◆

Hence, an interpretant exists always only to the extent that the corresponding psychic states (i.e. the domain of μ) are accessible for interpretation.

Axiom IV. For a psychic system engaged in communication, the dynamics of the communication process are given by a pair of sequences of basic semiotic components defined recurrently as follows:

$$A = \{M^A, P^A, F^A, \Xi_{objects}\}, \tag{4.1}$$

and

$$\Omega = \{M^\Omega, P^\Omega, F^\Omega, \Xi_{signs}\}, \tag{4.2}$$

where A is the model of the psychic system that includes M^A, a set of semiotic morphisms μ_{t+1}, P^A, a set of probabilities for each μ_{t+1} in M^A, F^A, a set of semiotic morphisms f_t, $t=1,...,K$, $\Xi_{objects} = \overset{M}{\underset{m=1}{Y}} Object_m$, and M is the number of the interpretants by the psychic system prior to the communication. Ω is the model of the social system with analogously defined M^Ω, P^Ω, and F^Ω, and $\Xi_{signs} = \overset{N}{\underset{n=1}{Y}} \Xi_{objects_n}$, where N is the number of psychic systems constituting the social system. ◆

It can be observed that A and Ω correspond to the representations of (2.1) and (2.2), respectively. μ-type morphisms are to define the internal dynamics – state transition – of the psychic (social) system caused by interpretation (evolving, in the case of social systems), and P is to reflect the indirect character of state representation (i.e. potentially multiple meanings of the same object or potentially multiple objects of the same sign). f-type morphisms are to specify the process of "externalising" the system's inner state. $\Xi_{objects}$ is, in effect, the psychic system's language that reflects the individual's communication experience, and Ξ_{signs} is the language of the social system. The cognitive and social dynamics of the communication process are specified with the morphisms of A and Ω, respectively.

Axiom V defines communication as the interaction – coupling – between the two self-organizing systems, where one system – psychic – may be affected by signs and produces objects (behaviour), and another system – social – may be affected by objects and produces signs (see Figure 3). Both systems are defined in a quite deterministic manner, but their numerous constituents and sensitivity to the initial conditions (i.e. the history given with $\Xi_{objects}$ and Ξ_{signs}) make the communication process, although controllable in principle, hard to model and predict. The coupling of the systems is specified with M^A (the psychic) and F^{Ω} (the social) semiotic morphisms. The rôle of the social system is considered to filter, or authorize, communication out of behaviour but, on the other hand, to buffer behaviour against the uniformity of socio-cultural norms. The social system is not to impose a "standard" of communicative behaviour, but rather to propagate regularities accounting for the possibility of coordinated behaviour.

(Closure) Theorem. A communication is orthogonally closed:

   a) *pragmatically* through the laws of nature in the sense that given an interpretant *Interpretant$_t$*, it is only the physical laws that determine its object *Object$_t$* so that *Object$_t$* = *Object$_t{}^{\perp\perp}$*;
   b) *semantically* through the psychic system in the sense that $\Xi_{objects} = \Xi_{objects}{}^{\perp\perp}$, and
   c) *syntactically* through the social system in the sense that $\Xi_{signs} = \Xi_{signs}{}^{\perp\perp}$.

Proof:

   a) If there is exactly one object *Object* with a single interpretant, the closure is self-evident. Let us then consider two psychic states $\alpha \neq \beta$ characterized by two objects *Object$_1$* $\neq$ *Object$_2$* with the same interpretant *Interpretant*. Whenever physically possible, one can define *Object$_3$* $\subset$ *Object$_1$* $\cup$ *Object$_2$* characterizing some γ, $\gamma \neq \alpha$ and $\gamma \neq \beta$, that has the same interpretant. Since *Object$_3$* $\cap$ *Object$_1$* $\neq \varnothing$ and *Object$_3$* $\cap$ *Object$_2$* $\neq \varnothing$, the state γ cannot be determined orthogonal to α or to β. Furthermore, for all the states δ, $\delta \perp \alpha$ and $\delta \perp \beta$, with objects *Object$_4$* having interpretants different from the *Interpretant*, *Object$_4$* $\cap$ (*Object$_1$* $\cup$ *Object$_2$*) = $\varnothing$, $\delta \perp \gamma$ as $\delta \cap \gamma = \varnothing$. Hence, extending to an arbitrary number of

Objects, given a set of psychic states and a distinction of these states by an interpretant, ultimately it is only the physical laws determining the psychic states – *the ultimate pragmatics of the situation* – that limit the possible *Objects* of the interpretant.

b) Provided that $Object_m = Object_m^{\perp\perp}$ for $m=1,...,M$, then $\Xi_{objects} = \Xi_{objects}^{\perp\perp}$, as $\Xi_{objects} = \overset{M}{\underset{m=1}{Y}} Object_m$ by definition.

Hence, given a psychic system and a distinction classification of its states by interpretants, it is only this classification – the *semantics* of the *Objects* – that determines the objects for the psychic system.

c) Provided that $Object_m = Object_m^{\perp\perp}$ and $\Xi_{objects} = \Xi_{objects}^{\perp\perp}$, then $\Xi_{signs} = \Xi_{signs}^{\perp\perp}$, as $\Xi_{signs} = \overset{N}{\underset{n=1}{Y}} \Xi_{objects_n}$, $n=1,...,N$, by definition. Hence, tautologically, the possible signs for the social system – the *syntax* of the *Signs* – are determined by the *Objects* of the psychic systems constituting it. ◆

It follows directly from the above theorem that psychic states corresponding to every physically possible *Object* should, in principle, uniquely be determined as characteristic of the given communication situation, but also that the *Object* corresponding to each psychic state does not have to be unique. Besides, the theorem dictates that every single communication is orthogonally closed only to a degree. Indeed, given a communication situation, its pragmatic closure can be established if one considers a typically huge number of *Objects* – in fact, all possible *Objects*, which are to express the physical frames of the situation and to establish the interpretant that is the corresponding psychic state (e.g. a perception or emotion). The latter is not a practical case unless one considers learning by trial and error or a similar process, and *Objects* are the result of some relations (not necessarily conventions) developed from individual experience rather than exhaustive representations of the psychic state. Furthermore, semantic closure is hardly obtainable, because to exist, it requires the definition of all the *Objects* for all the psychic states. This is unrealistic owing to the spatio-temporal dynamics uniquely allocating each psychic system every time, the indirect character of interpretant assessment, and the natural cognitive limitations (e.g. the memory limits). This, as well as the fact that social systems are generally dynamic in respect to their psychic constituents, makes the achievement of syntactic closure unfeasible, too. Hence, *every single communication is uncertain*.

The goal (or motivation) of a communication for a psychic system can be understood as *to reach a certain psychic state through perturbations by signs*. To initiate communication, the psychic system has to build a "model" of the corresponding social system – i.e. it has to make some assumptions, or anticipations, about the social language, as well as a "plan" or "strategy" for the interaction; it also has to interpret some of the Ξ_{signs}. On the other hand, as soon as the psychic system is involved in communication, it becomes part of the social system so that some of its *Objects* may be interpreted and thus become elements of Ξ_{signs}. It can be shown that having defined the orthogonal syntactic (semantic) closure, one can always reconstruct the state(s) of the social (psychic) system, though not the system itself, as there will always be an uncertainty caused by the "externality" – in respect to the social (psychic) system – of the pragmatic closure. The better the reconstruction, the more precise the corresponding model of Ξ_{signs} ($\Xi_{objects}$) and, naturally, the more efficient – for the psychic system and in the sense of minimizing the requisite interaction – the communication process built on the model.

Lemma I. Given a communication situation with a pragmatic uncertainty *Const* independent of time, a natural limitation on the minimal (communication) requisite interaction for a psychic system engaged in the communication is determined by the degree of the communication closure $E_{O,M}$. The latter is inversely proportional to the communication uncertainty and can be estimated using the following formula ($E_{O,M} \in [0,1]$, $E_{O,M}=1$ is for   the   absolute certainty)

$$E_{O,M} = k_s \sum_{i=1}^{M} \left(\sum_{j=1}^{M} \frac{N_{Int}(Object_i \cap Object_j)}{N_{Int}(Object_i \cup Object_j)} - 1 \right) + k_c \sum_{i=1}^{O} \left(\sum_{j=1}^{O} \frac{N_{Int}(Sign_i \cap Sign_j)}{N_{Int}(Sign_i \cup Sign_j)} - 1 \right) - Const =$$

$$= k_s \sum_{i=1}^{M} \left(\sum_{j=1}^{M} \frac{N_{Int}(Object_i \cap Object_j)}{N_{Int}(Object_i) + N_{Int}(Object_j) - N_{Int}(Object_i \cap Object_j)} - 1 \right) +$$

$$+ k_c \sum_{i=1}^{O} \left(\sum_{j=1}^{O} \frac{N_{Int}(Sign_i \cap Sign_j)}{N_{Int}(Sign_i) + N_{Int}(Sign_j) - N_{Int}(Sign_i \cap Sign_j)} - 1 \right) - Const,$$

(5)

where M is the number of *Objects* produced by the psychic system in the given communication, O is the number of *Signs* received by the psychic system, $N_{Int}(Object_i)$ is the number of interpretants by the psychic system for the same object $Object_i$, $N_{Int}(Object_i \cap Object_j)$ is the number of interpretants for both $Object_i$ and $Object_j$, $N_{Int}(Sign_i)$ is the number of interpretants of the same sign $Sign_i$ in the social system, $N_{Int}(Sign_i \cap Sign_j)$ is the number of common interpretants of $Sign_i$ and $Sign_j$, k_c and k_s are normalizing coefficients, and *Const* is a constant determined by the degree of pragmatic closure. Note that generally, $M \neq O$.

Proof:
    Let us first consider α, a set of psychic states corresponding to a certain communication situation. Let $Object_\alpha = f(\alpha)$ be the result of the externalisation of α (see Axiom IV). If the object $Object_\alpha$ uniquely determines the situation, we shall then expect, owing to Axiom II, that

$\mu(Object_\alpha)=\alpha$; otherwise if $\mu(Object_\alpha)=\alpha'\neq\alpha$, the communication is not pragmatically closed. In the latter case, the pragmatic uncertainty (as opposed to the closure) Up is directly proportional to L, the number of different interpretants of $Object_\alpha$ (i.e. distinct psychic states resultant from $\mu(Object_\alpha)$), and it defines the minimal requisite interaction (i.e. externalisation/interpretation trials) to describe the situation so that each of the interpretants corresponds to a physical distinction of the situation. Let us now consider a sequence of objects $Object_i$, $i=1,...,M$, determining a communication situation. The semantic uncertainty of the sequence Us depends upon the corresponding F^A and is directly proportional to the total number of interpretants of the objects but, by the Context Principle, it is inversely proportional to the number of common interpretants of the objects. Given a sequence of signs $Sign_j$, $j=1,...,O$, describing a communication, the communication syntactic uncertainty Uc depends upon the corresponding F^Ω and is directly proportional to the total number of interpretants of the signs but is inversely proportional to the number of common interpretants of the signs. It is obvious that $(Us + Uc)/2 \geq Up$ (equal when $\Xi_{signs} \subseteq \Xi_{objects}$, F^A and F^Ω are isomorphisms, and M^Ω preserves all the elements on which F^Ω are defined), and $E_{O,M}$ can now be obtained through normalizing transformations, as a difference of the left and right parts of this inequality. ◆

It should be noted that $E_{O,M}$ as an estimation of the minimal requisite interaction is not generally applicable to an on-going communication unless the principal parameters of the social and psychic systems remain constant from the time of estimation and including the time of communication.

$E_{O,M}$ can also be seen as a measure inversely proportional to the density of meaning (i.e. interpretants) for the psychic system in the given communication: lower values of $E_{O,M}$ (and higher uncertainty) are obtained in the case of general or explorative communication, while a communication on a specific subject typically produces a higher $E_{O,M}$ (and lower uncertainty).

The probabilities necessary to define the dynamics of the psychic system (see Axiom IV) can be estimated based on the following axiom:

Axiom V. For a psychic system in a state $\gamma \subset \Xi$, the real number $\Pi(\gamma,\alpha)$, where Π is an operator measuring the semantic distance and α is resultant from μ, is inversely proportional to and, in this way, determines the probability of obtaining the interpretation α when μ. For $\alpha \not\subset \Xi$ and $\alpha \perp \gamma$, $\Pi(\gamma,\alpha)=\infty$; furthermore, $\Pi(\gamma,\alpha)=0$ for $\alpha=\gamma$. ◆

If we disregard the dynamics of the psychic system (i.e. the meaning change) and for a sufficiently large number of observations, or interpretation trials, M, the semantic distance can be estimated using the notion of semantic closure:

$$\Pi(\gamma,\alpha) \cong \frac{1}{M} \sum_{i=1}^{M} \left[\frac{N_{Int}^{i}(Object_{\gamma}) + N_{Int}(Object_{\alpha})}{N_{Int}^{i}(Object_{\alpha} \quad Object_{\gamma})} \quad 2 \right]. \qquad (6)$$

One can show how formula (6) draws on a generalization of the Bayes axiom for conditional probability (Heylighen, 1990). It is apparent that the probabilities for the model of the social system can be analogously estimated.

Given $C=\{S_1,S_2,...,S_K\}$ a time-sequence characterizing semiosis processes of a communication, the behavioural coordination COR of the involved psychic systems can be estimated using the following formula:

$$COR(t) = k_b \sum_{i=1}^{K} \frac{N_{Int}(Sign_t \quad Sign_i)}{N_{Int}(Sign_t) + N_{Int}(Sign_i) - N_{Int}(Sign_t \quad Sign_i)} - 1, \qquad (7)$$

where $t=1,...,K$, and k_b is a normalizing coefficient.

$COR(t)$ shows how the syntactic uncertainty is changed through communication: as behavioural coordination produces contextual relations between signs, it should reduce the number of distinct psychic states associated with the given communication situation.

PILOT STUDY

Typically, to initiate communication with or within a distributed information system, a user must formulate a query representing her or his goal in terms of the system (social) language. This query can then be submitted to a search engine, which is often part of the system, and the user is suggested to browse across hyperlinks generated by the search engine to find and retrieve information of interest. Otherwise, to locate a particular resource, the user can be suggested to browse through a pre-defined hyperlink tree or network that reflects the social language. In both cases, the communication is considered successful if the information obtained through the interaction assists the user in achieving her or his goal or preferred state.

Previously, we have argued that there are two major problems in designing user interfaces of distributed information systems (Kryssanov *et al.*, 2002): 1) how to make the system language comprehensible to every user, given that this language has internal social dynamics resulting from the changing contents of the system and/or the shifting consumption trends in the community of the system users, and 2) how to reduce the number of interactions necessary to obtain information of interest, which may become unacceptably large for information systems comprising numerous digital documents, as in the case of the World-Wide Web or a corporate memory system.

In an attempt to find ways to resolve these problems, we have developed an adaptive user interface for a multimedia distributed information system. The interface dynamically builds models of the user's psychic states in terms of Ξ_{signs}, the language of the social system, for which the information system stands, and helps the user minimize the number of user-computer interactions necessary to reach the user's goal-state. In other words, the interface helps to increase the efficiency of communication.

With the developed interface, a user initiates communication by producing an *Object* – submitting a query to a search engine seen as an interface of the information system, which then generates a hit list composed of hyperlinks to digital documents. These documents contain *Signs*, not necessarily text, which may bring (through interpretation) the user's psychic system to its goal or preferred state. Thus, the hit list reflects the user's goal state but it also represents the state of the social system associated with the search engine at the time of the query. Based on training examples of the relevant and non-relevant documents pointed to by the user (i.e. a distinction classification), the interface develops some $F^{A'}$ that is to map the user's psychic state onto a language having a syntactic uncertainty for the given social system lower than in the case of F^A "intrinsic" to the user. The morphisms are used to create filtering rules, which are applied to select links from the hit list to the documents that are likely to be relevant. In the course of communication, the training-filtering cycle can be repeated until the user obtains a manageable volume of information and/or reaches the goal state. The detailed process is in five stages:

1. **Initial search**: A user inputs a query – keywords as *Objects*– to the system. An initial hit list is generated.

2. **Evaluation of results**: The user estimates the relevancy of the first N (usually ≤ 10) documents from the list. The system stores the relevant pages as positive training examples and the non-relevant documents as negative training examples.

3. **Analysis of training pages**: Made in two steps:

    a) <u>Generation of extended keywords</u>: Extended keywords are *Signs* that are results of $F^{A'}$. To develop $F^{A'}$ based on the training examples, the TFIDF method (Joachims, 1997) is used.

    b) <u>Generation of literals for filtering rules</u>: By utilizing the extended keywords, the system constructs conditional parts for filtering rules.

4. **Generation of filtering rules**: With a learning algorithm, the system generates a set of filtering rules.

5. **Selection of the relevant documents**: The system selects the documents satisfying the filtering rules from the hit list.

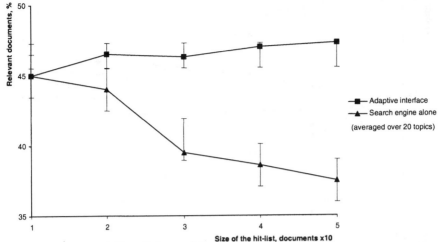

Figure 4. The efficiency of the communication process

To estimate the efficiency of the developed adaptive interface, two retrieval experiments have been made. In the first experiment, a fixed number of digital documents from the top of a hit list returned by a conventional search engine were judged regarding their relevancy to the goal-state. A set of filtering rules was build, based on training examples provided by the user, and the rules were applied to select the same number of documents from the original full-length hit list. The relevancy of the selected documents was then judged. Google (http://www.google.com) was used as the test search engine, and 20 different topics were chosen as *Interpretants* for 20 different goal-states. Relevance judgment in each case was made by the same person.

Figure 4 shows the results of the experiment. It can be seen that the adaptive interface can increase the efficiency of communication by decreasing the number of necessary user-computer interactions in the case of high syntactic uncertainty (i.e. in the case when the same keywords are used to index a vast number of documents).

In the second experiment, we have estimated the behavioural coordination by calculating *COR(t)* for communication conducted by an experienced system user (the expert), by a user with no *a-priori* knowledge of the system language (the non-expert), and by a non-expert using the adaptive interface. To calculate *COR(t)* (see formula (7)), keywords were used as *Signs* by assuming that the indexed documents correspond to *Interpretants* (i.e. one interpretant per every distinct document). Figure 5 depicts the results of the experiment for the first 5 *Signs*: the thin marked lines show the behavioural coordination for a typical single communication by the three users, and the bold show the average of over 20 communications on different topics. It should be understood that while *COR(t)* is discrete by its very nature, the lines were drawn to show the characteristic trends.

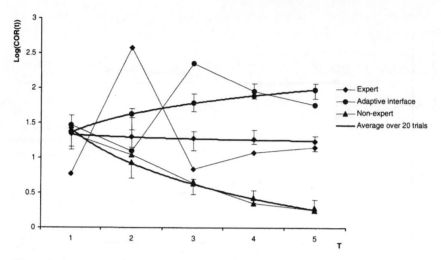

Figure 5. Communication as behavioral coordination

The figure shows that the (syntactic) uncertainty of communication by the expert quickly converges to certain value as in this case, there is no or almost no learning of the social language, and this value is likely to correspond with the minimal requisite interaction for the user for the given system. In the case of the first non-expert, the uncertainty of communication is increased through observation that may mostly be due to learning about the system (social) language. Finally, the uncertainty of communication by the non-expert with the adaptive interface quickly converges to low values corresponding to better behavioural coordination compared to the first non-expert. For the latter, the question remains if the interface is "too adaptive" so that it filters out too many relevant documents not covered by the training samples. This, however, does not refer to the communication process, but to the ability of the user to provide "good" training examples.

There are two main lessons learnt from the pilot study: 1) the conceptual framework formulated in the previous sections provides useful guidelines for designing and understanding user interfaces, and 2) the developed axiomatic basis allows the derivation of meaningful characteristics quantitatively describing communication as a socio-cognitive process.

RELATED WORK AND CONCLUSIONS

The proposed system-theoretic semiotic theory of communication rests on the "dynamic semiotics" conceptual framework introduced by Peter B. Andersen (Andersen, 2002). In our study, however, we pursued a more pragmatic goal – to develop a theoretical basis that could be applied for the design and analysis of user interfaces of distributed information systems. In this chapter, we, in fact, presented a novel theory for the study of communication, and the work by Francis Heylighen (Heylighen, 1990), which discusses representation problems in modern physics, influenced us to formulate the basics of the theory as axioms that are about semiosis of communication, though not about representation or re-representation. Our concept of *Objects* is somewhat similar to Gibson's *affordances* – behavioural patterns of physical or biological significance (Gibson, 1979), while our *Signs* might be thought of as *norms* – the social counterpart of affordances (i.e. socially created patterns of behaviour) – one of the key concepts developed by Stamper's organizational semiotics school (Stamper, 1996). In a sense refining Stamper's idealistic claim about subjectivism of perceived reality, we argue that no communication is possible without shared, physically grounded experience. Nevertheless, this is not to say that we adhere to an "extremist" collectivist point of view that communication is in principle irreducible to individualistic level descriptions, as advocated by N. Luhmann (Luhmann, 1995). Rather, we attempt to explain how social behaviour emerges from purely deterministic individual accounts, and how this behaviour affects individual experiences.

Philosophically speaking, our work does not generally deny the canonical concept of "ever unbroken" semiotic triad (Peirce, 1998), though it comes to a principally new level of description of semiosis processes (specifically – communication semiosis) by focusing on the synchronous development of its elements – object/interpretant and sign – separately, as products of the different psychic and social complex systems. In this way, we support the seemingly "revisionist" statement that "not all triadic sign systems are complete" (see Gazendam, this volume) by discriminating between the personal and the social sign systems and allowing for their independent dynamics. We also show how the definition of communication as coordinated behaviour builds on the existence, in principle, of completed semiotic triads.

One may consider this work as an effort to systematize and lay a scientific foundation for the analysis of the current technological trends in user interface design. The technique of creating "individual profiles" (Pretschner & Gauch, 1999) is frequently used to utilize subjective semantics of a single user. To elicit and make use of the language of a particular social group, the technique of "collaborative filtering" (Terveen & Hill, 2001) is employed. The application of these techniques to the development of adaptive interfaces is particularly based on some empirical and/or "common sense" considerations rather than on a theory or model of human-computer interaction. The system-theoretic semiotic explanation offered in this chapter gives an integral framework for the analysis and application of the adaptive techniques in user interface design. One warning should accompany this framework though: by definition, communication is possible only when the psychic system is coupled with the social system, i.e. when the user undergoes self-adaptation (due to Axiom II) rather than adaptation to the environment. The social system should also self-adapt to preserve the coupling. Reasoning in this way makes the adaptation-oriented techniques questionable in the sense of the necessity to examine what really reflects a particular individual or collaborative profile (e.g. adaptation *vs.* self-adaptation) and how it may influence communication.

The main contribution of the presented study is a new communication theory that offers a uniform and consistent basis for the description of the communication process, its goal, dynamics, and overall efficiency. While the current formulation of the theory mainly focuses on communication phenomena at the "micro" level (as for a psychic system), in our future research we plan to elaborate it so as to define the time-development of the social system – i.e. to specify communication at the "macro" level. The development of methodologies and principles for the practical application of the theory is another important direction for future work.

ACKNOWLEDGEMENT

The presented study has been made within the Universal Design of Digital City project of the Core Research for Evolutional Science and Technology programme funded by the Japan Science and Technology Corporation.

REFERENCES

Andersen, P. B. (2002). Dynamic semiotics. *Semiotica, 139*, 161-210.

Andersen, P. B. (2001). What semiotics can and cannot do for HCI. *Knowledge Based Systems, 14(8)*, 419-424.

Beaudouin-Lafon, M. (2000). Instrumental interaction: An interaction model for designing post-WIMP user interfaces. In T. Turner, G. Szwillus, M. Czerwinski, & F. Paterno (Eds.), *Proceedings of the CHI 2000 conference* (pp. 446-453). Amsterdam.

Condon, C. (2000). *A semiotic approach to the use of metaphor in human-computer interfaces.* Unpublished Ph.D. Thesis, Department of Information Systems and Computing, Brunel University.

Di Paolo, E.A. (1998). An investigation into the evolution of communication. *Adaptive Behavior, 6(2)*, 285-324.

Eco, U. (1976). *A theory of semiotics.* Bloomington: Indiana University Press.

Gibson J. J. (1979). *The ecological approach to visual perception.* Boston: Houghton Mifflin Company.

Goguen, J. A. (1999). Social and semiotic analyses for theorem prover user interface design. *Formal Aspects of Computing, 11*, 272-301.

Heylighen, F. (1990). Classical and non-classical representations in physics II: Quantum mechanics. *Cybernetics and Systems, 21*, 477-502.

Joachims, T. (1997). A probabilistic analysis of the Rocchio algorithm with TFIDF for text categorization, *Proc. of the 14th International Conference on Machine Learning ICML97* (pp.143-151).

Kryssanov, V. V., Okabe, M., Kakusho, K., & Minoh, M. (2002). Communication in Digital Cities. *Artificial Intelligence and Knowledge-Based Processing, 101(535)* [The IEICE Technical Report], 33-40.

Luhmann, N. (1995). *Social systems.* Palo Alto: Stanford University Press

Maturana, H., & Varela, F. J. (1980). *Autopoiesis and cognition: The realization of the living.* Dordrecht: D. Reidel Publishing Company.

Nadin, M. (2000). Anticipation: A spooky computation. *Int. J. Computing Anticipatory Systems, 6.*

Peirce, C.S. (1998). *The essential Peirce: Selected philosophical writings.* Bloomington: Indiana University Press.

Pretschner, A., & Gauch, S. (1999). *Personalization on the web* (Technical Report ITTC-FY2000-TR-13591-01). Lawrence, KS, The University of Kansas, Information and Telecommunication Technology Center (ITTC).

Schmidt-Isler, S. (2000). The language of digital genres: A semiotic investigation of style and iconology on the World Wide Web. In E. Sprague (Ed.), *Proceedings of the 33rd Hawaii International Conference on System Sciences.* Los Alamitos: IEEE Computer Society.

Shannon, C. E., & Weaver, W. (1963). *The Mathematical Theory of Communication.* University of Illinois Press

Sonesson, G. (2002, to appear). *The act of interpretation. A view form semiotics.* Sâo Paolo: Galáxia.

Stamper, R. (1996). Signs, information, norms and systems. In B. Holmqvist, P. B. Andersen, H. Klein, & R. Posner (Eds.), *Signs of work* (pp. 349-399). Berlin: De Gruyter.

Saussure, F. de (1974). *Course in general linguistics.* Glasgow: Fontana.

Souza, C .S. de (1993). The semiotic engineering of user interface languages. *Int. J. of Man-Machine Studies, 39,* 753-773.

Terveen, L., & Hill, W. (2001). Human-computer collaboration in recommender systems. In Carroll, J. (Ed.), *Human-Computer Interaction in the New Millennium.* Addison-Wesley.

Part II

Behaviour-oriented approaches

Chapter 3

Website interfaces as representamina of organizational behaviour

M. Cecilia C. Baranauskas, Kecheng Liu and Samuel Chong

ABSTRACT

Due to the increasing sophistication of the Internet, the role of computers as mediators has become more apparent through their applications interfaces. Despite the fact that computers have always been considered as symbolic machines, only in the last decade Semiotics has attracted the attention of researchers in studying interfaces and human-computer interaction. This chapter summarizes some of the main contributions in the field of Semiotics and Interfaces, while pointing out the needs of broadening the referential framework to cope with social issues involved in the new interfaces being created for Internet applications. We draw upon concepts of Organizational Semiotics to propose a framework to analyse interfaces of e-commerce applications focusing on aspects that include the underlying organization that the interface represents. Hereby we shed light on aspects that are not apparent in other approaches.

1. INTRODUCTION

The computer made its entrance in our culture as a tool for the exclusive domain of specialists: physicists, programmers and hardware engineers. As a consequence, the first thirty years of the computer history were marked by the design centred in the technology: people's interaction with computational artefacts had to fit a machine-centred perspective. That scenario changed radically in the last two decades; computers became integrated in most of the human occupations and were adopted by a wide spectrum of users, not to mention the widespread use of the Internet, which diversified and amplified the reach of computational applications.

In the very beginning, the areas of Human Factors in computer systems and Ergonomics grew as a result of the difficulties that computer scientists and engineers faced when they needed to consider the relationship between the systems that they were building and their potential users. Human Factors as a field of research was defined by that time as *an unruly mixture of theoretical issues and practical problems* (Shneiderman and Thomas, 1983). Since then, the central problem of psychologists, professionals of human factors and computer scientists, has been to develop theories and models of the human behaviour adequate for interactive systems. In the attempt to understand and accommodate human abilities of learning, memory constraints, and problem solving in interactive systems, aspects of the user's human nature have been considered mainly by the cognitive approaches (Card et al., 1983; Norman and Draper, 1986; Laurel, 1990), in the way of extending and refining theories of Psychology. These theories, in the eighties, led to a paradigm shift in software interface design: from a focus on the technology to the user centred perspective. In this new approach, the users' needs were to drive the design of the interface, and the needs of the interface should drive the design of the remaining system.

Norman and Draper (1986) have proposed the Theory of Action to understand how people interact with computer systems. According to that theory, people have goals expressed in terms relevant to them (psychological). On the other hand, the mechanisms and states of the system are expressed in terms relative to it (physical). The discrepancy between the psychological and the physical variables he named "gulfs", should be observed in the design, analysis and use of systems. The designer should diminish the gulfs, moving the system closer to the user; i.e. building interfaces capable of matching the user's psychological needs.

The user-centred approach taken to its extreme and misled view, allied to the sophistication of the available technological resources for designing interfaces, has confused rather than simplified the user's life. The web shows good examples of this type of phenomenon. In general, moved by commercial pressures, many websites present all types of features in their interfaces. Thereby adding to the already chaotic organization of elements in the interface affecting the user's performance.

The computer is no longer an exclusive tool for specialists, and as the sophistication of the software through the Internet increases, the demand for interpretability grows. Secretaries and managers cannot have their time wasted with difficult interpretations of the application interface; not to mention ordinary people using the Internet at home. They need to access their bank account balance, or get a new book for the weekend, or they just want to buy food without going physically to the supermarket: a good interface is a prerequisite for the new e-business enterprises survival.

Internet applications have changed the nature of using and interacting with computers. From their early conception as tools computers are more and more mediating our actions through their software interfaces. Even though computers belong to the class of symbolic engines, only in the last decade the symbolic nature of computers has attracted the attention of groups interested in studying interfaces and human-computer interaction through Semiotics. This chapter summarises some of the main contributions in the field of Semiotics and Interfaces, while pointing out the need for broadening the referential framework to cope with social issues involved in the new interfaces being created for Internet applications. We draw upon Organizational Semiotics concepts to propose a framework for analysing interfaces of Internet applications, including aspects such as the underlying organization that the interface represents. Furthermore, we point out other aspects that have not been made explicit in other approaches.

The chapter is organised as follows: Section 2 presents a brief chronological view of the main paradigms contributing to our understanding of human-computer interfaces. Section 3 presents the semiotic framework of Organizational Semiotics, which is used as a foundation for our approach to the interface analysis. Section 4 shows our understanding of the interface as a representamen in a triadic relation with an object it refers to and an interpretant. Section 5 refers to the OS theoretical foundations with regard to our understanding of communication as sharing to propose a framework for interface analysis. Section 6 illustrates the application of the framework and Section 7 comments on related work.

2. USER-COMPUTER INTERACTION ISSUES: A BRIEF RETROSPECTIVE VIEW

In the very beginning, the computer was considered a tool to facilitate human tasks with reliability and speed. The development of cognitive theories applied to the human-computer interaction provided us with a vision of the computer as a cognitive tool enabling people to extend their capacity of understanding, memorisation and decision-making. In the semiotics perspective, computers are seen as *media* (Andersen et al., 1993) in the same way as books, cinema, theatre, television, etc. The computer is a *medium* through which signs can be manifested for use in communication. We understand that the cognitive and the semiotic points of view are not antagonistic, but that they represent different perspectives for the same phenomenon.

The traditional cognitive approaches focus on the human nature of the user interacting with the interface, his motor system, his perception, learning and other mental processes. The semiotic approaches facilitate an interpersonal, social, cultural perspective, focusing on the representation, communication and signification of the elements in the software interface.

The cognitive tradition to the user interface
The tradition that has characterised the research in Human-Computer Interaction field is based on the cognitive approach. Cognition refers to the process by which we become conscious of things or, put in other words, the way in which we acquire knowledge. This includes

understanding, the ability to memorise, reasoning, attention, learning, and the creation of new ideas. The main objective of the research using this approach has been to understand and to represent the way in which humans interact with computers, in terms of the way knowledge is exchanged between them. The theoretical basis for this approach rests on Cognitive Psychology, which explains how humans reach their objectives in performing cognitive tasks that involve information processing. Thus, humans are characterised as information processors. The basic idea is that the information enters and leaves the human mind through an orderly series of processing steps (Preece et al., 1994, p. 62). The human model as a processor of information has influenced the development of several models of human-computer interaction as, for example, GOMS (Card, Moran and Newell, 1983) and the Theory of Action (Norman, 1986).

The cognitive approach can be applied with success to many problems of a human-computer interaction nature. However, there is an emerging consensus that this approach has its limitations. The information loop is closed, so it is difficult to take into consideration phenomena that exist out of that loop (Kaptelinin, 1996, p. 105). For example, the purely cognitive approach does not provide a basis to take into consideration phenomena of linguistic nature and interaction among groups of people.

Semiotic approaches, on the other hand, allow to consider not only the immediate aspects of the human-computer interaction but, also, the underlying aspects of the cultural and social context in which the interaction happens.

Semiotic approaches to interface analysis

Semiotics is the science of the signs which is aimed at examining the constitution of any phenomenon of the signification and creation of meaning. The Peircean School of Semiotics, one of the most influential, defines a sign as anything that stands for something else for somebody under certain aspects or capacities (Peirce, 1932).

Interface has been widely defined under several points of view. For Andersen (1997, p. 201), *interface is a collection of computer-based signs, i.e., all parts of the system processes that are seen or heard, used and interpreted by a community of users.* This definition presents a relationship between the perceptible parts of a computer system and its users. To illustrate the idea of a computer-based sign, he exemplifies this with the "pencil" present in most drawing applications, which differs from the concrete tool in the sense that it is not being used primarily as a physical object, but as a sign.

> *The pencil of the drawing program is no real pencil that can be used to chew on, it merely stands for a pencil, represented by a collection of pixels on the screen.* (Andersen, 1997, p. 1)

Andersen proposes a paradigm change for the interface concept that involves our understanding of the computer science itself: from the computational system seen as a self-sufficient mathematical object, the focus is gradually moved toward the relationships between the system and the work context. In this sense, *the role of the computer system is basically that of a medium - a physical substance in which signs can be manifested, one that can be - and is - used in communication* (Andersen, 1997, p. 333).

Our understanding of communication is not limited to its physical sense of information transmission, but presupposes that the signal transmitted rouses an interpretative answer in the receptor, as discussed in Eco (1976:8-9). Thus in our understanding of human-computer interface, processes of signification turn into focus. This perspective seems to fit in with the new scenario of using the Internet technology, where the function of communication among people through the interface plays a fundamental role.

Having recognised the fact that computers are basically sign processors and that Semiotics is the science of the signs and their function in society, we can make use of semiotic principles to improve the communication function of the interfaces. In this direction, Jorna (1996) suggests three perspectives to be differentiated in the analysis of the information contained in the interface of computational systems: high level theories about the interaction among task-computer-user, general structure of the information in the screen and elements inside that structure of presentation. While the signs on the screen *instigate users to accomplish actions* (Jorna, 1996, p. 241), the amount of signs in the interface influences the time required for human processing, and the type of signs affects the species of involved processes (Nadin 1988). Therefore, the type and number of signs that compose the interface, as well as the ways of inferring aspects in terms of their interpretability should be considered in a semiotic framework for interface analysis.

Current literature concerning methods for user interface analysis and evaluation has not paid sufficient attention to the social and organizational aspects that surround the user experience. The need to take into consideration social aspects involved in the design and use of software applications seems to be much more significant with the Internet as medium of communication. Communication is essentially a social affair. As pointed out by Cherry (1980, p.3), when people are in communication with one another, they are associating, cooperating, and forming an "organization". This chapter aims to integrate some Organizational Semiotic principles into the user interface analysis, as a way of illustrating aspects of communication and signification brought about by the organization that the interface represents.

3. ORGANIZATIONAL SEMIOTICS AS A THEORETICAL FOUNDATION

Organizational Semiotics is a discipline that explores the use of signs and its social effects within a social setting. An actualist position has been accepted as the basic philosophy for developing organization semiotics as a discipline (Stamper 2000, Chong 2001). In contrast to the realist account, which assumes that the world consists of an absolute truth and can be readily observed and expressed, the actualist account of the nature of reality assumes a world to which we have access only via our actions or behaviour mediated by signs. In this work we are considering the semiotic approach of Stamper (1973), which is based on the works of Peirce (1932) and Morris (1985) and which has evolved into a set of semiotic methods for Information Systems. Stamper, quoted in Liu (2000), proposed a new paradigm for Information Systems Design grounded in the *information field* concept. As opposed to the concept of *information flow*, which is the basis for most of the conventional information systems approaches, the information field paradigm helps us to obtain a macro perspective for system design. This paradigm is based on the analogy with the several internal and external fields an object is subject to (gravitational, electromagnetic, tensional, etc.). In the same way, human agents involved in the use of computational systems are all governed by the forces of information fields and therefore behave accordingly. These forces are present in the forms of formal and informal rules, beliefs, cultural habits and conventions, which can be called norms. Underlying this approach, there is a stance that rejects the position taken by many practitioners in the field according to which information systems are seen as devices for representing and interacting with an objective reality. On the opposite, Stamper's approach is based on the assumption that the world is socially and subjectively constructed. This subjective view of information systems is in line with assumptions we have to make when considering the user experience enabled by an interface.

The Organizational Semiotics approach takes a step towards an understanding of the whole organization, stressing the distinctions as well as the interdependent links between the organization, the business process and the IT system (Liu, 2000). Organization is taken here in a broad sense, meaning a group of people, a society, a culture, which not only share rules of language, custom, habit, but also participate in the social construction of these rules. According to Stamper's approach, an organization can be characterised by a structure of three embedded layers: the informal, the formal and the technical, which Stamper (1992) names "the organizational onion". The whole organization is regarded as an informal information system in which its culture – values, beliefs, habits and pattern of behaviour of each individual member – plays an important role. It is in this layer that meanings are established, intentions are understood, beliefs are formed, commitments are made and responsibilities are negotiated through discussion and physical actions. Inside the informal layer there is the formal information system layer, where literate culture dominates by means of rules that specify how the work should be done and how the tasks should be performed. In this layer, form and rule replace meaning and intention. The third layer concerns the technical system that is placed inside the formal layer to automate part of the formal system. It presupposes well-defined work processes, clearly understood human responsibilities for the jobs and explicitly specified rules for operations. Therefore, in analysing the user interface of computer applications, we must be aware that the system is a reflex of the formal and informal layers of the organization that it represents.

Thus, on the one hand, we have the subjective reality constructed by the user through his/her experience using the interface. On the other hand, the interface is a reflex of the formal and informal layers of the organization it represents.

Besides syntactics, semantics and pragmatics of the original Semiotics, which deal with structures, meanings and usage of signs, Stamper has added three other divisions: physics, empirics, and social world (Figure 1). The physics and empirics are concerned with the physical aspects of signs and their statistical properties when different media are involved. Together with syntactics, they constitute the infrastructure to support the other three layers: semantics, pragmatics and social world. The three lower layers will answer questions referring to how signs are organised and expressed, as well as the physical properties they have, while the upper layers are concerned with the use of signs, how they function in communicating meanings and intentions, and the social consequences of using signs.

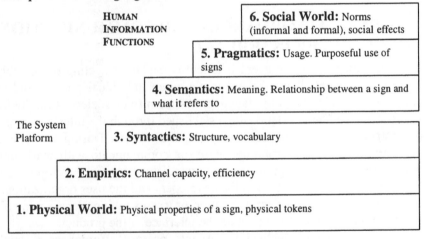

Figure 1. Stamper's semiotic framework (adapted from Liu (2000), p.27)

Here, we acknowledge the discussion with regard to the distinction made by Stamper between pragmatics and the social world, carried out by some authors. Goldkuhl and Agerfalk (2000, p.8) argue that *"these two levels are so intertwined that distinguishing them is probably not only conceptually inelegant, but also misleading"*. The same authors explain their arguments stating that pragmatic intentions are usually directed from one actor to another and so they are social by nature. Taking intentionally arranged signs related to action, it is impossible to study the pragmatic level of the semiotic framework without relying on the social world level (Goldkuhl and Agerfalk, 2001). This theoretical discussion has also been extended to the distinctions between semantics vs. pragmatics, which *"may sound clear enough in theory, but when it comes down to practical applications there is often disagreement about where the line should be drawn..."*(Goddard, quoted in Falkenberg, 2000, p.58). We recognise the difficulty of making a clear cut between these layers (pragmatics and social world, semantics and pragmatics); nevertheless, the distinction seems to be useful to a certain extent, in our case study, as a way of guiding our analysis to different foci. From the user interface standpoint, these six layers determine different aspects of the experience a user will have as an active participant (an agent) in the interface signs system. As discussed by Stamper (1993:12), society can be understood as people and groups of people behaving according to shared norms, and "communication" is a reflection of the generation of "community" or shared norms. By making salient the sixth layer we should be able to analyse the "social communication" between the two communities (end-user and organization), according to the extent to which they make explicit responsibilities and shared norms.

The two main categories of the construction blocks of the world from the OS perspective are the concepts of *agent* and *affordance*. Despite having a context-sensitive definition, in the next section we discuss the concepts of the OS and the HCI standpoints.

4. AGENTS, AFFORDANCES AND COMMUNICATION THROUGH THE INTERFACE

In the OS framework, an agent is an entity capable of acting responsibly in an environment. It can be as simple as an individual person, and as complex as a cultural group, language community or society (Liu, 2000). In the agent-computer relationship established through the interface, many other agents, besides the user, play important roles. During the design process, designers and usability engineers communicate with marketing people; the customer support team intermediates between developers and users; external consultants help the developers and the user organizations, etc. The interaction and communication processes taking place among all these agents also have an impact on the interface of the product.

Behaviour affords behaviour. Agents possess affordances through their patterns of behaviour and, at the same time, they are subjects of the affordances of the objects they interact with. The concept of a*ffordance* has been mentioned by influent authors in the HCI field (Norman, 1988; Winograd, 1996; Preece et al, 2002; Shneiderman, 1998) usually to refer to the affordances of objects. Nevertheless, the richest and most elaborate affordances of the environment for the humans are provided by other people, as they interact with the observer and with one another (Gibson 1968, 1979; Michaels & Carello 1980).

The concept of "affordance" was first proposed by Gibson, in the ecological approach to visual perception, for designating the behaviour of an organism made available by some combined structure of the organism and its environment. *The affordances of the environment are what it offers the animal, what it provides or furnishes, either for good or ill* (Gibson, 1979, p.127). As an example, the terrestrial surface affords support, if it is horizontal, flat, sufficiently extended and firm for the human body, while a surface of water in a swimming pool affords sinking-into-it. In the same way, artefacts of our culture afford its use. For example, the shape of a doorknob affords the type of movement we should make in order to open the door. In the same way, a button in the desktop interface can be perceived with the affordance of pressing it; the difference here is that the interface button is not a real button, but it stands for one: it is a sign.

Understanding how we could take advantage of this concept in the context of interface design still needs further investigation. There seems to exist a correspondence between the concept of norm (in the social level) and the concept of affordance in an individual level, as norms are social constructs that drive, coordinate and control our actions inside an organization.

The important thing is that the properties of the object (for example its surface), when measured as an affordance (of support in this case), have to be measured in the relative context of the agent (the animal in this example), and should not just be treated as physical properties alone. In the same way, affordances in interfaces should be measured in the context of the users, and should not just be treated as sign properties alone. This explains why different cultures provide different affordances, hence different perceptions of reality. Semiotic approaches derived from Peircean theory support this relativeness in the core concept of the sign as a triadic relation between the *representamen*, the *object* it refers to, and the *interpretant*.

Affordances in the interface could be perceived in the ways the user and the system communicate. As discussed by Eco (1976:8-9) any flow of information from a source to a destination is a process of communication, even the transfer of a signal from one machine to the other. But signification is the highest level of semiotic interaction, in which the destiny has to be a human being and the signal is not a mere stimulus, but arouses an interpretative answer in the receptor. Thus, inspired by Eco, we believe that communication is possible without signification, but signification presupposes communication. In this sense, we stress the use of the concept of communication not as a message-passing mechanism, but as *sharing;* i.e., a process of signification shared by a community. As stated by Cherry, (1980, p.30) *communication is an act of sharing*. The word communication comes from the Latin *communico* and means *to share*. As this author argues, we do not "send" messages; we always "share" them. Messages are not goods or commodities, which can be exchanged or sent from one person to another. When someone tells you something, s/he still owns that information, and the both of you have shared it, although not necessarily with equal interpretants. Whereas goods are sent or exchanged, messages are always shared. Thus, communication means a sharing of elements of behaviour, through the existence of sets of rules of sign usage. This notion of communication as *sharing* (not restricted to transmission) is in line with Stamper's concept of communication, as discussed in the previous section. According to this understanding of the concept of communication, we can say that there is communication between the user and the system through the interface. During the interface design, several other types of communication take place towards the common objective, which results in the interface design. Besides the user-system communication, other groups are also engaged in some type of communication through different channels: designers communicate with users, designers talk to marketing people, the customers support mediates between developers and users, external consultants help both users' and developers' organizations. A Fractal Model of Communication (FMC), proposed and discussed elsewhere (Salles et al., 2000, Salles, 2001), captures the structure of the communication process involved among agents in the system design process. It stresses the fact that the interface is a primary message and, in order to design it, other fractionated messages should be carefully designed, and appropriate channels should be chosen to convey them. Figure 2 illustrates the main concepts of the fractal model of communication.

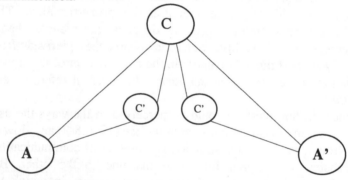

Figure 2. The Fractal Model of Communication

In this diagram, nodes represent the agents participating in the communication (A and A') and the channels (C and C'). The links are bi-directional, which means that the agents share messages. Nodes C' represent the fractal nature of communication. Different foci of the design process can be highlighted: the designer-user communication (A-A') using the interface as a messageon a first level, as the interface is the message conveyed by the computer (which is the first channel). The designer-artefact communication, in the sense discussed by Schön (1996) (A-C), and the user-system communication (A'-C) are represented on a second level of the fractal, having C' as channels.

In the next section, we draw upon this semiotic basis to propose a framework to analyse website interfaces while taking into consideration the organizational dynamics behind them.

5. AN OUTLINE OF THE PROPOSED FRAMEWORK FOR WEBSITE INTERFACE ANALYSIS

The first aspect to highlight in the semiotic framework is our understanding of agents and communication. In e-commerce, for example, users (clients/customers) communicate with the store through the website. This corresponds to the level 1 in the fractal geometry of the communication process, illustrated by Figure 3. Thus, according to the Peircean definition of sign, we have here a triadic relation between the website as the representamen of an object (the store) for an interpretant (the sense made by an user agent), as shown in figures 3a, and 3b.

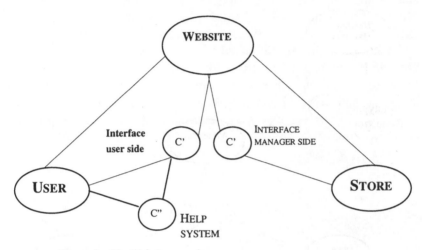

Figure 3a. The Website as a sign

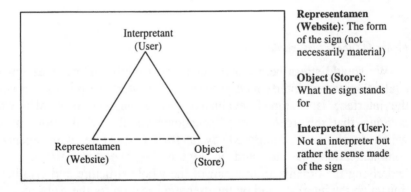

Figure 3b. Triadic Relationship Between Website, Store and User

On the second level of the fractal geometry, the user communicates with the website through interface features (the user side). The store communicates with the website through interface features (the manager side). To illustrate other levels of this geometry, we could say that the user communicates with the interface through the help system. This type of repeated pattern may grow or shrink, as we need to move the focus of analysis to different aspects of the interface.

More important to observe is that other agents are involved and participate in this communication process. We must be aware that during the creation of the website, the design/usability team communicates with the website through, for example, heuristic evaluation, prototype evaluation, etc. This extension in the diagram is illustrated in Figure 4a. Incidentally, the triadic relation can be adapted in a recursive fashion to a few levels to reflect the direct orientation towards the extensions, as shown in figure 4b.

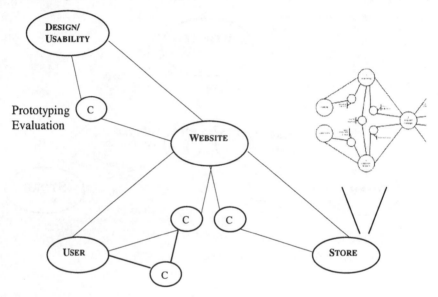

Figure 4a.Other agents participation

We should stress here our understanding of the interface design and evaluation as two intertwined processes of an iterative process, in which the interface is designed, evaluated and redesigned. It is also worth noticing that the agent "Store" encompasses the whole organization, which is, in fact, composed by a fractal structure with agents in communication, as indicated in Figure 4a. Therefore, the dynamics underlying the organization is part of the whole structure and also has an impact on the interface and on the user signification for the website.

When considering the context of Internet applications in general and a website for e-commerce in particular, the traditional approaches for user requirement analysis and elicitation cannot be straightforwardly applied. Considering the wide reach of the Internet as a media, it is much more difficult to have a clear understanding of who the users are and what they need.

Looking at the website as a representamen for "store", a business organization, the most important question we have to answer from the interface point of view is: *Does the interface afford appropriate actions?* To answer this question we can apply Stamper's semiotic framework to understand how each layer, which constitutes part of the semiotics of the interface, informs and contributes to communication in the interface. More important, this question should be answered from the perspectives of the several agents in communication with the website: the user, the usability team, the design team, etc. and the agents on behalf of the company.

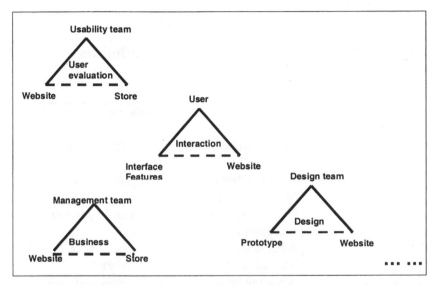

Figure 4b. Recursive Fashion of the Triadic Relation.

Starting from the layers that constitute the infrastructure of the system, the *physical world, empirics, and syntactics* tell us about the physical properties of the sign, its physical tokens, the channel capacity and efficiency, and the structure and vocabulary of the interface. Considering the context of Internet applications, the *physical world* layer can be used, for example, to answer questions about the infrastructure of Internet access and the compatibility to different browsers. In the *empirics* layer, factors that interfere directly in the user experience, such as time spent on downloading, percentage of http errors and time spent on updating actions could be investigated. The *syntactic* layer should be used to tell us about the typology of signs used in the interface, its composition and factors that influence its interpretability.

The three upper layers concern the human aspects involved in the meaning negotiation, usage, and social implications of the sign system; the relationship between the signs in the interface and what they refer to; and the purposeful use of signs and its social effects. The *semantic* layer can tell us about the affordances of a web site and how those affordances reflect the business substantive area. Also the determiners for the affordances can be listed which informs us about aspects of redundancy, unpredictability, the use of metaphors as shorthand of expression of meaning, and absences and contradictions present in the site. The layer of *pragmatics* can tell us about the "silent messages beneath the surface" (ideological content), and the business mechanisms implied by the interface compared to the real practice, for example. Finally, the *social world* layer concerns affordances at the social level, informal and formal norms afforded by the interface, and the social commitments and obligations of the parts implied by legislative aspects of the business.

Drawing upon the semiotic framework proposed, Table 1 summarises a set of guidelines to inspect an e-commerce website interface.

Table 1. Guidelines to inspect an e-commerce website interface

Semiotic Layers	Inspection Guidelines
1. **Physical world** Signs and their physical properties	▪ Does the site inform about the technology needed/used? ▪ Are the webpages compatible for different browsers? ▪ Are there features concerning accessibility for people with special needs?
2. **Empirics** Signs and their statistical properties	▪ Is time spent on downloading and updating acceptable? ▪ What is the percentage of errors? Are there web links or addresses that do not work?
3. **Syntactics** Signs and their relations to other signs	▪ What can be said about the typology of signs and computer-based signs used in the interface? ▪ What can be said about the relationships among signs in the interface concerning layout/navigation?
4. **Semantics** Signs and their relation to the meaning perceived by users	▪ What are the functions afforded by the website? Do they reflect the business substantive area? ▪ What can be said about the use of metaphors in the website? Are there contradictions, absences, asymmetries?
5. **Pragmatics** Signs and their effect on users	▪ What can be said about ideological content for the website? Are there advertisements present? In what ways? ▪ What can be said about the mechanisms for buying? Do they reflect the aspects of the commerce practice? ▪ Are there effective means to find specific products? Are there possibilities of returning or

	substituting products?

6. Social World
Signs and their
relation to social
implications
	▪ What laws regulate the use of the site?
	▪ What can be said about the formal rules
	  supported by the interface? Must the user
	  subscribe to become a customer?
	▪ What are the implications of the operations
	  afforded at the social level? What can be said
	  about the social commitments and obligations of
	  the parts? Are they symmetric?

6. INSTANTIATING THE PROPOSED FRAMEWORK TOWARDS THE ANALYSIS OF AN E-COMMERCE WEBSITE

As an example of applying the proposed framework, an inspection of a supermarket website in the UK, here called *T.com* was conducted using the *Help* as a representamen for the interface features and the pages of the website itself. Even though it is beyond the scope of this chapter to show the complete analysis, the following discussion illustrates some findings of applying the framework.

The physical world layer

At the *physical* layer, the direct relevance of knowing the physical properties of signs in *T.com* website is that one could design more efficient devices and infrastructure for storage and transmission. For example, for the website to function with technical precision, one has to obtain the right cable connection, network infrastructure, data storage devices and so on.

Concerning this layer, the site presupposes the user has already everything necessary in terms of infrastructure of communication for his connection, as s/he is already in the site, even if s/he is using the web from an Internet Café, for example. Nevertheless, some information related to the physical level can be found in the *Help Section,* concerning security issues of payment through the Internet, and in the *General Terms and Conditions* document, concerning excluded services and the organization's liability. The sentences below suggest some of the physical aspects revealed in the website that are supporting the business:

" *...our Secure Server Software encrypts your credit card information to ensure your transactions with us are private and protected as they travel over the Internet. We accept orders only from Web browsers that permit communication through Secure Socket Layer (SSL) technology...* "

" *the services provided by the T.com site do not include the provision of computer or other necessary equipment to access the T.com Site. To use the T.com site you will require Internet Connectivity and appropriate telecommunication links. We shall not be liable for any telephone or other costs that you may incur".*

Considering the website as a physical channel for shopping online, it is worth noticing that there are no special features in it to facilitate the use by disabled people, or considerations related to the elderly, who would benefit from shopping from home.

The empirics layer

The main objects of study at the *empirics* layer are the channel capacity, optimal sign transmission, correctness of transmission, reduction of noise in transmission and so on. The collection of signs can be seen as a number of signs that have to be transported from one location to another, regardless of the meaning they may carry. Concerning this layer, some errors are found in a "Quick Tour" link, in the bottom of the Home Section. Through this link the novice user can have a look at and experience the whole structure of the site. Besides finding oneself at a very discreet place in the page, some errors and unexpected inconsistencies were found, such as:

  o   The blue tabs in the quick tour, which should be indicating possibilities of navigation in the site, do not correspond to the blue tabs in the website.
  o   The quit button in the quick tour returns to the beginning of the tour, trapping the user.
  o   The quick tour link in the quick links section of the shopping page links to another page related to graduate careers!

The syntactics layer

The *syntactics* layer is concerned with the formal structure, logic and language of signs. This layer is concerned with the rules for composing simple signs into a more complex sign. With regards to syntactics, we could say that the syntactical signs in the case study afford "clicking". The types of signs used in the site are mostly from the interactive category. Furthermore, the links with graphical representation are mostly iconic, facilitating the user's interpretation. The actor and object types are also present, providing a good feedback for the user's actions on the interface. Some examples of the sign types found in the site are illustrated below:

  o   Interactive signs: links and buttons.
  o   Actor signs: the progress bar; the change of colours when we pass the mouse through the interactive signs; the change in the cursor shape when passing the mouse through interactive signs (the arrow and the hand); the tips in the links (hints).
  o   Object signs: texts that are not links. E.g. 30 October 2001 in the *Today at T Section*.

o Layout signs: the blue tabs that are not links; e.g. *Shopping Directory*, *More to Explore*. The drawn lines to separate the items.

Redundancy is present on the syntactical level: in the identical regions of a number of pages, we found at least 4 types of representations for each link representing the categories of goods the user can buy: 2 graphical (iconic and symbolic signs), with hints and 2 textual. E.g.:

The semantic layer

The *Semantic* layer is concerned with issues related to the meaning of signs within the constructivist principle, i.e., meanings are constructed and continuously changed by people using syntactic structures to organise their actions. Concerning this layer, first of all, we could say that the frontier between the .com and the physical store (supermarket) is not clear. In some sections (e.g. the *Help Section*), the user is encouraged to think in the site as the equivalent supermarket and some of the metaphors used contribute to this. In other sections (e.g. *Terms & Conditions*) it is suggested that they are separate organizations, owned and operated by different registered companies.

At the semantic layer, we are equally interested in the different metaphors used for representing the meanings of the terms. Choosing the wrong metaphor could have an adverse effect leading to a different meaning. "Warehouse" seems to be an important concept in the website, as its redundancy is the largest. Only in the *Home Section,* the word appears 22 times! The concept of a warehouse as explicitly shown in the site could suggest other types of business interaction, much closer to buying from a catalogue than being in a virtual supermarket. Other metaphors present in the website include:

- o The site is presented in the *Help Section* as a set of seven stores. However the seven stores are not distinguished among the links and there is no explicit representation for them in the interface. Also, the concept of "store" is used in some places to indicate the real store (the supermarket) as in the figure below:

More to explore
_____

▶ T   **store locator:** Find your nearest T₁   store.

- o In the site, "Navigation" is presented in the *Help Section* as "moving around" the stores. Blue tabs along the top of the page are presented as important "locations". However, they are not related to the stores of the website or to the "departments" of the real supermarket.
- o Quick links on the left side of the pages are presented as a "quick" move to the different stores or different departments in a store. How quick? Quick seems to mean here more accessible, as they are all located on the left side of any page and the user does not need to scroll to find it. However, it means more redundancy, and more "clicking" affordance.
- o The basket metaphor is used to choose the goods the user wants to buy. There are some inconsistencies between information presented in the *Help* of the *Home Section* and the *Help* of some stores, concerning how to buy. A "buy" button is referred to in the *Help* of the *Home Section*, while, in fact, the button to put things in the basket is labelled "add".
- o Putting things in the shopping basket is easier than removing it. The reverse operation (to remove items from the basket) uses a different procedure: change quantity to 0 and click on recalculate/update basket. Because there is an "add" button to add things in the basket, the user probably would expect a "remove" one to do the opposite operation. There is no symmetric relation between the meaning and representation of these operations.

The pragmatics layer

The *pragmatics* layer is concerned with the relationships between signs and the behaviour of responsible agents, in a social context. Regarding *pragmatics*, the site uses the concept of "stores" as department stores in a supermarket. However, the stores are neither distinguished in the site or in its *Home Section*, nor in the *Shopping Section*, and the list of the 7 online stores is different in different parts of the *Help Section*. This set of stores seems to reflect the structure of the business organization. What is also reflecting that structure is that the customer needs to register separately for 2 subsets of the stores. *Personal Finance* could be interpreted from the *Help Section* as one of the "stores". Also, among the stores it is the only one with a distinguishable place in the interface: it is one of the 7 that are represented with a blue tab on the top. Nevertheless, the *Personal Finance* is not a store; actually, it is a different organization with its proper regulations and a different style of webpages. Some other inconsistencies related to the pragmatical aspects of the interface include:

- o   The "search engine" is only present when the user is "inside" one of the stores to buy something, and it searches only through the contents of the store the user is in. This support does not seem to correspond with the intentions of a user entering the website.
- o   Some concepts common to the two types of organization, *T.com* and *T supermarket*, are not applicable to both. For example, there is no way of using vouchers online. The vouchers sent by post in the "normal" mailing can only be collected in a supermarket.
- o   The customer cannot return items to a *T* store, or to the closest supermarket. If the user needs to return something, for example, a product bought from the music warehouse, s/he needs to contact some special customer service team by telephone or email. This also suggests that the .com and the supermarket are different organizations.
- o   The changing of details does not directly involve filling in forms, as it is the first time the user gets registered. If the customer changes address, for example, s/he will have to phone or email the site in order to change it.

The social world layer

The *social world* layer consists of norms of many kinds, related to beliefs, expectations, commitments, contracts, laws and culture. No intentional sign can be fully understood without considering its potential and actual social effects on the human agents. Concerning this layer, there are some social implications for shopping online, and the interface itself is the way to have access to that knowledge.

The *General Terms and Conditions* for *T.com* is a written document containing the regulations and is accessible through the last link at the bottom of the home page (and at the bottom of the shopping page as well). Even though it cannot easily be located in the interface, considering its physical location on the page, the document itself stresses its importance for the user:

"Please, read them carefully as they affect your rights and liabilities under the law. If you do not agree to these Terms and Conditions, please

do not register for or use the T.com Site. Please, note that to use any of the services provided on the T.com Site you are required to register as an authorised user on the site."

In addition to the *General Terms and Conditions*, there is also the *Product Terms & Conditions* for 10 different types of products.

To get authorisation to use the site as a customer, i.e. buying products, the user has to register. This should be done by using a blue tab (on the top) *Register &Sign in*. When starting the registration process, the user encounters the *Privacy Policy*, a document explaining the privacy police of the organization and providing options to let the user choose how his/her personal data will be used. However, the text states that, even if the user has mentioned that s/he does NOT want to be contacted or receive information , the user will nonetheless receive communications of the whole range of .com service:

"These may include but are not limited to details of new products, special offers, Internet developments and other .com services."

The "Privacy Policy" form and the "Terms and Conditions" document are signs in themselves and, as therefore, the framework can be applied to them to reveal more detail, as we move closer. Some brief considerations about the social implications the General Terms and Conditions document has:

o Social commitments and obligations of the parts are not symmetric. For example, commitments of customers are secured by their payments (by credit cards or T's accounts of the customer), while commitments of the store are not explicit; the website does not provide access to "the rights of the customer". Furthermore, some important operations, such as the possibility of returning goods, are only found as a FAQ in the *Help Section* and provide no clear answers. There is no mention of the possibility of substituting products. The email is the channel for anything that is not covered by the *Help Section*. Other signs of this asymmetry include issues concerning liability, as illustrated below:

   "The T.com Site is provided by T.com without any warranties or guarantees. You must bear the risks associated with the use of the Internet."

   "In particular, we disclaim all liabilities in connection with the following:

   Incompatibility of the T.com Site with any of your equipment, software or telecommunications links

> Technical problems including errors or interruptions of the T.com Site
>
> *Unsuitability, unreliability or inaccuracy of the T.com Site*
> *Inadequacy of the T.com site to meet your requirements.* "

The interface inspection, as proposed in this work, could consider the perspective of analysts and be part of the process of designing and developing the website. The same framework based on the semiotic layers could be adapted to a context of user testing, where the analysts would be observing users interacting and buying online. Also, the same framework could be applied to different levels of the fractal geometry shown in Figure 4 in order to get a more complete picture of the interface issues of a website. The analysis could focus on the *Help System*, for example, as it is also a sign (a representamen for the website features). More importantly, the same framework could be applied at the level of the organization to capture the different perspectives of the groups whose work affects or is affected by the design of the website.

1. COMMENTS ON RELATED WORK

Methods for analysis and evaluation of websites have mostly been derived from the approaches based on the traditional heuristic evaluation of user interfaces, and do not capture the complexity and organizational dynamics behind the website. Contributions from semiotic approaches have appeared very recently. Despite not addressing the context of Internet applications, Connolly and Phillips (2001) have shown insights offered by OS that help to deepen theoretical and practical appreciation of established user-system interface design principles.

An other approach to website evaluation based on Semiotics was proposed by Vile in a personal communication (Vile, 2000;Tim and Vile 1999). He applied the Social Semiotic text analysis (Hodge and Kress, 1988) to evaluate websites of e-commerce business.

The Social Semiotics proposal draws upon Saussure's work on diachrony and transformations, and on reflections of the own authors to construct its principles (Hodge and Kress, 1988, p.35). In the Social Semiotics framework, the smallest unit of meaning that can have an independent material existence is the *message*. The material existence of a message is determined by the existence of at least two signs organised into a syntagmatic structure. Thus, a *sign* is a portion of the syntagmatic plane that is treated as a unity. It can be ranged within a continuum between "transparent" and "opaque". Semiotic phenomena have both social and referential dimensions, and such should, must be described in terms of both: a mimetic and a semiosic plane. The *mimetic plane* implies some version of reality as a possible referent. The *semiosic plane* implies some semiotic events linking together producers and receivers, signifiers and signifieds into a significant relationship. The semiosic plane is the context for the mimetic plane and the mimetic plane is constituent part of the semiosic plane. The interaction of both is necessary for the social production of meaning.

The Social Semiotics approach uses the word *text* to refer to a structure of messages or message traces which have a socially ascribed unity, and it proposes six principles for text analysis, briefly described here. The *semiosic determination* concerns the conditions for the semiosic plane to be fixed before analysis of the mimetic plane. The *mimetic anchorage* concerns the specification of the world of referents. The *ideological content* is related to the competing versions of reality implied by the text. The *analytic anchorage* concerns the position of the analyst in a semiosic structure that incorporates the text. *Homology* refers to possible homologies between mimetic and semiosic structures, syntagmatic and paradigmatic structures, etc. Also, patterns of *redundancy and absence*, and *contradictions* should be investigated in the text.

While it is not the focus of this work to go deeper into the analysis of the SS approach, we must highlight in what ways our approach differs from it. First, we state that our framework for interface analysis derives from a different school of Semiotics. We draw upon the work of Stamper (1973), which is based on the works of Peirce and Morris. As so, the differences between the theories start with the fundamental concept: the sign. As discussed earlier in this chapter, the Peircean definition of the sign as a triadic relation among the *representamen*, the referred *object* and the *interpretant* is in line with our concept of the interface. We understand the interface (or the website) as a *representamen* of an object (the store) for an *interpretant* (the sense made by the agent or user). The social dimension of the sign, besides being implicit in the core definition of sign, is made explicit in the Stamper's extended layers, mainly the sixth layer - *the social world*. Furthermore, this understanding of the sign supports the core concept of affordances in interfaces not being treated as a sign property alone, but as a measure in the relative context of the users. Second, the SS concept of a message having a direction seems to be only appropriate with regard to understanding communication by sending electronic signals at the empirical level. In our scenario, an agent (the user) is in communication with another agent (a store for example) through a computational interface. This type of communication, as discussed in our previous work (Baranauskas *et al.* 2001, Baranauskas *et al.* 2001), is much more like a conversational process. Thus, our concept of communication as sharing differs fundamentally from the concept of the school that understands communication as a message passing mechanism.

8. CONCLUSION

The Internet considered as a medium has generated the need to broaden the referential framework of user interface analysis, taking into consideration the semiotic nature of the interface in its social aspects.

Apart from some literature in HCI and CSCW, which acknowledges social aspects of usage context, methods for user interface analysis and evaluation have not paid sufficient attention to the social and organizational aspects that underlie the interface design and influence the user signification to Internet applications. Drawing upon input from Organizational Semiotics, this chapter proposes a framework for user interface analysis of websites, and illustrates its use for websites of e-commerce. Our findings point out issues concerning the organization and the business that should be afforded by the interface and should be taken into consideration in the analysis, design and evaluation of websites. The proposed framework enables the analysis of the affordances in the interface through different levels, and from different perspectives, moving the focus to the organization itself by including other groups and responsibilities associated with the website design.

ACKNOWLEDGEMENTS

This work was partially supported by grants from Brazilian Research Council (CNPq 301656/84-3). The authors thank the editors and the anonymous referees for their constructive and helpful comments.

REFERENCES

Andersen, P. B., Holmqvist, B., & Jensen, J. F. (eds) (1993). *Computer as media*. New York: Cambridge University Press.

Andersen, P.B.(1997). *A Theory of Computer Semiotics*. Updated ed. of 1990. New York: Cambridge University Press.

Baranauskas, M.C.C., Salles, J.P., & Bigonha, R. S. (2001). Looking Inside: understanding communication in the organisational context of software design. In *Proceedings of the IFIP WG8.1 Working Conference on Organisational Semiotics: evolving a science of information systems*, Montreal, p.248-249.

Baranauskas, M.C.C., Salles, J.P., & Bigonha, R. S. (2001). Bringing Interface Design and Software Development Processes Together: How Organisational Issues Impact Product's Usability. In *Proceedings of IHC2001, IV Brazilian Workshop on Human Factors in Computational Systems*. Florianopolis, SC, Brazil.

Card, S. K., Moran, T. P., & Newell, A. (1983). *The Psycology of Human-Computer Interaction*. Hillsdale: Lawrence Erlbaum Associates.

Cherry, C. (1980). *On Human Communication*. London:The MIT Press.

Chong, S. (2001) *DEON: A Semiotic Method for the Design of Agent-Based E-Commerce Systems*, PhD Dissertation, Staffordshire University.

Connolly, J.H., & Phillips, I.W. (2001). User-System Interface Design: an Organisational Semiotic Perspective. In *Proceedings of IFIP WG8.1 Working Conference on Organisational Semiotics*, Montreal, QC.

Eco, U. (1976) *Tratado Geral de Semiótica*. Translation from *A theory of Semiotics*. Sao Paulo: Editora Perspectiva, 1980.

Gibson, J. J. (1968) *The Senses Considered as Perceptual Systems*, Allen & Unwin.

Gibson, J. J. (1979) *The Ecological Approach to Visual Perception*, Mifflin Company.

Goldkuhl, G. (2001) Exploring the Explanatory Power of Actability – The Case of Internet-based Software Artefacts. In *Proceedings of IFIP WG8.1 Working Conference on Organizational Semiotics, Montreal, QC, July 23-25*.

Goldkuhl, G., & Agerfalk, P.J. (2002). Actability: a Way to Understand Information Systems Pragmatics. In K. Liu, R.J. Clarke, P.B. Andersen, R.K. Stamper (eds.), *Coordination and Communication Using Signs: Studies in Organisational Semiotics 2*. Kluwer Academic Publishers, Boston/Dordrecht/London.

Hodge,R., & Kress, G. (1988). *Social Semiotics*. Cambridge: Polity Press.

Jorna, R.; & Van Heusden, B. (1996). Semiotics of user interface. *Semiotica*. V. 109, n. 3/4, p. 237-250.

Kaptelinin, V.(1996). Activity Theory: Implications for Human-Computer Interaction. In Nardi, B. A. (ed.), *Context and Consciousness – Activity Theory and Human-Computer Interaction*. Cambridge: The MIT Press, p. 103-116.

Laurel, B. (1990). *The Art of Human-Computer Interaction*. Reading, MA: Addison-Wesley.

Liu, K. (2000). *Semiotics in Information Systems Engineering*, Cambridge University Press.

Michaels, C. F. & Carello, C. (1981) *Direct Perception*, Englewood Cliffs, Prentice Hall

Morris, C. (1985). Signs and the Act. In R.E.Innis (ed), *Semiotics – An Introductory Antology*. Indiana University Press, Bloomington. p. 178-189.

Nadin, M. (1988). Interface design: A semiotic paradigm. *Semiotica*. V. 69, n.3/4, p.269-302.

Norman, D.A., & Draper, S. W. (1986). *User Centered System Design in New Perspectives on Human-Computer Interaction*. Hillsdale: Lawrence Erlbaum Associates.

Norman, D.A. (1988). The design of everyday things. New York:Basic Books.

Peirce, C. S. (1932). *Collected Papers of Charles Sanders Peirce*. Charles Hartshorme e Paul Weiss (eds.), Vol. II: Elements of Logic; Third Printing. Cambridge,MA: Harvard University Press, 1974.

Preece, J., Rogers, Y., & Sharp, H. (2002). *Interaction Design – Beyond Human-Computer Interaction*. John Wiley & Sons, USA.

Salles, J.P., Baranauskas, & M.C.C., Bigonha, R.S. (2000) A Communication Model for the Interface Design Process. In *Workshop on Semiotic Approaches to User Interface Design, CHI2000*.

Salles, J.P. (2001). *O Modelo Fractal de Comunicação: Criando um Espaço de Análise para Inspeção do Processo de Design de Software*, Unpublished PhD thesis, UFMG, Brasil.

Schön, D & Bennet, J, (1996) Reflective Conversation with Materials, in: Winograd, T, (ed.), *Bringing Design to Software* ACM Press.

Shneiderman, M. L., & Thomas, J. C. (1983). The Humanization of Computer Interfaces (Introduction). *Communications of the ACM*. V. 26, n. 4, p. 252-253.

Shneiderman, B. (1998) *Designing the User Interface: Strategies for Effective Human-Computer Interaction (3rd ed)*. Reading, MA: Addison-Wesley Publishing Company.

Stamper, R. K. (1973). *Information in Business and Administrative Systems*. John Wiley and Sons, New York.

Stamper, R.K. (1992). Language and Computer in organised behaviour. In Riet, R.P. and Meersman, R.A. (eds.), *Linguistic Instruments in Knowledge Engineering*, Elsevier Science, Amsterdam, 143-63.

Stamper, R.K. (1993) Signs, Norms and Information Systems. In *ICL/University of Newcastle Seminar on "Information", UK*.

Stamper, R. K. (2000) *Invited Speech*, Fifth Internation Workshop on the Language-Action Perspective on Communication Modelling, 14th – 16th September, Aachen, Germany.

Tim, F. & Vile, A. (1999) Semiotics for E-Commerce: Shared Meanings and Generative Futures, In *Proceedings of the BIT'99 Conference, Manchester Metropolitan University, UK, 3rd & 4th November.*

Vile, A. (2000). The e-Commerce Experience, a View through the Semiotic Lens. Invited Seminar at the Staffordshire University, Stafford, UK.

Winograd, T. (1996). (ed.), *Bringing Design to Software* New York: Addison-Wesley Publishing Company.

Chapter 4

Improving Business Modelling with Organizational Semiotics

Zhiwu Xie, Kecheng Liu and David Emmitt

ABSTRACT

Organizational semiotics and its derived methods are mapped to object oriented paradigm. Expressed in Unified Modelling Language, the mappings make improvements to the business modelling using the Rational Unified Process. It facilitates a converging process for reaching semantic representation with clear definitions of responsibilities, which delivers an agreed business model.

1. INTRODUCTION

Understanding the business itself is the foundation for any successful software development. For the information systems analysts and designers, successful communication with the domain experts so as to properly understand, interpret, and apply their business knowledge into software design and implementation has always been a challenging part of the job.

Ronald Stamper's semiotic ladder model (Stamper 2000) can be used to illustrate the difficulties. Since all communications are conducted via signs, any block through the ladders, either physical, empiric, syntactic, semantic, pragmatic, or social, could more or less fail to convey the right knowledge.

Various techniques have been proposed to tackle the problem, among which Unified Modelling Language (UML) (OMG 2002) is one of the most noticeable developments. Its standardisation and widely acceptance by the industry may partially attribute to its success to address the needs for a unified modelling notation system within the object orientation community. UML exposes the possibility of seamless transition between the object oriented software design and implementation. Rational Rose and some other UML compliant tools have partially implemented the functionality of code generation from a properly designed UML model, and vice versa, reengineering from the source codes to UML models. This has considerably eased the communication and understanding difficulties between the software designers and the programmers.

Applying the UML to the business modelling, however, is a different story. Mapping the stakeholders' natural language expressions and domain knowledge into a fixed set of notations is never an easy task. UML has been and will still be under extensive examination, evaluation, and revision (Kobryn 1999, Krogstie, 1999), so that the notations' semantic leaks can be gradually eliminated and expressiveness improved.

Even though, how to apply this more and more complex notation system into the practical business modelling remains a problem. We can neither expect the domain experts to think in the OO paradigm nor express themselves in the software terms. Whether their knowledge can be smoothly transferred to the system analysts and designers relies not only on the notation system, which is only a tool, but also on how people use it to communicate.

A modelling process guides the people involved on how to use the notations to get the best results. Although UML is supposed to be process neutral, the "three amigos", Grady Booch, Jim Rumbaugh, and Ivar Jacobson, always advocate a "use-case driven, architecture-centric, iterative, and incremental process", which apparently refers people to Rational's commercial product, Rational Unified Process (RUP) (Jacobson et al. 1998, Kruchten 2000). Along with UML, RUP has nowadays gained the biggest market share.

In this chapter, RUP is taken as a representative business modelling process for those currently used in the information systems development. We propose a series of organization semiotics improvements to RUP, and believe the similar improvements may be applied to most other popular object oriented business modelling methods and processes. Although the process has been changed, the notations used remain UML. This consistency may help users to understand and learn this new approach.

We first present our observations on the business process modelling on an actual IT development project. The modelling process was under Rational consultancy and supposed to conform strictly to the RUP. Out of our observations, a few questions are raised and analysed, followed by a brief introduction on the organizational semiotics and methods derived from it. We believe that the organizational semiotics and the derived methods is an appropriate theoretical foundation both to understand the observed phenomenon and to improve the process. The improvements are then proposed and summarised.

2. CASE STUDY

We were involved in a UK Police Information Technology Organisation (PITO) development project aimed at defining the core functional requirements of a generic Crime solution for the Police Service in England and Wales. The scope of the business area included Crime Reporting, Crime Management and Crime Investigation (at high level only). Historically, individual Force Crime legacy IT systems were developed independently of each other and legacy functionality was not anchored to a standard Crime business process.

The approach taken was to initially reverse engineer the functional requirements from a typical Force Crime legacy system and to express these as use-cases using the RUP method. This served as a baseline of functionality available to support Crime business processes in a typical police force. Next, the Crime business area was modelled via a series of PITO moderated workshops, each attended by Crime domain experts from England & Wales. The core business workflows were identified and analysed, translated into System use-cases, from which the core Crime functional requirements were elicited.

As mentioned previously, RUP was strictly abided by throughout the process. The major RUP business modelling activities and artefacts are described in the definitive books by Jacobson et al. (1998) and Kruchten (2000), as well as in Rational's RUP website at http://www.rational.com/products/rup.

Our observations on the project raised a handful of questions, which are reported as following, using the examples transformed from the project[1].

2.1. To what extent a common vocabulary is feasible?

In RUP, it is stated that:

In business modelling you must define a common vocabulary using the most common terms and expressions in the problem domain. You should then consistently use the common vocabulary in all textual descriptions of the business. In this way, you keep the textual descriptions consistent and avoid misunderstandings among project members about the use and meaning of terms. You should document the vocabulary in a glossary.

It implies that:

- a common vocabulary exists in the domain, and
- the definitions can be compiled relatively independently to the modelling, therefore
- the textual definitions can help to avoid misunderstandings in the modelling

Our observations, however, reveal that these implications can be oversimplified.

---

[1] The examples used in this chapter have been altered for confidentiality reasons.

Firstly, meaning seeking for those vocabularies is always part of the modelling itself and has to be done in parallel with other modelling activities. On one hand, the business analysts usually lack the expertise to collect and compile the glossary independently. They need the help from the domain experts, either through workshop discussions or via separate communications. On the other hand, only via the other modelling activities such as business use case analysis etc., the context and real meanings of the term can be revealed.

We observed that only during later workshops, when the reporting and assessing of a crime were discussed, the meaning of the fundamental term "crime" used in the domain began to emerge. It has very little to do with the normal meaning of a crime, e.g., anti-law violence and offence, court judgement to guilty, etc. For the police forces, a crime becomes a crime far earlier than any court judgements are made. It does not even need to have a suspect. When a crime related incident is initially reported to the police, e.g. via the Command and Control application, a crime record will be initiated, provided that the offence (as reported) qualifies as a crime, i.e. via the Home Office counting rules. The crime related incident would then be cross-referenced to the crime report. A crime number is allocated to the recorded crime, which is then assessed i.e. as to its potential for further investigation.

From an outsider's view, the term "crime" is used as an alias of "crime record", or is perceived as a crime record. There is no right or wrong in it, only one has to be aware of these hidden usages. The analysis and modelling activities is the right path leading to the discovery of these meanings and cannot be separated from them.

Second, a common vocabulary may not always exist. In many cases, although all domain experts know what they are referring to, there are just no terms to name them. Once a term was needed to describe the actor of the "Record Crime" use case. This actor can be either a patrolling police officer, one on duty at the police station, one at the police crime reporting centre, or much more others. The ranks and business roles of the actors vary so much and the use cases are so many to enumerate that a common acceptable definitive term is needed. But it just does not exist in the business domain. The domain experts and business analysts had to create a term "Crime Recorder" for this purpose. From the workshop attendees' view, the term may explain itself for the time being. But the problem is that the potential users of the system might not accept these purposely created terms. Moreover, unless we enumerate all possible occasions, the term still depends on the definition of the use case to get its meaning, which can be a deadlock. Similar problems are not uncommon in many other development processes. In many cases, due to different perspectives and backgrounds the domain experts even can not reach an agreement on the terms within themselves, which also leads to term creations.

The third question is, whether a textual definition is sufficient and efficient. This is related to the above two questions. Since a globally accepted definition for a term does not likely to exist in the business domain and most accepted definitions are contextual, a textual definition can be too lengthy to include all the contexts, and may introduce even more undefined terms. On the other hand, if word meanings are tightly related to the modelling activities expressed mostly in graphical notations, keeping the definitions textual does not seem to be economic.

The vocabulary issues may seem too trivial to be of any significant importance. However, in most workshops we participated, the word meaning discussions were always the lengthiest, but not necessarily the most fruitful part. For most of the difficult business terms, the discussions resulted in either compromising the wordings or clarifying the contexts where the terms were used. These contexts, however valuable for the modelling process itself, are not required to be recorded and documented either in the glossary or in the modelling of an RUP compliant project.

2.2. To what extent a common workflow is feasible?

RUP states that:

The workflow of a business use case describes what the business must do to provide the value the served business actor requires. The business use case consists of a sequence of activities that, together, produce something for the business actor. The workflow often consists of a basic flow and one or more alternative flows. The structure of the workflow is described graphically with the help of an activity diagram.

It implies that a commonly accepted deterministic workflow exists in all business domains, which we feel suspicious in many cases. Take the "allocate crime" use case as an example. During the workshops the domain experts presented many possible workflows for it but strongly suggested the business analysts not to formalise them. In some police forces, there are police officers whose specialty is to allocate crime to the investigating officers. He/she allocates crimes according to the nature of the crime, the investigator's skills profile, availability and the current crime workload, as well as other factors. But many other police forces have different methods to allocate crime; some are very informal, but still effective and efficient. Their variations can be inexhaustible. If we only record those formal workflows and use them as the standard business procedures, the organization operation may lose its elasticity and balance.

Another problem associated with the workflow is at the decision-making forks. When deciding which path to take, the business workers must explicitly identify the business rules underneath. For the purpose of decision automation, RUP only recognises those "solid", formal laws and regulations as part of the business rules. This dramatically reduces its ability to model the business processes. For example, the business rules for assessing crime can be very informal and non-deterministic. The domain experts pointed out that the home office counting rules determine which crime related incident are formally reported as crimes, i.e. prior to being screened before resources can be allocated to it. These are the formal and deterministic rules. However, under what condition who should assess a specific crime is beyond the formal rules and up to the situations. These kind of informal, non-deterministic workflows, although extremely common in the domain, are largely ignored by the RUP.

2.3. Where does the business modelling end?

This can be partitioned into two questions. The first, at what detail and granularity level should the business modelling maintain? The second, where do the modelling iterations stop?

During business modelling, the business analysts are usually submerged in the floods of information from the domain experts. What to include in the model and what not to has always been a problem. The business analysts have to rely on their instincts to make the decisions, which is potentially error prone. For example, a common practice in the business modelling is to avoid modelling a class' attributes and operations, since they are considered too trivial to be specified in the business level. Only those significant structural relationships such as inheritance and aggregation are important enough to be recorded. Therefore, although a Crime Recorder creates a Crime can be explicitly expressed by inserting a function call "record" in the class specification of the "Crime Recorder" class with a "Crime" type return parameter, it was ignored. In this manner, much important domain knowledge is lost. We cannot blame the business analysts for this, because there are no criteria to decide what information is important.

RUP is an iterative process. Even in business modelling, navigating to and from business use cases and business object models can reveal their differences, hence complement the lost information and yield a better model quality. However, since the granularity of the modelling itself is difficult to decide, we will have difficulties to decide when the use cases and object models are fully synchronized and compatible. The iterations can be endless.

To summarise, the quality of the RUP models need to be further enhanced by introducing:

- facilities to rigorously analyse and define the meanings of the business entities
- use of notations that help to reach and disseminate the common understanding of the business entities
- method to reveal the fundamental and essential relationships among the business entities
- method for responsibility-oriented workflow analysis
- criteria for the level of details of the activity descriptions
- criteria for the termination of the iterations

We propose that organizational semiotics and the methods derived from it can help to understand the problems specified and provide guidance for improvements.

3. ORGANIZATIONAL SEMIOTICS APPROACH

Peirce founded semiotics as the "formal doctrine of signs" (Hartshorne, 1960). A sign is defined as something that stands to someone for something else in some respect or capacity. Organizational semiotics and the analytical methods (Stamper 1996, 1997, 2000, Stamper et al. 2000, Liu 2000, Liu et al. 1996) offer a theory to understand business organizations, with or without the supporting computerised information systems. Organizations are deemed as systems where signs are created, transmitted, and consumed for business purposes. Adopting the concept of sign enables us to study the organization in a more balanced way, taking account of both the technological issues and the human and social aspects of information resources, products and functions.

Organizational semiotics adopts a subjectivist philosophical stance and an agent-in-action ontology. This philosophical position states that, for all practical purposes, nothing exists without a perceiving agent and the agent engaging in actions. Any knowledge must be represented in the form of:

Agent behaviour

The classical distinction between entity, attribute and relationship disappears to be replaced by the concepts of agents (a responsible person, a group of person, or an organization), affordances (the potential actions or behaviours of the agents) and norms (the socially defined patterns of behaviour) related to their antecedents to indicate the ontological dependency.

3.1. Semantics analysis

Ronald Stamper adopts the concept of affordance from the perceptual psychologist James Gibson, who defined "the affordances of the environment" as "what it offers the animal, what it provides or furnishes, either for good or ill..." (Gibson, 1979). Based on the theory, since a person perceives things by recognising what he can do with them or to them, a thing can be defined as an "invariant repertories of behaviours, either substantive affordances or social norms" (Stamper 2000) that are available to the responsible person. For example, in the context of the crime management, an incident affords to be reported.

Reporting a crime related incident is a potential ability, which may or may not be implemented in the reality. However, once it is implemented, new possibilities emerge. A reported crime-related incident is evaluated against the home office counting rules, to determine whether or not a crime has occurred. If that incident is reported as a crime, it will then be assessed as to its potential for further investigation, i.e. screened. This shows that affordances have dependency relationships among them. In organizational semiotics this relationship is called ontological dependency.

Using Stamper's notation, the relationship is shown below, with the antecedents on the left side and the dependencies on the right, and the solid line denotes the ontological dependency:

incident – crime

Ontological dependency does not only show the logic relationship between the concepts. What's more important is that it shows the dependencies get their meaning from the existence of the antecedents. Since the existence of the dependencies would not be possible without the existence of the antecedents, the lifecycle of the dependencies are always included by that of the antecedents. The existence of the antecedents thus forms a context for the dependencies.

Semantic analysis helps us to build a more rigorous context of communication. This method defines the word meaning in two ways, first, defines who-do-what by specifying the responsible agents and the repertoire of behaviours, and second, defines under which circumstances these behaviours can be implemented by specifying the ontological dependencies and norms.

3.2. Norm analysis

Norm, which is defined as the shared pattern of behaviour, exists in a community and governs how members behave, think, make judgements and perceive the world. The shared norms, formal or informal, explicit or implicit, define a culture or subculture. A subculture may be a team who know how to work effectively together, and their norms include a solution to their organizational problems.

Four types of norms exist, namely evaluative norms, perceptual norms, cognitive norms and behavioural norms. Each type of norms governs human behaviour from different aspects. In business process modelling, most rules and regulations fall into the category of behavioural norms. These norms prescribe what people must, may, and must not do, which are equivalent to three deontic operators "is obliged", "is permitted", and "is prohibited". Hence, the following format is considered suitable for specification of behavioural norms:

    whenever <condition>
    if <state>
    then <agent>
    is <deontic operator>
    to <action>

With the introduction of deontic operators, norms are more flexible than the business rules recognised by RUP, and provide more expressiveness. For those actions that are "permitted", whether the agent will take an action or not is seldom deterministic. This elasticity characterises the business processes, therefore is of particularly value to understand the organizations.

If we know the various norm-subjects who are the agents in the organization and we know the specific norms they should obey, then we can deduce what information individual or group agencies in the organization will need and what they produce for others to use.

4. AN ORGANIZATIONAL SEMIOTICS EXTENSION

In this section, semantic analysis and norm analysis methods are incorporated into RUP. The purpose of the case study is to illustrate how the existing components of RUP can be improved by semiotics methods, rather than extending RUP to gain insights of the organizations. For this reason, although organizational semiotics is very powerful to disclose the social aspects of the information systems, this is largely not covered by this chapter.

4.1. Semantic analysis

Our observations in the case study show that the meanings of terms depend on the context in which they are used. Organizational semiotics provides a unique way to build the contexts.

First, a business term is associated with two important elements, the agent(s) who perceives and uses it, and the possible actions the agent(s) takes upon it. The meanings of a business entity can be reached by specifying the actions different agents take upon it. In object oriented methods, the functionalities of an agent can be modelled as his/her functions or behaviours. Using UML, figure 1 shows part of the potential actions different agents can take on a crime, e.g., a crime recorder creates a crime from a crime-related incident. A Crime Allocator allocates to it resources such as budget, personnel, and vehicles, a Crime Auditor audits it to generate statistic data, etc. No direct link with the court and law can be found in the figure, and the fact that a crime can be audited to create statistic data more or less suggests its documentary nature. The above information enable us to understand the term "crime" in the context of crime management business much better than a dictionary definition like:

crime: an act or the commission of an act that is forbidden or the omission of a duty that is commanded by a public law and that makes the offender liable to punishment by that law; especially : a gross violation of law... (Except from Merriam-Webster's Collegiate Dictionary)

We must keep in mind that unlike a normal object oriented analysis, in semantic analysis only responsible agents are allowed to perform actions. A printer may seem to have the ability to print, but in semantic analysis the responsibility of printing must belong to a responsible person or organization.

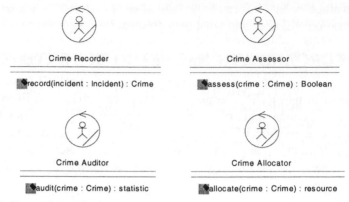

Figure 1. Define a crime: affordances

Figure 1 may suggest some similarities to the business use case analysis, which is already included in RUP. Figure 2 shows some business use cases that are relevant to the definition of the term "crime". Both of them are related to the behaviour descriptions. However, the primary question asked in use case analysis is how different users use the system, rather than what kind of actions different responsible agents can take upon one business entity. A business entity is not necessarily part of the use case, and in those circumstances like inter-system transactions, a computer or computer system is qualified as a user.

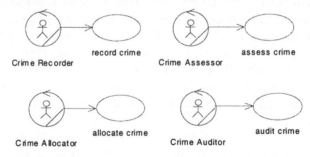

Figure 2. Define a crime: use cases

Another important contribution from the semantic analysis is the concept of ontological dependency. While the affordances define what kind of behaviour can possibly be implemented by whom, ontological dependencies define the context for the behaviours to happen. For example,

Society – Law – Home Office Counting Rules – Crime

denotes that a crime exists in the context of the home office counting rules, which in turn depends its existence on law. The law system is also defined in the context of a society. Although a Crime is not a specific type of Home Office Counting Rule (no inheritance relation between them), its existence depends on the existence of the later. If the legislation is to be changed, the home office counting rules as well as the definition of crime in the crime management system will all need to be revised. In some cases, the police forces will have no ground to create a certain type of crime, because it is not deemed as crime any more by the revised counting rules. These ontological dependencies contains important business knowledge, but are usually overlooked by most traditional information systems modelling process.

In object oriented system design, a possible modelling element that can reflect these non-inheritance ontological dependencies is the nested class. If B is a nested class of A, its definition is within that of the class A, therefore for any B object to exist, an A object must be created beforehand, and the A object can only be destructed after B ends its lifetime. Outside the scope of class A, B will not have any meaning. Also, no B object can be accessed from outside of an A object. Using UML, the above scope definitions are shown in Figure 3.

Society   Law   Home Office Counting   Crime
             (from Society)   Rules   (from Home Office Counting Rules)
                                  (from Law)

Figure 3. Define a crime: ontological dependencies expressed as nested classes

However, some ontological dependencies such as
Incident – Crime
can be modelled as inheritance relations (as shown in Figure 4). Due to the constructor and destructor grammar of an object oriented language such as C++, the life time of a crime must always be within that of an incident, therefore automatically conforms the requirements of an ontological dependency relationship. The Crime class is modelled as the subclass of the Inheritance class only because from the object oriented view, a crime can be deemed as a particular type of incident.

Incident   Crime
(from Home Office Counting Rules)

Figure 4. Define a crime: ontological dependency expressed as subclass

4.2. Norm Analysis

Although the term crime has been defined from the perspective of affordances and ontological dependencies, one important aspect we have not touched till now is the business rule. People are not totally satisfied to only knowing a crime can be created by recording the assessed incidents etc. How the assessment is being done can provide more help for people to understand it.

Norm analysis is used instead of the rigid business rule collecting and documentation in RUP. Liu and Ong (1999) proposed to extract norms from activity diagrams. Here we use the same notation but stick to the semantic analysis framework. We gather the agents' potential actions on a particular business term, then we analyse and record the agents' norms for each of the actions. Figure 5 shows part of the norms a crime recorder used to decide whether to create a crime or not.

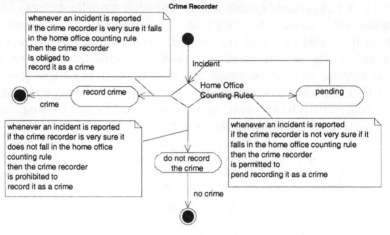

Figure 5. Define a crime: norms

4.3. Granularity and iteration

Question may arise why the iterations of business modelling must be put to an end, now that the organizations and their business will inevitably change with the time and the environment. The answer is that although changes are inevitable, business models must be delivered on time so that the IT systems construction can start to implement the models. Since a large portion of the activities involved in the business modelling are related to the processes of reaching consensuses among the domain experts and the business analysts, a method is much needed to help the modellers to reach consensuses quickly and efficiently enough to both effectively capture the business and catch up with the changes, instead of engaging themselves into non-stoppable arguments on the details, which in not uncommon in many business modelling projects.

For the granularity and iteration problems encountered in the RUP, organizational semiotics methods give a simple and straightforward solution. All analysis and modelling tasks must be strictly restricted to the level of agents, affordances, ontological dependencies, and norms. In the business modelling, there's no place for those automated jobs people delegate to the computer, e.g., dialogue boxes popping up, windows opening and closing, etc. However, as shown in figure 2, those crucial operators, parameters and visibility tags that show affordances and ontological dependencies must be kept. It's also noteworthy that within the business domain, most ontological dependencies should be implemented rather than left open. For example, while "crime" is within the scope of both "home office counting rules" and "incident", the question how they are related should be answered. Some of the questions, such as how the home office counting rules are related to law, or how people is related to society, can be very difficult to answer and implemented. But if the question is within the business domain, it cannot be avoided.

If the granularity of the business modelling is strictly kept to the level of answering questions like who does what based on which rule, the convergence of different views in the model will be very fast, therefore the semiotics methods can be used as the iteration criteria.

Organizational semiotics methods do not attempt to build an invariant business model which can last forever, but instead, provide a mechanism that helps the iterations induced by the changes converge to a relatively stable model that can be delivered to the system analysts and modellers.

SUMMARY

In this chapter, semantic analysis and norm analysis are mapped to object oriented paradigm and expressed in UML to improve the RUP. To summarise, the following improvements are made:

- While identifying the major business actors, business workers, and the boundary of the business, the connotations and denotations of these business entities must be analysed in terms of affordances and ontological dependencies.
- The ontological dependency relationships must be reflected on the business object models in terms of class creation and destruction. Two possible mappings to the object oriented methods are inheritance relationship and nested class.
- Responsibility analysis takes the form of Norm Analysis, which not only covers the behavioural norms, but also the perceptual norms and many others although not explicitly stated, exists as untold rules. An important source to extract these norms is the workflow description of the business, although semantic analysis remains the framework for doing norm analysis.
- While describing business use cases as a sequence of transactions performed by the business worker, the level of abstraction must be strictly kept to the level of their affordances, ontological dependencies, and norms. Once in different views of the models these elements are synchronised, the iterations come to an end.
- Improving the conventional methods with organizational semiotics facilitates a converging process for reaching semantic representation with clear definitions of responsibilities, which delivers an agreed business model.

Further validation of the improvements will be conducted in the near future.

ACKNOWLEDGEMENTS

The work reported in this chapter was partly supported by the Police Information Technology Organisation (PITO) during Inspector David Emmitt's secondment with PITO.

REFERENCES

Gibson, J. J. (1979). *The ecological approach to visual perception.* Boston: Houghton Mifflin

Hartshorne, C. & Weiss, P. (eds.) (1960). *The collected papers of Charles Sanders Peirce.* Harvard: Harvard University Press

Jacobson, I., Booch, G. & Rumbaugh, J. (1998). *The unified software development process.* Reading, MA: Addison-Wesley.

Krogstie, J. (1999). *UML, a good basis for the development of models of high quality?* Retrieved June, 2002, from http://dataforeningen.no/ostlandet/metoder/krogstie.pdf

Kruchten, P. (2000). *The rational unified process: an introduction.* 2nd edition, Addison Wesley.

Kobryn, C. (1999).UML 2001: a standardization odyssey. *Communications of the ACM, 42(10),* 29-37.

Liu, K. (2000). *Semiotics in information systems engineering.* Cambridge: Cambridge University Press

Liu, K., Ades, Y., & Stamper, R. (1994). Simplicity, uniformity and quality: the role of semantic analysis in systems development. In Ross, M., Brebbia, C.A., Staples, G., & Stapleton J. (Eds), *Software quality management, volume 2: building quality into software* (pp219-235). Computational Mechanics Publications.

Liu, K., & Ong, T. (1999) A modelling approach for handling business rules and exceptions. *The Computer Journal, 42(3),* 221-231.

OMG (2002). *Unified modelling language specifications, version 1.4.* Retrieved June, 2002, from http://www.omg.org

Stamper, R. K. (1996). Signs, information, norms and systems. In Holmqvist, B., & Andersen, P. B. (eds.), *Signs of work: semiotics and information processing in organisations* (pp 349-379). New York: Walter de Gruyter.

Stamper, R. K. (1997). Organisational semiotics. In Mingers J. & Stowell F. (eds.) *Information systems: an emerging discipline?* (pp267-283). London: McGraw-Hill.

Stamper, R. (2000). Organisational semiotics - information without the computer? In: Liu, K., Clarke, R.J., Andersen, P.B., Stamper, R.K., (Eds), *Information, organisation and technology, studies in organisational semiotics.* Amsterdam: Kluwer.

Stamper, R. K., Liu, K., Hafkamp, M., and Ades, Y., (2000) Understanding the role of signs and norms in organisations, - a semiotic approach to information systems design. *J. of Behaviour and Information Technology, 19(1),* 15-27.

Chapter 5

Linking Intention and Processes in Organizations

Andy Salter

ABSTRACT

This chapter addresses how the intention of an agent responsible for an instance of a pattern of behaviour determines the processes by which the instance is started or finished.

An organization may be modelled using the concepts of Semantic Analysis which determine the relationships between agents and affordances - the patterns of behaviour available to the agents. These relationships may be represented in an ontological schema. A particular, the individual occurrence of affordance, is started and finished by processes resulting from communicative acts on the part of an agent

This chapter considers how the norms which initiate the processes leading to the start or finish of particulars may be triggered by substantive or communicative acts committed by or on behalf of an agent. In authorising the commitment of the act the agent has some intention to achieve something, the completion of a specific process. Different intentions on the part of authorising agents lead to triggering different norms and initiating different processes.

Modelling norms and processes which derive from different intentions recorded in communicative acts has two benefits. First it assists in the provision of semantic understanding of an organization; secondly it enables the model to incorporate changes to the organization in the form of changes to single rules or norms by which particulars may start or to complete changes in the affordances available to the agents.

The aim of the chapter is to demonstrate how the different intentions of the authorities initiating the start or finish of a particular may be used to define which norms and processes are selected to execute the start or finish. The concepts presented in this chapter are illustrated using an example of a library where members may borrow books or 'reserve' books with the intention of borrowing when the book is available.

1. INTRODUCTION

MEASUR is a set of techniques introduced by Stamper, Althaus, & Backhouse (1988) using concepts developed within the emerging field of Organizational Semiotics (Andersen 1997, Clarke 2000, Stamper 2001).

Using these techniques it is possible to represent organizations in terms of the agents from which the organization is made up, and the affordances, patterns of behaviour available to these agents. The approach looks for the meaning behind the interaction of the agents and approaches the whole organization as an information system rather than merely the data manipulated within it (Carvalho, 2000; Falkenberg et al., 1998). Semantic Analysis, one of the methods contained within MEASUR, can be used to determine the agents and affordances which represent an organization. The ontology charts, semantic schema in the form of a graphical representation of the organization, are part of the output of Semantic Analysis indicating the relationships between the potential patterns of behaviour which are afforded the agents within the organization. The affordances represented in the charts are termed 'universals'. 'Particulars' is the term given to specific instances or individual successful realisations occurring for each universal.

The charts of affordances use the concept of ontological dependency to represent some of the semantic meaning of the organization. Affordances are dependent on either one or two antecedents which must exist before the pattern of behaviour represented by the affordance becomes available to the agent. This is represented on the semantic schemas in a left to right relationship. Affordances to the right connected to those on their left are dependent on them. In the same way the particulars maintain ontological dependency.

The particular of any universal is dependent for its existence on the particulars of the universal which is antecedent to it. To derive the full meaning available for particulars, each particular requires the antecedents on which it is ontologically dependent, the times of start and finish of the particular, the authorities responsible for those starts and finishes and the intention of the authority when they authorised the start or finish of the particular. This information is important because the start or finish of a particular is the result of a process governed by norms. There may be a number of possible norms governing the same particular start or finish, the selection of which may be determined by the time, the authority or the intention of that authority. A different combination of these factors at the start or finish leads to different processes taking place.

The beginning of a process to start or finish a particular may be initiated in one of the following ways:

- a substantive act – physically placing a library book on the librarian's desk; or
- a semiological/communicative act – asking the librarian to place a hold on a book.

Taking the concepts of speech act theory (Austin, 1962; Searle, 1969) and communicative action (Dietz, Goldkuhl, Lind, & Reijswoud, 1998; Goldkuhl & Röstlinger, 1999), both of these ways may be considered as communicative acts. The concept here is similar to that illustrated by Goldkuhl in which *'both communicative and material actions may be described as instrumental, social and comprehensible'* (Goldkuhl, 2001). Communicative acts may result from substantive acts. The substantive act communicates an intention on the part of the agent authorising the act. The intention, which comprises part of the communicative act, defines the processes that the agent intends will be initiated by the act. The same act with a different intention may lead to a different process although the eventual outcome may be the same. By exploring the semantics of an organization in this way it is possible to derive understanding of the meanings of the interactions between agents within an organization. The theory behind the method is that,

"meanings are relationships between words and patterns of behaviour (in context) which they represent. Any norms that are appended to the ontological structure serve only to refine the kernel of meaning" (Stamper, 1996).

The application of authority and intention to the norms and processes helps to define the context of the relationships.

The start or finish of a particular, therefore, occurs in time and has a responsible authority who has some intention in initiating the process involved in the start or finish. If the process relating to the start is completed successfully then the particular will start. Once started the particular remains invariant until such time as a second process is initiated, following a similar procedure involving a communicative act which, if successfully completed, leads to the finish of the particular. Attached to each universal is a set of norms and processes which determine how a particular of the universal starts and finishes. These concepts will be demonstrated using a library management system (LMS) which need not be an electronic or IT system, it may be a physical record set (cards in a box).

2. SEMANTIC ANALYSIS AND THE ANALYSED DOMAIN

Semantic Analysis is a method which determines the relationships between agents and affordances. The analysis consists of four stages.

1) The problem is first defined, usually from a written description but always in discussion with the users and domain experts.
2) A linguistic analysis looking for verb and noun phrases, applied to the domain description results in a list of potential candidate affordances.
3) These potential affordances can then be grouped together in accordance with their ontological dependencies.

4)   In the final stage of Semantic Analysis a complete ontological chart can be produced which gives an indication of the structure of the organization.

The methods of Semantic Analysis have been explained in detail elsewhere, for example Liu, (2000); Stamper, Althaus & Backhouse (1988).

Agent and Affordance

Affordance is the term introduced by Gibson (1986) given to a collection of patterns of behaviour which define an object or a potential action. Affordances are the acts or behaviours permitted by objects, places and events (Michaels & Carello, 1981, p42). As examples, chairs, benches and stools afford sitting on; an object with a handle affords grasping. These concepts, which were applied to animals and the environment, can be extended to the social environment and organizations in terms of the patterns of behaviour available to members of a society.

The patterns of behaviour are defined within the context of the society and shared by members of that society. A cup for example can be defined as an affordance because it is associated with a set of patterns of behaviour including being able to contain things, the ability to be placed upright on a fairly horizontal, level surface, the possibility to be drunk out of in an acceptable manner (Stamper, 1985). A contract is an affordance that is determined by the patterns of behaviour of the material it is presented on (paper or electronic) and the behaviour it generates in the parties that are affected by it. Certain patterns of behaviour may, then, be recognised by the agent and classified as affordances, the concepts of which may be shared with other agents. In the social world the concept of affordance, patterns of behaviour, may include contracts, copyright and other 'legal' relationships (Stamper, 1996) and an organization may be modelled in terms of the properties of an environment, an agent and the kinds of actions supported in the interactions between agents (St. Amant, 1998).

Agents themselves are affordances, they exhibit patterns of behaviour, for example a person is born, dies, is able to manipulate (other persons and things) and is able to communicate. What makes agents different is that they can take responsibility both for their own actions and the actions of others.

Norms

Norms are the rules which determine how social organisms interact and control affordances (Liu, Sun, Dix, & Narasipuram, 2001; Sergot, 1998; Stamper, 1985). They include explicitly stated rules and regulations, for example a member may only borrow 7 books at any one time, and unstated, implicit social rules by which members of social groups including organizations interact; for example users of the library will wear clothes when visiting the library.

Affordances exist in time; they have a start and a finish and remain invariant during the period in between. Norms control the start and finish of each occurrence of an affordance; they may determine whether an occurrence of an affordance is successfully started or does not come into existence at all, and in the same way control if, how and when an occurrence of an affordance finishes. Norms govern the behaviour of agents within the organization. They may be represented by the general form:

If condition **then** consequence.

If the person is a member of the library **then** the member may borrow books.

The start or finish of the particular only occurs if the norm has a successful outcome, if the actions determined in the norm do not occur then the particular will not start, or will not finish (Salter & Liu, 2002).

The analysed domain

The domain to be analysed and modelled is as follows. The affordances of 'person', 'library' and 'book' exist and are defined by society. All affordances are defined within the context of 'Society' which gives the affordances the meanings by which we interpret them. Person and library are termed agents. These are affordances which can make and be responsible for, decisions which affect themselves and others. These agents will be the authorities who determine whether or not particulars of affordances may be started or finished. The existence of person and library enables a pattern of behaviour which is termed 'employ'. Books exist and may therefore be 'stocked' by a library. A person may borrow books which places the person in the role of 'borrower'. It is feasible for any 'person' to borrow books from a library although there may be norms which govern whether the person has to be a member or not before being allowed to borrow. A member may also 'reserve' a book for their use. This is represented as a semiological act, with which the 'reserve' indicates the intention of the person to 'borrow' the book at some future point in time. These concepts are explored further in Barjis, Dietz, & Liu, (2001) and Stamper (2001).

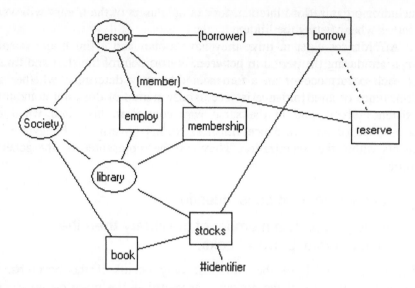

Figure 1. Ontology chart for a library domain

Figure 1 presents an ontology chart, a graphical representation of the library domain being considered (agents are represented as ellipses). The chart represents the ontological dependencies of the domain, for there to be membership, the library and the person must both exist, a library may stock books and a person may borrow stocks in the role of borrower. This is a brief sketch of the relationships between the affordances represented in the chart, more details of the methods used for representation may be found in Liu (2000); Stamper, Althaus, & Backhouse (1988).

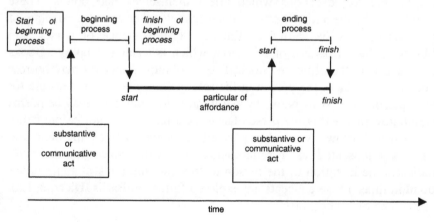

Figure 2. The start and finish of a particular

3. PARTICULARS, THE INDIVIDUAL OCCURRENCES OF UNIVERSALS

Further semantics of the organization may be derived when the information represented in the chart is considered with respect to the particulars, the individual occurrences of the universals shown in the chart. Each particular, dependent on the existence of its antecedents, exists in time. It has a start and a finish which may be determined and recorded. These starts and finishes are governed by norms and are the results of processes which occur before the start and finish of the particular. Nothing comes into or goes out of existence except as the result of some process which may be started by a substantive or communicative act (see Figure 2).

The substantive or communicative process, governed by norms, that begins an affordance finishes when the affordance starts or it may finish without success. The process itself may consist of other norms and may involve the start or finish of other particulars of the same or other affordances. If the process is successful the end of the start results in the creation of a particular of the affordance.

Any particulars of agents or affordances that are involved in the processes including those agents that are the authority for the start or finish of the particular must exist as particulars for the process to complete – this is a necessity of the ontological dependency. For example, for a particular of the affordance 'membership' there must exist particulars of the antecedents of membership, thus there must be a particular of person (i.e. 'John') and a particular of 'library' (i.e. ''Thompson library'). Given the existence of these particulars it is possible to start a particular of the affordance 'membership'. The start may be a communicative act "I (John) want to become a member of the library". This act triggers a norm:

if a person wants to become a member of the library, **then** the librarian should register the person for membership.

Note that the librarian, the agent responsible for enacting the norm must also exist as a particular, this is a prerequisite of the norm, if there were no librarians, or equivalent, there would be no agent to authorise the membership and the particular could not start. This norm leads to a process by which the person may be asked to give details about themselves and perhaps to prove their identity. If all of these details are accepted, the process finishes successfully and the particular of membership starts. The particular may be represented using the notation (Stamper *et al.*, 1988):

membership (John, Thompson library)

The act which triggers the norm responsible for the beginning of the process which may ultimately lead to the start or finish of the particular may be substantive or communicative.

4. ACTS LEADING TO THE START OR FINISH OF A PROCESS

Substantive acts

A substantive act involves the physical movement of an object. The act will have been authorised, at some point, by an agent who may or may not be involved in the actual movement of the object. The act will however be a reflection of the intention of the agent authorising the act. Thus, a person places a library book in a 'returns' box by the library door. The intention of the person is to return the book to the library, to end the particular of the book loan thereby having it recorded that the borrower no longer has the book and may borrow another book. This act may be done without any form of direct verbal communication or discourse between the borrower and library. It initiates a process which continues when the librarians open the box, the book is scanned, the library management system records the fact that the book has been returned and the borrower's record is altered to indicate that the book has been returned to the library. If the box is never opened, the process is not completed and the book remains recorded as being borrowed by the member. The particular does not finish.

Semiological or communicative acts

A semiological act occurs when there is the transfer of a sign between two parties. The sign may be in written or electronic form, a piece of paper or electronic message with a representation of the book that is required, the title or ISBN number. The process is thus begun by a communicative act between the member and the library (librarian). The member may signal that they wish to 'reserve' a book, that they wish to borrow the book and would like the library to reserve the book for their use. The act triggers the norm:

> ***whenever*** a person is a member, ***if*** the member wishes to reserve a book ***then*** the librarian should reserve the book.

The norm begins the process which involves the librarian determining if the book has been borrowed in which case they must indicate that the book is requested on the library management system (so that when the borrower comes to return the book the system notes that it may not be renewed and is to be placed on hold). If the book is recorded as 'on the shelf' then the librarian should go to find the book, remove it from the shelf to the hold shelf and then indicate on the library management system that the book is on hold.

5. INTENTION

Which norm is triggered to begin the process of starting or finishing a particular is defined by which agent (defined as the 'authority') initiates the act and what the intention of that agent is. There is thus a direct link between intentions, norms and processes initiated by the norms. Returning a book to the library involves a range of intentions, leading to different processes. The borrower may return the book intending to become eligible to borrow another book finishing the particular of the affordance 'borrow'. The substantive act of returning the book leads to the librarian checking the book against the library management system (LMS) records. If the check reveals that there is no problem with the return or the borrowers details, fines outstanding etc, then the LMS records that the book has been returned and the particular is finished.

It may be the intention of the borrower to renew the loan of the book. In this case the beginning of the ending process is the same as for return, the LMS checks the details of the book against the records, if the details are validated then the process continues by finishing the particular of borrow and triggering the start of a new particular of borrow, the ending process connects to a beginning process.

In the case of borrowing a book which has been 'reserved' by the library, the beginning of the start of the particular of 'borrow' is initiated by a communicative act in which the person communicates the intention to borrow the book which they previously asked to be 'reserved'. The process continues by the librarian validating the person's membership card and determining if the member may borrow the book. If the norms governing the start of the particular are successful then the particular may start and the member may borrow the book. The same process resulting in the start of the particular for borrow results in the finish of the particular for the affordance 'reserve':

> **whenever** a book is placed on hold, **if** the person placing the hold borrows the book **then** the librarian should remove the 'reserved' status from the record of the book on the LMS.

The processes may thus be represented as series of norms selected from norm fields (Stamper, 2000a) depending on authority and intentional considerations. Sometimes the links may not be obvious, a norm governing the length of time a book may be held may govern the start of a particular to 'borrow' a book.

The intention of the authority initiating the processes may be overridden by temporal effects. For example if the hold has expired due to the passage of a certain period of time after the 'hold' was placed then the particular of the affordance 'hold' may have finished. The book may be returned to the library shelves and be available for borrowing by any member.

6. PROCESSES

The start and finish of a particular may be the result of a complex process which involves several steps possibly including the start or finish of particulars of other affordances. Renewing a book that has been borrowed is the combination of finishing one particular of the affordance 'borrow' and starting another using the same antecedents but with different temporal data. The start of a particular relating to borrow may be connected to a book that is reserved – the beginning process for a particular of the affordance 'borrow' would in this case include the ending process for a particular of the different affordance 'reserve'.

The beginning and ending processes are governed by norms. For a start or finish to occur the series of norms attached to the process must all be completed. For example the start of a particular of the affordance borrow. The particular is started by the substantive act of the person taking the book to the librarian, The authority is thus the person; the intention is to borrow the book.

This substantive act triggers the norm:

> **if** a person intends to borrow a book **then** the
> librarian may issue the book.

The execution of the norm begins the beginning of a borrowing process in which the librarian determines if the person is eligible to borrow the book. Are they a member of the library? Have they exceeded their borrowing allowance? Are there fines outstanding against the person which prevent them from borrowing further books? The librarian asks the person to produce a membership card as a result of the following norm being embedded in the beginning process:

> **if** a person wishes to borrow a book **then** the
> person must produce a valid membership card.

If the member cannot produce the card then the norm is not successfully completed and therefore the process within which the norm is embedded does not complete successfully. In this case the particular of the affordance 'borrow' does not start.

If the person produces the card then the librarian may validate it thereby validating that person's membership and their eligibility to borrow books. The process continues by triggering the norm:

> **if** a member wishes to borrow a book **then** the
> librarian must check that the book is available for
> borrowing.

The book will have some form of identifier which enables the librarian to determine if the book is a reference work or if a hold has been placed on the book which prevents it being borrowed. If the book is available and the member is eligible to borrow it then the process continues by allocating the book to the member and recording on the LMS that the book has been borrowed – the start of a particular. The substantive borrowing is a social relationship capturing a number of rights and obligations for the parties to it. This is a semiological representation of the fact that the borrower has borrowed the book.

This example of the start of a particular of the affordance 'borrow' is relatively simple, the only authority responsible for the substantive act which begins the start of the process leading to a potential start of a particular is the borrower, their intention is to borrow the book. If the intention had been to renew the book loan then the process might start with the norm:

> **whenever** a member has borrowed a book, **if** the borrower wishes to extend a borrowing **then** the borrower must inform the library that they wish to renew the book loan.

The process involved here will include checking that the book has not been requested by another member, that the borrower is still eligible to borrow the book, to finish the current particular of 'borrow' and to start a new particular with altered temporal data.

7. CONNECTIONS DUE TO ONTOLOGICAL DEPENDENCY

Ontological dependency also has a considerable effect on the processes and the connection of affordances. Any particular which is dependent on an antecedent must finish when the antecedent does. Thus, for example, if a person indicates to the library their intention to finish their membership of the library then any particulars dependent on that particular of membership must also finish. The ending process for the membership therefore includes the processes of checking for any unfinished particulars of other affordances dependent on the particular of membership. Ending processes will then be triggered for these particulars. Note the sequence resulting from the ontological dependency – all particulars which are dependent for their existence on a particular to which an ending process is applied must finish before the ending process can complete and the particular finish. If the member does not return any borrowed books, leaving a particular of the affordance unfinished, the ending process for the particular for membership will remain unfinished allowing the library to apply whatever norms are triggered temporally by the unfinished particulars of borrow or reserved, etc.

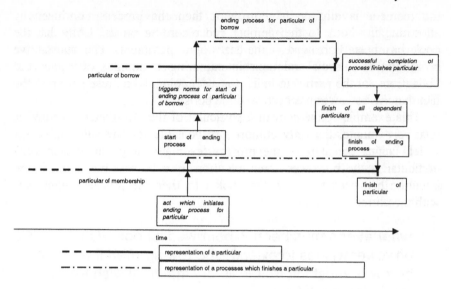

Figure 3. Finishing a particular of 'borrow' requires the finish of dependent particulars

Figure 3 represents how these processes would be related in time. The diagram starts on the left with time passing to the right. Particulars which are ontologically dependent appear above their antecedents and must exist within the time of the antecedent. The intention of the agent authorising the finish of a particular thus extends to the finish of any particulars dependent on it.

8. CHANGE IN ORGANIZATIONS

The information resulting from modelling the organization using Semantic and Norm Analysis, at the universal and particular levels may be recorded in a semantic temporal database (STDB) (Liu, 2000; Salter, 2001; Stamper, Althaus, & Backhouse, 1988). The STDB may also record information on the agent that initiated the norm leading to the beginning or ending process and the intention of the agent in doing so. This facility allows for changes to the organization to be recorded at a wide variety of levels. At the lowest level, single rules or norms may be changed or added so that new intentions on the part of agents may be included. Novel methods of communication may be incorporated by the addition of the relevant norms and complete affordances may be added to the ontological model without disruption of the existing schema and underlying STDB. Existing database and schema remain unaffected by changes until agents act in a way to finish particulars using the new information and processes.

9. CONCLUSION

To model organizations accurately requires the capture not only of the flow of data within the organization, but the relationships between the agents who are the members of the organization and the affordances, the patterns of behaviour available to them. The behaviour of these agents is governed by norms which initiate processes. Semantic details of the organization only become apparent when the agents responsible for invoking these norms and their intention when doing so are derived. Ontology charts represent the links between the agents and the affordances at a 'universal' level. The start of each particular, the individual realisations of each universal, involves a process which is initiated by a substantive or communicative act triggering a norm. Where several norms relate to a beginning process the selection of the norm which triggers the process will be determined by which authority is responsible for triggering the norm and their intention when doing so. Ontology charts as semantic schema present a level of meaning within the context of an organization. Further levels of meaning may be derived from the details of the particulars themselves, the norms involved, the particulars, the authorities responsible for the initiation of the particular and the intention of those authorities. Where there are several different processes which lead to the same effect, the start or finish of a particular, the authority and their intention make it possible to determine which route or process is required. Changes to an organization may be reflected in the model at the level at which the changes are made. Thus the change of a single norm may be represented or the addition of a completely new affordance to the organization may be easily recorded and applied.

REFERENCES

Andersen, P. B. (1997). *The Theory of computer semiotics*, Cambridge University Press, Cambridge.

Austin, J. L. (1962). *How to do things with words.* Oxford: Oxford University Press.

Barjis, J., Dietz, J. L. G., & Liu, K. (2001). Combining the DEMO methodology with semiotic methods in business process modelling. In K. Liu, R. J. Clarke, P. B. Andersen, & R. K. Stamper (Eds.), *Information, organisation and technology.* Dordrecht: Kluwer Academic Publishers.

Carvalho, J. A. (2000). Information Systems? Which one do you mean? In E. D. Falkenberg, K. Lyytinen, & A. A. Verrijn-Stuart (Eds.), *Information system concepts: An integrated discipline emerging* (pp. 259-276). Dordrecht: Kluwer Academic Publishers.

Clarke, R. J. (2000). *An Information System in its Organisational Contexts: A Systemic Semiotic Longitudinal Case Study*, Ph. D. Thesis, Wollongong, .

Dietz, J. L. G., Goldkuhl, G., Lind, M., & Reijswoud, V. E. v. (1998). The communicative action paradigm - an agenda. Paper presented at *The Third International workshop on the Language Action Perspective on Communication Modelling* (LAP'98), Stockholm June 25-26, 1998.

Falkenberg, E. D., Hesse, W., Lindgreen, P., Nilsson, B. E., Oei, J. L. H., Rolland, C., Stamper, R. K., Assche, F. J. M. V., Verrijn-Stuart, A. A., & Voss, K. (1998). *A framework of information systems concepts - the FRISCO report (web edition).* IFIP. Available: http://www.leidenuniv .nl /~verrynst/frisco.html.

Gibson, J. J. (1986). *The ecological approach to visual perception.* New Jersey: Lawrence Erlbaum Associates.

Goldkuhl, G. (2001, July 21-22, 2001). Communicative vs material actions: Instrumentality, sociality and comprehensibility. Paper presented at the *Sixth International Workshop on the Language-Action Perspective on Communication Modelling* (LAP 2001), Montreal, Canada.

Goldkuhl, G., & Röstlinger, A. (1999). Expanding the scope — From language Action to generic practice. Paper presented at the *Language Action Perspective*, 1999, Copenhagen.

Liu, K. (2000). *Semiotics in information systems engineering*. Cambridge: Cambridge University Press.

Liu, K., Sun, L., Dix, A., & Narasipuram, M. (2001). Norm-based agency for designing collaborative information systems. *Information Systems Journal, 11*, 229-247.

Michaels, C. F., & Carello, C. (1981). *Direct perception*. Englewood Cliffs, NJ: Prentice-Hall, Inc.

Salter, A. (2001). *Semantic modelling and a semantic normal form* (SOCTR/01/01): Staffordshire University, School of Computing.

Salter, A. & Liu, K. (2002). Using semantic analysis and norm analysis to model organisations. Paper accepted to the *ICEIS 2002*, Cuidad Real, Spain.

Searle, J. R. (1969). *Speech Acts - An essay in the philosophy of language*. Cambridge: Cambridge University Press.

Sergot, M. (1998). Normative positions. In P. McNamara & H. Prakken (Eds.), *Norms, logics and information systems* (pp. 289-308). Amsterdam: IOS Press.

St. Amant, R. (1998). *Affordances for acting in direct manipulation interfaces* (Technical Report TR-98-04): North Carolina State University.

Stamper, R. (1985). Knowledge as action: a logic of social norms and individual affordances. In G. N. Gilbert & C. Heath (Eds.), *Social Action and Artificial Intelligence* (pp. 172-191). Aldershot, Hampshire: Gower Press.

Stamper, R. (1996). Signs, information, norms and systems. In B. Holmqvist, P. B. Andersen, H. Klein, & R. Posner (Eds.), *Signs of Work: Semiosis and Information Processing in Organisations* (pp. 349-397). Berlin: Walter de Gruyter & Co.

Stamper, R. (2000a). New directions for systems analysis and design. In J. Filipe (Ed.), *Enterprise Information Systems* (pp. 14-39). Dordrecht: Kluwer Academic Publishers.

Stamper, R. (2001). Organisational semiotics - Information without the computer? In K. Liu, R. J. Clarke, P. B. Andersen, & R. K. Stamper (Eds.), *Information, Organisation and Technology: studies in Organisational Semiotics* (pp. 115-172). Amsterdam: Kluwer Academic Publishers.

Stamper, R., Althaus, K., & Backhouse, J. (1988). MEASUR: Method for Eliciting, Analysing and Specifying User Requirements. In T. W. Olle, A. A. Verrijn-Stuart, & L. Bhabuts (Eds.), *Computerised Assistance During the Information Systems Life Cycle* (pp. 67-116). Amsterdam: Elsevier Science.

Chapter 6

Deriving use case from business process models developed using Norm Analysis

Boris Shishkov, Zhiwu Xie, Kecheng Liu and Jan L.G. Dietz

ABSTRACT

Bridging software design and business process investigation appears to be a crucial research problem in modern software development. With respect to the UML-based software design, a fundamental question to be answered in solving the mentioned problem, is: How to find all relevant use cases, based on sound business process modelling? The adoption of business process modelling as a basis for identification of use cases has been studied by different researchers – it has been studied how use cases could be derived based on DEMO and Petri Net business process models. The goal of the this chapter is to tackle the problem from a new perspective in order to study the appropriateness of placing a use case model on a semiotic analysis. This could be helpful for identifying strengths of semiotic models, which could be useful for deriving use cases. We consider in particular Norm Analysis to be a proper semiotic tool for this purpose. We demonstrate the derivation of use cases based on Norm Analysis by means of a case study.

1. INTRODUCTION

UML (OMG, 2000) appears to be the standard language for conducting software design (Mallens et al, 2001). UML reflects the ideas of some of the most outstanding researchers and practitioners within the software community. Probably for this reason UML is widely accepted within the community and most of the current research on software design relates to UML. Rumbaugh, Booch and Jacobson state that the UML is meant for "visualizing, specifying, constructing and documenting the artefacts of a software intensive system" (Booch et al, 1999).

With regard to the design of software (including UML-based) that is intended to support contemporary business processes, a fundamental goal should be its alignment to prior investigation of these processes. The lack (in many cases) of such an alignment, on a consistent basis, is considered by Shishkov & Dietz (2002) as a major reason for the great percentage of software project failure (Liu, 2000). Actually, we observe two opposite phenomena (Shishkov, 2002).

On the one hand, we observe software being developed without prior (consistent) investigation of the (business) processes to be supported by it.

This means that the business requirements are poorly determined and the software design model does not have its roots in a business process model. Therefore, the developed software inadequately supports the business processes to their needs, and although its quality might be high from a software point of view, the effectiveness of its support to the target business processes remains low.

On the other hand, although in many cases sound business process modelling is conducted prior to the design of software, the business process model is only partially used, since it is not straightforwardly transformable into a relevant input for the software design. This undermines the full employment of the software and ICT possibilities in solving the particular business problem(s).

Therefore, the two outlined tasks need to be aligned in a better way, as claimed by Shishkov & Dietz (2002). The business process investigation and the development of ICT (software) applications for the support of the business processes should be considered as one integrated task.

Different researchers address issues related to the aforementioned problem. Dehnert & Rittgen present a formal representation for describing business processes (Dehnert & Rittgen, 2001). Its results could be of particular significance, especially if the work is further developed towards relating the representation to software design. Olivera, Filho and Lucena introduce an approach for conducting software design, based on business requirements analysis (Olivera et al, 2001). The approach appears to be consistent regarding the software related issues. However, it does not provide a straightforward mapping of a business process model into a software design model. Hikita & Matsumoto suggest a framework for the development of adaptive systems (Hikita & Matsumoto, 2001). It is investigated how the appearance of additional requirements could be easily integrated into the system's construction. But again, the framework does not provide a consistent mechanism for building a design model on the basis of business process investigation. Therefore, it might be concluded that further knowledge is still required in the direction of an application design that is based on business process investigation.

Narrowing the outlined problem by considering in particular the UML-based design of software (that supports business processes), our goal should be to find out how to derive use cases based on a consistent business process model (because it is well known that use cases are modelling constructs that serve to link the application domain (the business world) to the software domain, (regarding UML-based software development). We take into consideration that the software community still lacks consistent guidance for use case identification. Sound and complete methods for the construction of UML Use Case diagram (Jacobson et al, 1992; Fowler & Scott, 2000; Shishkov & Dietz, 2001) on the basis of business process investigation are still needed.

Adopting the business process modelling as a basis for the identification of use cases has been studied by different researchers; Shishkov & Dietz (2002) have been investigating use case derivation based on DEMO. Shishkov & Barjis (2002) have been investigating use case derivation based on a Petri Net business process model. The goal of the current chapter is to tackle the problem from the perspective of Semiotics in order to study the appropriateness of basing a use case model on a semiotic one. This could be helpful for identifying some advantageous features of semiotic models, which could be useful for deriving use cases. We consider Norm Analysis (NA) to be a proper semiotic tool for this purpose. We demonstrate the derivation of use cases based on NA through a case study.

In this chapter, the basic concepts regarding NA and use cases are discussed in Sections 2 and 3, respectively. Section 4 studies how use cases could be derived based on NA. In Section 5, we explore a case example related to a hotel reservation system, in order to demonstrate the suggested NA-based use case derivation. Section 6 contains the conclusions.

2. BUSINESS PROCESS MODELLING BASED ON NORM ANALYSIS

When studying organizations from the perspective of the behaviour of agents it is necessary to specify the norms based on which this behaviour is realized. Norms (Stamper et al, 1997) are the rules and patterns of behaviour, either formal or informal, explicit or implicit, existing within a society, an organization, or even a small group of people working together to achieve a common goal (Liu et al, 2001).

Norms are determined by society or collective groups, and serve as a standard for the members to coordinate their actions. An individual member uses the knowledge of norms to guide his or her actions. If the norms can be identified, the behaviours of the individuals, hence their collective behaviours, are mostly predictable. From this perspective, specifying an organization can be done by specifying the norms (Stamper, 1992).

Four types of norms exist, namely evaluative norms, perceptual norms, cognitive norms and behavioural norms. Each type of norms governs human behaviour from different aspects. In business process modelling, most rules and regulations fall into the category of behavioural norms. These norms prescribe what people must, may, and must not do, which are equivalent to three deontic operators "is obliged", "is permitted", and "is prohibited". Hence, the following format is considered suitable for specification of behavioural norms:

whenever <condition>
if <state>
then <agent>
is <deontic operator>
to <action>

It is essential to recognise that norms are not as rigid as logical conditions. If a person does not drink water for a certain duration of time he cannot survive. But an individual who breaks the working pattern of a group does not have to be punished in any way. For those actions that are "permitted", whether the agent will take an action or not is seldom a determining factor. This elasticity characterises the business processes, therefore is of particular value to understand the organizations.

A NA is normally carried out on the basis of the results of the Semantic Analysis (for information on Semantic Analysis interested readers are referred to (Liu, 2000)). The semantic model delineates the area of concern of an organization. The patterns of behaviour specified in the semantic model are part of the fundamental norms that are embedded in the ontologically determined relationships between agents and actions without imposing any further constraints. However, NA could also be successfully related to other modelling tools, e.g the UML activity diagram, Petri net, etc.

In general, a complete NA can be performed in four steps: 1) Responsibility analysis; 2) Proto-norm analysis; 3) Trigger analysis; 4) Detailed norm specification. Responsibility Analysis enables one to identify and assign responsible agents to each action. The analysis focuses on the types of agents and the types of actions. In an organization, responsibilities may be determined by the organizational constitution or by common agreements in the organization. Proto-norm Analysis helps one to identify relevant types of information for making decisions concerning a certain type of behaviour. After the relevant types of information are identified, they can be used as a checklist by the responsible agent to take necessary factors into account when a decision is to be made. The objective of this analysis is to facilitate the human decisions without overlooking any necessary factors or types of information. Trigger Analysis aims at considering the actions to be taken in relation to the absolute and relative time. The absolute time refers to the calendar time, while the relative time makes use of references to other events. The results of trigger analysis are specifications of the schedule of the actions. The detailed Norm Specification concerns the specification of norms in two versions, a natural language and a formal language. The purposes of this are (1) to capture the norms as references for human decision, and (2) to perform actions in the automated system by executing the norms in the formal language.

For those norms identified in the business processes, some refer to the major authorities and responsibilities of the major figures in the organizations. These norms govern some trivial, relatively less important norms or those of lower priorities, from the perspective of organizational functionalities. This strongly suggests that the possible hierarchies exist not only in the organization structure, but also in the norms. Liu et al (2001) use the terms framing norms, contractual norms, etc. to express the hierarchies.

3. THE IMPORTANCE OF USE CASES IN THE UML-BASED DESIGN OF SOFTWARE

With regard to the UML-based design of software, use cases have a crucial role in capturing the functional requirements that have to be fulfilled by the application software. These modelling constructs represent the system's functionality, by defining its behaviour without revealing its internal structure. They are incorporated in UML through the UC diagram – an essential UML diagram. The UC diagram has a fundamental role in the UML development process, showing actors and UCs together with their relationships (OMG, 2000). The diagram itself is a graph of actors, a set of UCs, and the relationships between these elements (associations, generalizations, etc.). It also might include some interfaces. By representing the potential UCs for the system to be built together with the relevant actors, the diagram provides the starting point in system modelling.

However, it is still a question how to properly identify UCs that correctly reflect the model of the processes to be supported by the developed software. Solving this problem would also bring a solution to the problem outlined in the introduction, regarding the alignment between software design and business process investigation, because if the UC model stems from a business process model, then the software development could be consistently placed on prior business process investigation. For this reason, the current section stresses upon UCs, outlining the most up-to-date concepts about these modelling constructs. In the following sections, the relation between the UC model and business process modelling is explored, particularly from the perspective of Semiotics.

As for UCs, exploring them should not be limited to UML, since they have appeared independently of UML. Anyway, Jacobson, who introduced UC (Jacobson, 1992), has further developed his ideas about UC in the direction of UML (Booch et al, 1999). It should also be noted that Cockburn has developed his own consistent UC perspective (Cockburn, 2000) which, although complementing the concepts of Jacobson in some respects, reveals slight contrasts with regard to other issues. Therefore, when considering the modern UC theory, one should take into account not only the fundamental concepts of Jacobson, but also e.g. the UC perspective of Cockburn (which adds elicitation value). The concepts of Jacobson and Cockburn are briefly outlined below.

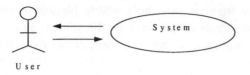

Figure 1. UC concept of Jacobson

Regarding **Jacobson's conceptual views**, also shared by Fowler (Fowler & Scott, 2000), in a UC *"a user performs a behaviourally related sequence of transactions in a dialogue with the system"*. This perspective is illustrated in Figure 1 and according to it, a UC is a typical user/computer system interaction. It captures some user-visible function. This view suggests that developers of good UCs identify the users' goals, not the system functions.

Jacobson provides descriptions of several UC formalisms: 1) The basic UC consists of structured text description, including alternative and exceptional behaviour. Scenarios may also be used to explain different perspectives of use. 2) There are two UC stereotypes - <<include>> and <<extends>>, and actor inheritance hierarchies. 3) There is a contract, specifying an object's interface in detail. Actors may provide a contract that involves multiple UC. Conversely, a UC may provide a contract that multiple actors use. 4) A stimulus from an actor will cause the system to leave its current state and carry out some tangible amount of work, which is associated with pre- and post-conditions.

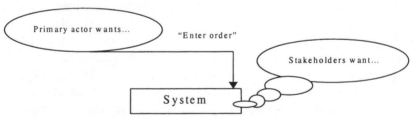

Figure 2. A UC as seen by Cockburn

Cockburn's concept adds elicitation value to the fundamental UC theory. His work (Cockburn, 2000) has existed among the most ambitious material in the domain since 1992, when Jacobson introduced UC. According to Cockburn, a UC describes a system's behaviour. His view is illustrated in Figure 2.

In his model, Cockburn defines at the most generic level a *system* and *actors* (both having responsibilities and behaviour). He is interested in just these actors, situated outside the system, and starting from these actors he chooses those whose interests should be protected by the system. Cockburn calls these actors *stakeholders*. The *primary actor* (or *user*) is one of the stakeholders, the one who has the goal and who initiates the system's activity. The system should satisfy this goal but at the same time it should protect the interests of the stakeholders.

The primary actor's *goal* drives the UC. The primary actor should be determined as well as the goal level; a goal may contain sub- and sub-sub-goals. Three most widely used goal levels are suggested – user goal (the goal the primary actor has in trying to get work done), summary goals (involving multiple user goals), sub-function goals (those required to carry out user goals).

Besides determining the goals, it is essential to exactly determine what system is under discussion. This is called *scope*. Functional scope refers to the services that the system offers. Design scope is the set of systems, hardware and software, that the developer is charged with in his designing and discussing. It is important that the writer and reader are in agreement about the design scope for a UC. Cockburn suggests as fundamental: "*Enterprise*" scope – the UC describes a person's interaction with an organization, "*System*" scope – the UC describes a person's interaction with hardware/software, "*Subsystem*" scope – refers to situations where we describe how a piece of a system works.

A UC may also include other elements – action steps, scenarios, preconditions, etc.

The outlined perspectives need to be **compared** considering the purposes behind them.

Aiming at looking inside UC, Cockburn has built a concept that allows developers to keep interest not only in the user of the system (the primary actor) but also in the other stakeholders. For this reason, the model of Cockburn seems more complete than the model of Jacobson. At the same time, the graphical representation of the Cockburn model is unsuitable for presenting a multitude of UC.

The latest developments in Jacobson's UC concept are put in the perspective of UML. For this reason, instead of focusing on the complete representation of a UC, the concept emphasizes on features that allow developers to show relationships which cover a large number of UCs and actors. This is the main function of the UC diagram. Thus, Jacobson extracts the gist – actors, pieces of functionality and their relationships.

Jacobson and Cockburn form their UC perspectives starting from different angles. This indicates that UC needs further exploration in order to provide options for both complete insight and flexible multi-UC representation.

However, in the current chapter, basing our study on the concept of Jacobson (reflected in the UML), we also take into consideration the ideas developed by Cockburn.

4. DERIVING USE CASES FROM NORM ANALYSIS

As stated in the introduction, we claim that NA can be useful in bridging UML-based software design and business process investigation. Our arguments are as follows:

(a)   NA is an effective and proven tool for investigating (in combination with Semantic Analysis) business processes;

(b)   UCs mark the starting point in UML-based software design;

(c)   Regarding a business system under study, NA specifies the rules according to which the behaviour of agents is realized;

(d)   UCs represent the functionality of a system by defining its behaviour.

Hence, in trying to align software design and business process investigation, we claim that deriving UCs from a NA model would be useful, and is placed on sound theoretical foundation, since both modelling tools reflect behaviour within business/software systems (norms describe rules of behaviour; UCs represent pieces of functionality). This is actually the relation between the OS-based NA and the use case modelling. Hence, deriving use cases from such a Semiotic model has sound theoretical foundation.

In this section, we suggest how to base UC-derivation on NA (Figure 3).

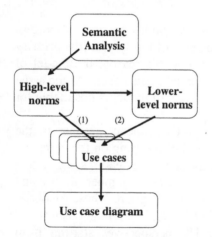

Figure 3. Deriving Use cases from Norm Analysis

It is clear that before deriving UCs from norms, we need to produce a consistent and complete set of norms, reflecting the considered business system. The first step in doing this, as shown on the figure, is to conduct Semantic Analysis and construct an Ontological chart. On this basis, it is possible to straightforwardly derive the High-level (HL) norms which include: Framing norms (these fundamental norms (concerning the model) which, as explained in Section 2, govern the general responsibilities underneath) and the rest of the higher priority norms. The HL norms can easily be derived based on Semantic Analysis, and this is well-known in the Semiotic theory.

Once the HL norms are identified, one could proceed with the identification (based on them) of UCs that reflect essential behaviour (Dietz, 1994). These UCs should be straightforwardly identifiable since both they and HL norms concern essential business system behaviour.

Taking into consideration that in order to produce a complete UC model, we need not only the UCs reflecting essential behaviour but also those UCs reflecting behaviour elaboration, our development process also suggests to further elaborate on the HL norms an go towards lower-level norms (e.g. Behaviour norms). These norms are valuable in deriving from them UCs that reflect elaboration of essential behaviour.

In summary, our suggested development process is claimed to be a contribution to the knowledge on aligning software design and business process investigation (in general) and on deriving UCs from business processes (in particular). According to the process, some UCs are straightforwardly derived from HL norms, others from lower-level norms. This is illustrated in Section 5 using a case example.

5. THE HRB CASE

A system, representing a Hotel Reservation Broker (HRB) is modeled in order to illustrate the NA-based UC derivation. Since the goal is just illustrative the developed case is fictitious. However, real hotel reservation systems were considered beforehand in order to thoroughly understand and reflect the problems related to such systems.

HRB matches the data about clients' required accommodation and hotel offers. Both the hotels and clients need to register in order to use the service for a selected period of time. The subscription fees for hotels are fixed depending on the chosen period and the hotel size; the fees are fixed for clients also, depending on the chosen period. Besides these subscription fees, both clients and hotels pay fixed fees when a match-making is realized. Further on, we refer to these fees as: a "reservation fee" (paid by a client) and a "hotel fee" (paid by a hotel). HRB accepts accommodation requirements from clients (e.g. check in/out dates, place, type of accommodation, price, etc) and accommodation information from hotels (e.g. number and type of rooms/beds available, etc.). Once HRB has received requirements from a client, if requested, it performs match-making on a real time basis. HRB provides the client with a list of available accommodation to select from. Once the client has accepted one of the offers, he pays the reservation fee. He also has to pay the costs of the selected accommodation. Then, HRB is obliged to guarantee the accommodation. HRB should contact the selected hotel and realize the actual booking of a particular room/bed. Then, the hotel has to pay to HRB the hotel fee. The hotel will be paid (by HRB) the costs of the reserved accommodation. Once this is done, the reservation is actually completed and the service is considered finished.

Further on, we design (using the UML UC diagram) the functionality of such a software broker, based on a consistent investigation of the business processes to be supported by the developed software application. This investigation is based on Semiotics and is performed in the first, second and third phases of our study. The fourth phase deals with the actual UC derivation.

First. Based on the textual description and after delimitation of the domain, an Ontology chart (or another suitable business process modelling tool) needs to be applied. Based on this, we should further identify the HL norms corresponding to the system outlined above. Because of the limited scope of this chapter we are not going to depict the Ontology chart. Conducting Semantic Analysis and producing an Ontology chart based on a textual description is well studied and demonstrated in (Liu, 2000).

Second. Based on an Ontology chart, the set of HL norms are identified (including the Framing norms (called for short "f-Norms" in this chapter) as well as the other higher-level norms). These are:

f-NORM 1
Whenever
<Client/Hotel has decided to use HRB>
If <The Client/Hotel initiates subscription>
Then <the Client/Hotel>
Is <Obliged to>
To <Pay the subscription fee>

f-NORM 2
Whenever
<The subscription fee is paid by the Client/Hotel>
If <The Client initiates the match-making>
Then <HRB>
Is <Obliged to>
To <Perform the match-making>

NORM 3
Whenever
<The match-making is completed successfully>
If <An accommodation is selected by the Client >
Then <the Client>
Is <Obliged to>
To <Pay the reservation fee>

NORM 4
Whenever
<The match-making is completed successfully>
If <An accommodation is selected by the Client >
Then <the Client>
Is <Obliged to>
To <Pay the accommodation costs to HRB>

NORM 5
Whenever
<An accommodation is selected by the Client >
If <The reservation fee and the accommodation cost are paid by the Client>
Then <HRB>
Is <Obliged to>
To <Guarantee the accommodation >

NORM 6
Whenever
<An accommodation is selected by the Client >
If <HRB has triggered the booking procedure with the corresponding hotel>
Then <the Hotel>
Is <Obliged to>
To <Pay the hotel fee to HRB >

NORM 7
Whenever
<An accommodation is selected by the Client >
If <HRB has triggered the booking procedure with the corresponding hotel>
Then <HRB>
Is <Obliged to>
To <Pay the accommodation costs to the Hotel >

NORM 8
Whenever
<The hotel fee is paid by the Hotel >
If <The accommodation costs are paid by HRB>
Then <the Hotel>
Is <Obliged to>
To <Reserve the accommodation >

Third. Based on the identified norms, it is possible to derive lower-level norms, as "behaviour" norms, for instance (we call this "norm elaboration"). As already stated, these norms are an important supplement to the basic identified norms for the purpose of UC derivation, because a complete UC model needs to reflect the behaviour elaboration as well. We have illustrated the norm elaboration with one norm derived from Norm 5:

NORM 5

Whenever

<An accommodation is selected by the Client >

If <The reservation fee and the accommodation costs are paid by the Client>

Then <HRB>

Is <Obliged to>

To <Guarantee the accommodation >

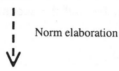

Norm elaboration

NORM A

Whenever

<An accommodation is guaranteed by HRB >

If <The accommodation is refused by the Hotel>

Then <HRB>

Is <Obliged to>

To <Return the accommodation costs, reservation fee, and penalty to the Client >

Fourth - development of a UML UC diagram, based on the built models. The diagram (Figure 4) shows UCs and actors typical for such an HRB. Since the purpose of this section is just illustrative, only some of the UCs and actors typical for such a system are considered.

Regarding the diagram, there are two actors represented on it: *Client* and *Hotel*. Concerning Client (Hotel) – he takes the decision, he has the responsibility, he has the goal to subscribe for using HRB and have his information matched up with relevant data about accommodation (potential clients).

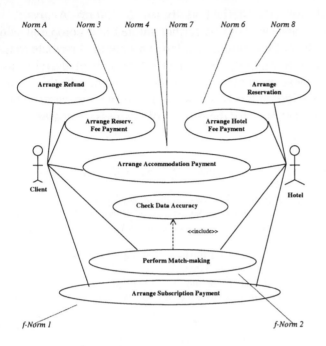

Figure 4. Use Case Diagram of HRB derived from NA

The diagram contains eight UCs: "Perform Match-making", "Arrange Refund", "Arrange Reserv. Fee Payment", etc. There is one <<include>> relationship ("Perform Match-making" requires "Check Data Accuracy").

It can be easily seen on the figure, which are the norms each of the UCs are derived from (dotted line). It can also be seen also that UCs are derived not only from HL norms but also from lower-level norms, which indicates that in designing a software system it is essential to reflect not only the essential behaviour (reflected by the HL norms) but also the behavioural elaboration regarding the considered business processes.

6. CONCLUSION

This chapter's goal, as stated in the introduction, is to contribute to the knowledge on use case derivation based on business process modelling. We further continue the investigation of Shishkov & Dietz in this direction, by studying how a use case model could be placed on a semiotic analysis. In particular, we have shown that use case derivation could be consistently realized based on a business process model that is developed using Norm Analysis. This has been demonstrated through a case study.

It was established that norms (both HL and lower-level norms) are a suitable source on which use case identification can be based. However, it should be noted as well that producing norms requires Semantic Analysis (or other business process investigation) to be conducted beforehand which is a drawback since it makes the modelling process more complicated.

The suggested use case derivation, based on Norm Analysis, is claimed to be useful and needs to be further studied and compared with the other existing ways of use case derivation. This could contribute to the efforts directed towards finding the most effective way of deriving use cases based on business process investigation. Succeeding in this would contribute to the design of good software, regarding the cases where software applications are built for the support of business processes.

REFERENCES

Booch, G., Rumbaugh, J., & Jacobson, I. (1999). *The Unified Modelling Language User Guide*. Addison-Wesley, USA.

Cockburn, A. (2000). *Writing Effective Use Cases*. Addison-Wesley, USA.

Dehnert, J. & Rittgen, P. (2001). Relaxed Soundness of Business Processes. In *the proceedings of the 13th Int. Conference on Advanced Information Systems Engineering, Interlaken, Switzerland*.

Dietz, J.L.G. (1994). Business Modelling for Business Redesign. In *the proceeding of the 27th Hawaii International Conference on System Sciences, Los Alamitos, USA*.

Dietz, J.L.G. (1999). Understanding and Modelling Business Processes with DEMO. In *the proceedings of the 18th International Conference on Conceptual Modelling (ER), Paris, France*.

Fowler, M. & Scott, K. (2000). *UML Distilled, Second Edition – a Brief Guide to the Standard Object Modelling Language*. Addison-Wesley, USA.

Hikita, T. & Matsumoto, M. J. (2001). Business Process Modelling Based on the Ontology and First-order Logic. In *the proceedings of the 3rd Int. Conference on Enterprise Information Systems, Setubal, Portugal*. ISBN: 972-98050-2-4.

Jacobson, I., Christenson, M., Jonsson, P., & Overgaard, G.(1992). *Object-Oriented Software Engineering: A Use Case Driven Approach*. Addison-Wesley, USA.

Liu, K. (2000). *Semiotics in Information Systems Engineering*. Cambridge University Press, London, United Kingdom.

Liu, K., L. Sun, A. Dix, M. Narasipuram. Norm-based Agency for Designing Collaborative Information Systems. *Info Systems Journal, 11, 2001*.

Mallens, P., Dietz, J.L.G., & Hommes, B.J. (2001). The Value of Business Process Modelling with DEMO Prior to Information Systems Modelling with UML. In *the proceedings of the 6th CAiSE/IFIP Int. Workshop on Evaluation of Modelling Methods in Systems Analysis and Design, Interlaken, Switzerland*.

OMG (2000). *UML, Version 1.3*. Object Management Group – www.omg.org.

Olivera, T.C., Filho, I.M., & Lucena, C.J.P. (2001). Using XML and Frameworks to Develop Information Systems. In *the proceedings of the 3rd Int. Conference on Enterprise Information Systems, Setubal, Portugal*. ISBN: 972-98050-2-4.

Shishkov, B. (2002). Business Engineering Building Blocks. In *the proceedings of the 9th CaiSE Doctoral Consortium, Toronto, Canada*.

Shishkov, B. &Barjis, J.(2002). Modelling of e-Business Brokerage Systems Using UML and Petri Net. In *the proceedings of the 17th IFIP World Computer Congress, Montreal, Canada*.

Shishkov, B. & Dietz, J.L.G. (2002). Modelling of e-Business Brokerage Systems Using DEMO and UML. Chapter 11, *Building blocks for Effective Telematics Application Development and Evaluation*. TU Delft Edition, Delft, The Netherlands. ISBN: 90 5638 092 3.

Shishkov, B. & Dietz. J.L.G. (2001). Analysis of Suitability, Appropriateness and Adequacy of Use Cases Combined with Activity Diagram for Business Systems Modelling. In the proceedings of the 3rd Int. Conference on Enterprise Information Systems, Setubal, Portugal. ISBN: 972-98050-2-4.

Stamper, R. (1992). Language and computer in organised behaviour. In Riet, R.P.v.d. and Meersman, R.A., (eds.), *Linguistic Instruments in Knowledge Engineering*. Elsevier Science, Amsterdam, The Netherlands.

Stamper, R., Liu, K., Hafkamp, M, & Ades, Y. (1997). Signs Plus Norms – One Paradigm for Organizational Semiotics. In *the proceedings of the 1st Int. Workshop on Computational Semiotics, Paris, France*.

Chapter 7

Towards an integral understanding of organizations and information systems: Convergence of three theories

Göran Goldkuhl and Annie Röstlinger

ABSTRACT

A need for an integrated theoretical understanding of organizations and information systems has been acknowledged. For this purpose three theories inspired by language action perspective are investigated. These three theories (Theory of Practice, Business Action Theory, Information Systems Actability Theory) deal with different but related subject matters. The theories have theoretical affinities but lack clear relations. The common theoretical thread of these theories is articulated in terms of socio-instrumental pragmatism. The different theories give substance and basis for steps towards development of an integral understanding of organizations and information systems. This includes the clarification, modification and convergence of the investigated theories.

1. INTRODUCTION

There is a widespread claim that computer-based information systems (IS) should be viewed and understood contextually. Information systems are parts of larger organizational work systems and the use of IS should give support to those broader work systems. However, it is often reported that information systems do not fit the organizational context which they are part of. Many approaches have been developed intended to overcome these deficiencies. One can, for example, regard much of process management and knowledge management approaches as attempts to bridge the gap between IS and the organizational context. The early process management approaches (e.g. Davenport, 1993) claimed the need for a joint development of IS and human resources. Similar claims can also be found in many approaches to knowledge management (e.g. Nonaka & Takeuchi, 1995).

One main problem is that there seem to be noticeable differences between theories concerned with IS on the one hand, and theories concerned with organizational issues on the other hand. Theories on IS can be oriented towards technological and informational aspects. Theories concerned with organizations are often oriented towards economic aspects including ways of allocating organizational tasks between people (issues of leadership, control, work structures etc). These different theories deal with different subject matters and their theoretical grounds are disparate and thus hard to relate and combine. Hence, our claim is that there is a need for theories that encompass both IS and organizational aspects.

Attempts have been made to create IS theories which are more context-sensitive, with ambitions to cover aspects of both IS and organization. There are also theories concerning work and organization which have been brought into the IS area. Such examples are Activity Theory (Nardi, 1996; Kuutti, 1996) and Actor Network Theory (Walsham, 1997). The IS character, however, seems not yet to have been sufficiently described in these theories. There are also examples of non-IS scholars who have tried to treat the relations between IS and organizational issues. The comprehensive work of Castells (1996) can be mentioned here. Although very illuminating, such theorising does not provide sufficient in-depth and integral understanding either of IS and organization and their complex relations.

Where should one search for an answer in this quest for an integral understanding of organizations and information systems? We turn our interest to another set of theories brought in from outside the IS area: Theories oriented towards communicative action. Inspired by language action (LA) theories (Austin, 1962; Searle, 1969; Habermas, 1984) there are several authors who have described the character of IS: E.g. Goldkuhl & Lyytinen (1982), Winograd & Flores (1986), Holm (1996), Schoop (1999) and Goldkuhl & Ågerfalk (2002). The communicative action approach has also been used to describe organizations. For example, Taylor & Van Every (2000) claim that communication is the very core of organizations. Organizations are constituted of and sustained through communicative acts (cf also Boden, 1994). Therefore, communicative action theories seem appropriate and promising to use as a common theoretical thread for understanding both IS and organization.

We turn our interest to a particular group of three theories developed inspired by communicative action theory. 1) Business Action Theory (BAT) is a theory concerned with the business interaction between customer and supplier (e.g. Goldkuhl, 1998). BAT describes six generic phases of business interaction and it acknowledges communicative actions as well as value exchange between the business parties. 2) Theory of Practice (ToP) is a theory concerned with workpractices (e.g. Goldkuhl & Röstlinger, 1999). It gives a relational and contextualised description of an organization or some part of it. It emphasises different "governance forces" of a workpractice, i.e. external assignments (from customers) and internal assignments (from management), external and internal norms and also instruments used in the workpractice (material as well as immaterial). 3) Information Systems Actability Theory (ISAT) views IS as action systems (e.g. Ågerfalk, 1999). The theory conceptualises different use situations: Interactive, automatic and consequential use situations. The communicative character of IS is emphasised by a recognition of both performative and propositional/conceptual aspects.

This last theory is thus oriented towards IS. The other two theories are oriented towards workpractices and business interaction, that is towards more organizational issues. These different theories share a common theoretical background, not only in communicative action theory, but also in more general action theory. Together, these three theories can potentially provide an integral understanding of different IS and organizational aspects. At the moment these three theories are not explicitly related to each other and therefore, as such, they cannot yet contribute to the desired encompassing view of IS and its organizational context.

Our claim is that the three theories together provide a potential for an integrated theoretical understanding of organizations and information systems. The purpose of this chapter is to investigate these three theories and to make explicit connections between them. The purpose is thus to take steps towards theory clarification and integration.

A common background in communicative action theory is one important theme connecting the three theories. The ambition to go beyond communicative action theory and incorporate aspects of material actions and artefacts, is another conjoining factor. Many actions in organizations are not communicative actions per se. There are many actions dealing with transforming and transporting material objects. A comprehensive IS/organizational theory must incorporate such material aspects. To have a theory on computer-based information systems which does not acknowledge the technical and material character of computers, seems to be self-contradictory.

The three theories offer a possibility to view information systems as *organizational sign artefacts with action capabilities* (Goldkuhl et al, 2001). This stance transcends a pure representational view on signs. The representational aspect of signs is acknowledged, but the action character of signs is emphasised (e.g. Austin, 1962). Using the semiotic ladder of Stamper (2001) as positioning instrument, we will focus on the pragmatic and social aspects of signs and communication.

There may be other candidates for theory integration to consider. In this chapter, however, we will not try to incorporate such theories. What we will do is to investigate and clarify the common theoretical thread of the three theories. One important reason for limiting ourselves to these theories, at this moment, is the closeness and affinity between them. They can be seen as members of the same theory family, however, concerned with different domains. It is an important task to make this theory family more congruent. But it should not be seen as an interest restricted only to the proponents of these theories. The theory clarification and integration are aimed at taking steps towards a coherent view on information systems and organizations[1].

In this chapter, the common theoretical thread of the three theories will be articulated in order to facilitate further theory integration. We will call this common theoretical background *socio-instrumental pragmatism*. Pragmatism means an emphasis on actions. We are not creating a theory of isolated human actions. Instead, the main interest will be on actions directed towards other persons, i.e. social actions. In our action view we will also acknowledge the importance of using material or immaterial instruments when performing actions. Therefore, our focus will be on socio-instrumental actions.

2. THREE ACTION ORIENTED THEORIES

2.1. Theory of Practice (ToP)

ToP is a theory concerned with workpractices. The kernel of the theory is a generic characterisation of workpractices made in a contextual and relational fashion. The model is built from the following four basic categories:

- actors in roles
- actions
- action objects
- relationships between actors/roles

The focus is on a workpractice and how it satisfies its clients through the production of products based on different prerequisites. A workpractice can be seen as a complete organization, or as some delimited part of an organization or as an integral part of (the interaction of) several organizations, or as some other meaningful unit of activities. ToP, as a theory and model, was presented in Goldkuhl & Röstlinger (1999) and later refined in Goldkuhl et al (2001). It is a theory developed with inspiration from language action theories; e.g. Searle (1969) and Habermas (1984). It has, however, a broader scope and other sources of inspiration that are described in Goldkuhl & Röstlinger (1999) and Goldkuhl et al (2001). The generic model of a workpractice is depicted in figure 2.1.

---

[1] This chapter should not be interpreted as a rejection of other theories and approaches. We have a great interest in different theories within an action perspective that contributes to the understanding of IS and organisations. It is a task for future research to perform further theory integration. It should, however, be noted that all the selected theories are eclectic frameworks built from different action-oriented theories.

The main result from a workpractice is products for clients[2]. There exist several different prerequisites for creating products. An assignment can be either an externally furnished product order or an internally created assignment, such as e.g. a job description. The base is "raw material" used for transformation into products. The need for economic compensation is also recognised in the model. Different norms and judgements have an impact on what is performed in a workpractice. Such norms and judgements are both externally furnished and internally created. The ability of a workpractice is also recognised in the model. This kind of workpractice ability is seen as instruments for action and it consists of knowledge, , artefactfunctionality and supporting descriptions like manuals. Knowledge and instruments always evolve over time through experiences from performed actions.

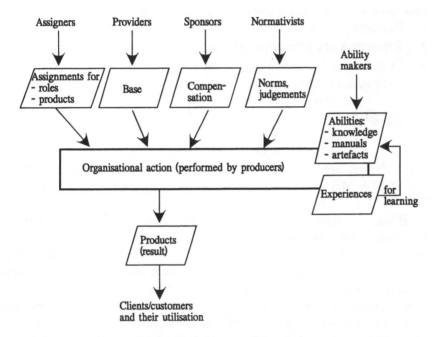

Figure 2.1 A generic model of workpractices – ToP model (from Goldkuhl et al, 2001)

The ToP model is claimed to be used as a basis for further theoretical development and in practical development and evaluation situations. In the latter cases the ToP model has been used as a template for making "workpractice definitions" of an organization or parts thereof. In Goldkuhl & Röstlinger (1999) and Goldkuhl et al (2001) examples of applications are presented (a web shop and municipal home care respectively). A ToP-based workpractice definition is said to be an instrument for governing and focusing business and IT design (ibid). ToP aims at being a theory on a generic level. It is said to be used as a basis for the development of theories with more restricted domains. One example is Nilsson (2000)

---

[2] The term "client" is used, as it is a more neutral term than "customer".

who, based on ToP, has developed an adapted theoretical model of knowledge management activities within organizations.

A workpractice is defined in the following way: "A workpractice means that some actor(s) - based on assignments from some actor(s) - makes something in favour of some actor(s), and sometimes against some actor(s), and this acting is based on material, immaterial and financial conditions and a workpractice ability which is established and can continuously be changed." (based on Goldkuhl et al, 2001).

2.2. Business Action Theory (BAT)

BAT is a theory on business interaction between customers and suppliers. It describes in a generic way how customers and suppliers interact when conducting business (the business logic). The business interaction is structured in six generic phases. These phases are:

* Business prerequisites phase
* Exposure and contact search phase
* Contact establishment and proposal phase
* Contractual phase
* Fulfilment phase
* Completion phase

BAT was presented in Goldkuhl (1998) and proposals for revisions and additions have later been presented in e.g. Axelsson et al (2000) and Goldkuhl & Melin (2001). The original phase model is depicted in figure 2.2.

Business interaction is considered to consist of business communication and exchange of value (products vs. money). The whole model is inspired by language action theories (e.g. Searle, 1969; Habermas, 1984). Inspiration comes also from other LA-based business interaction models, such as e.g. Action Workflow (Medina-Mora et al, 1992), where different generic communicative acts are identified and ordered in a generic way. The BAT model differs from other LA models (as Action Workflow). It starts earlier in the business process and it also includes material acts (exchange of value). Generic communicative acts - such as offer, delivery promise and claim (of supplier) and query, order and claim (of customer) - are identified and ordered in the phase model. BAT emphasises exchange between supplier and customer in each stage. The contract, as a mutual commitment made by both business parties, plays a central role in the business interaction. The phases before contracting can be seen as preparatory phases and after the contract has been established, fulfilment and assessment follow.

Later developments of BAT include separation between recurrent business transactions and long-term (frame) contracting (Axelsson et al, 2000) and introducing influences concerning corporate abilities (Goldkuhl & Melin, 2001). Lind & Goldkuhl (2001) have presented an architecture of generic layers as a conceptual development of BAT. The BAT model has been used as an instrument for the design and evaluation of business processes (examples are found in the papers referred to above).

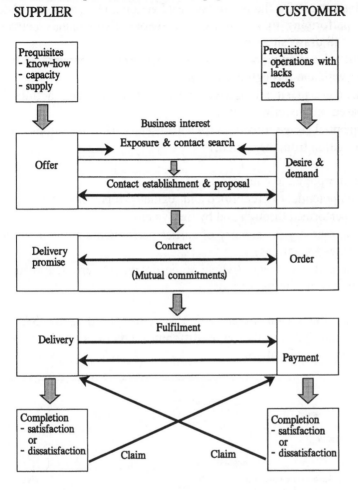

Figure 2.2 The BAT model of business interaction (from Goldkuhl, 1998)

2.3. Information Systems Actability Theory (ISAT)

What we here choose to call ISAT is a theory on information systems. The theory is based on the actability perspective on information systems. ISAT has been presented in many different publications, e.g. Ågerfalk (1999), Cronholm et al (1999), Ågerfalk et al (1999) and Goldkuhl & Ågerfalk (2002). The theory has been used as a basis for developing methods for information requirements analysis (Ågerfalk, 1999). It has also been used as an instrument for understanding and evaluating information systems. The actability notion takes a central position in the theory. Actability is defined in the following way: "An information system's ability to perform actions, and to permit, promote and facilitate the performance of actions by users, both through the system and based on information from the system, in some business context" (Cronholm et al, 1999). A computerised information system considered to be an "action system". It is both an instrument for the performance of action and a support tool for humans in performing their actions. The theory distinguishes between three types of IS usage situations:

- Interactive usage situation (where users performs actions interactively together with and through the system)
- Automatic usage situations (where the system performs actions by itself based on predefined rules)
- Consequential usage situations (where users performs actions based on information from the system)

An IS is interpreted to consist of:

- An action potential (a predefined and regulated repertoire of actions)
- Actions performed through and by the system
- An action memory (a memory of earlier performed actions including prerequisites for actions)
- Messages and documents (where some documents are action media for the user's interactive actions)

An information system as an action system, according to ISAT, is depicted in figure 2.3. In this figure, different kinds of actions (and thus usage situations) are visualised.

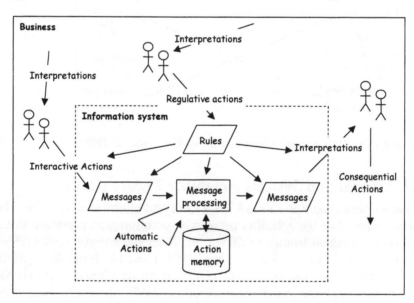

Figure 2.3 Information system as action (from Ågerfalk, 1999)

Actability can be compared to the usability notion, which is one key concept within human-computer interaction (e.g. Nielsen, 1993). ISAT gets some of its inspiration from the usability area, but it also tries to extend and transcend this view with regard to IS (e.g. Cronholm et al, 1999). Part of this broadening of views is the emphasis on actions performed by both users and IS. An IS is seen as an organizational action artefact (Goldkuhl & Ågerfalk, 2002). ISAT does not only focus on interactive situations, but also on automatic and consequential situations as described above.

The action view on interaction between human user and the computerised IS has led to a generic model of three phases: The Elementary InterAction Loop model – EIAL (Ågerfalk, 1999). This model is depicted in figure 2.4.

Figure 2.4 The Elementary InterAction Loop – EIAL (from Ågerfalk et al, 1999)

3. TOWARDS A THEORY INTEGRATION

3.1. Action translation between theories

As we have seen, the three aforementioned theories are concerned with partially different subject matters. However, they also cover similar kinds of phenomena. The theories partially use different concepts (terminology), which makes it somewhat problematic to compare them and to use them together. In our analysis of the theories, we have found it necessary to make them more comparable with each other. For that reason, we have applied a common example. The example (a web shop) is described through different organizational actions performed by different actors. We have used all three theories to look at these actions. This means that we have used the concepts from each theory to classify each action situation. In this sense, we made an "action translation" between the theories. We have created an example which covers phenomena valid for all three theories. The use of the simple example is meant to illustrate the three theories and relations between them.

We will describe the example briefly: An enterprise (here called eCompany) sells products through the Web. Their web site consists of product descriptions (standard offers) and purchase functions. Customers can register their order by filling in a form at the web site. After receiving orders, the IT system[3] of eCompany produces delivery directives. The IT system handles information about customer orders and products in inventory. The delivery directives are used by stock workers when they pick products from the inventory and deliver them to the customers. For further usage of this example, we have delimited four action situations:

1) Customer searching among available products at the web site
2) Customer registering an order through the web site
3) IT system handling orders and producing delivery directives
4) Stock workers picking products from the inventory and delivering them to customers.

We have made a classification of different aspects of the four action situations according to the three theories. This classification is documented in figure 3.1 below.

ECompany Example (Performed actions)	Business Action Theory (BAT)	Theory of practice (ToP)	IS actability theory (ISAT)
1) Customer searching among available products at the web site	Proposal phase; Product description on the web = supplier making offers to customers	Product description on the web = product repertoire (internal assignment); Web site = instrument for product orderers	Interactive action; Exposure and search for possible offers from eCompany/web site to customer/user
2) Customer registering an order through the web site	Contract phase; Customer sending order to supplier	Customer order = product order (external assignment); Web site = instrument for product ordering	Interactive action; Customer/user registering order; eCompany/web site receiving order
3) IT system handling orders and producing delivery directives	Fulfilment phase; Supplier preparation for delivery of products	IT system = instrument for transforming product orders (assignments)	Automatic action; Producing (communicating) delivery directives through updating action memory concerning orders and inventory
4) Stock workers picking products from the inventory and delivering them to customers	Fulfilment phase; Delivery of products to customer	Stock workers = producers; Inventory = base; Delivery from eCompany = products for clients and their uses	Consequential action; Stock workers/users picking and delivering products based on IT produced delivery directive

Figure 3.1 Illustrations of different aspects of the BAT, ToP and ISAT theories through a common example (eCompany)

---

[3] In the following we use the term IT system (and not information system) in order to emphasise our designation of systems based on information technology.

The ToP analysis has been focused on different *roles* and *action objects*. E.g., the IT system is seen as an instrument for transforming product orders, and the stock workers are identified as producers. We want to comment on the distinction between external and internal assignments. The customer order (as product order) is an externally generated assignment. The product description (as the product repertoire of eCompany) is an internally generated assignment, although it is, of course, exposed to potential product orderers (customers).

The different action situations of the example have been classified as different *IS usage situations* according to IS Actability Theory; i.e. interactive, automatic and consequential actions. Different actor roles (customers and stock workers) are identified as *IS users*. We have also identified different types of *information actions* performed by IT systems or users; e.g. exposing, searching, receiving, updating action memory, communicating.

In sections 3.2-3.5 below we will perform an analysis of differences, similarities and overlap between the three theories.

3.2. Relations between ToP and BAT

We will now focus on some relations between Theory of Practice and Business Action Theory. BAT is a two role model with focus on business interaction between two business partners (customer and supplier). ToP can be seen as a model of the workpractice of a producer (supplier), with relations not only to its clients (customers) but also to many other parties (especially those who create prerequisites for the workpractice). BAT is a reciprocal model and ToP is oriented towards one particular workpractice and how it satisfies its clients. One fundamental difference is that BAT describes business interaction in terms of commercial relations, whereas ToP tries to describe both commercial practices and non-commercial practices, i.e. it has a broader scope even in this sense. This is one explanation why the terminology differs. ToP has tried to use a more "neutral" terminology, while BAT has a clear business terminology. In the aforementioned example and in our elaboration on related issues, we applied a clear business focus and we will continue with such a focus below.

Both theories have an action and actor orientation. BAT runs on the organizational level. Supplier and customer organizations are seen as actors. There is no explicit connection to human actors. In ToP both organizations and humans are regarded as actors.

BAT describes the interaction between a supplier and a customer in more detail than ToP, but there are also clear correspondences between the theories. The customer order (in BAT) is described as one kind of assignment (product order) in ToP. The delivery from the supplier (in BAT) is described as the main result from the workpractice - the product (in ToP). Payment from the customer (in BAT) is one type of compensation (in ToP). These are the three parts where there is a clear correspondence between BAT and ToP. One can also say that parts of claims from customer (in BAT) can be interpreted as judgements (in ToP). Other actions described in BAT, such as e.g. supplier's offer, delivery promise and possible claims, are disregarded in ToP.

There are many aspects in ToP which are disregarded in BAT. Examples of this are internal assignments and bases from providers. In BAT the first phase is concerned with establishing prerequisites for conducting business. For the supplier this is said to be know-how, capacity and a supply. Parts of these business prerequisites can be compared with the workpractice ability of ToP. We think that this is one point where the two theories could converge and not use different concepts and terms. One proposal is that BAT should use the concept of organizational ability, since this concept is more theoretically articulated (Goldkuhl et al, 2001; Goldkuhl & Braf, 2002).

One way to conceive BAT in relation to ToP is to say that BAT is a magnification of some aspects in ToP. The latter is a more holistic and encompassing theory, covering both inter-organizational and intra-organizational issues, while BAT has an inter-organizational focus. BAT can be seen as focusing on how product orders are created and resolved. BAT describes how customers (product orderers/clients in ToP) and suppliers (producers in ToP) establish agreements and how these agreements are fulfilled and possibly questioned through claims. BAT can in this sense be seen as a business assignment theory and as such an extension of ToP in a similar way as the product theory of Goldkuhl & Röstlinger (2000) is considered as an extension and magnification of product aspects of ToP. One further development of BAT could then be to adapt it more clearly to ToP as a supporting sub-theory.

Is there no need for influence on ToP from BAT? We do think that there is something to be learned from BAT. There is in ToP only one thing that is thematised in the relation from producer/supplier to client/customer: The product as a result of the workpractice. Of course, the product should be seen as the main result, but there are other aspects which could also be considered important. There is not only a need for products; there is also a need for product descriptions. We propose to add product description as one result of the workpractice in the ToP model. For example, product descriptions are important supplements to products for an effective utilisation of them (often in the form of manuals). Following BAT, different communications from supplier to customer must include description of the product. An offer should of course, to some extent, describe the product that is offered.

3.3. Relations between ToP and ISAT

We will now focus on some relations between Theory of Practice and Information Systems Actability Theory. One important part of ToP is its emphasis on the abilities of the workpractice as important prerequisites. The ISAT view on information systems is that such systems hold and expose an action repertoire. The IS has powers to act (in an automatic way) and it also affords possibilities to users to interactively perform actions through the system. These different ingredients of the IS action repertoire are to be conceived as its actable ability. Such ability is part of the total ability of the workpractice, which is clearly acknowledged in ToP. The details of IS actability are, however, not described in ToP. These two theories seem to be congruent concerning organizational ability. ToP gives the broad view and ISAT presents a deepened view concerning IT abilities.

In ToP, IT systems are seen as instruments, meaning instruments for the producers in their performance of actions in order to create products for clients. In ISAT this instrumental view is acknowledged when such systems are viewed as supporting devices for human action (in interactive and consequential actions). But in ISAT IT systems (as artefacts) are also viewed as possibly independent performers of actions (in the automatic mode). This aspect is not explicitly recognised in the ToP model. We propose that ToP should adopt the differentiated view of IT artefacts as it is expressed in ISAT.

One of the strengths of ToP is that it gives a clear view of relations to different external actors (e.g. clients, providers, sponsors). The roles in ISAT are restricted to users of IT systems or other IT stakeholders. Other specific roles are not recognised. Concerning these matters we conceive ToP as a necessary complement to ISAT. When discussing IT systems in workpractices[4], we think that a more nuanced role apprehension is often needed than the one offered by ISAT. We think that ToP has an interesting potential regarding how to view and pursue the development of IS and thus a potential for ISAT on a theoretical level. The different categories of a workpractice, as they are described in the ToP model, should be cognizantly treated in the workpractice, and thus possibly by the support of IT systems. An IT system can hold and treat information about the different parts of a workpractice (e.g. its assignments, products, clients, norms)[5]. The workpractise categories could thus influence a proper theory of IS, or at least complement it when applied in design and evaluation situations. At the moment, ISAT does not consist of such workpractice categories.

On the other hand, we think that ISAT, with its notion of actability, has an interesting potential for ToP. In ISAT, actability is seen as an ability to perform and to support action. The domain of ISAT is IT system usage. This means that the notion of actability is restricted to such action. But this need not be the case. Why can actability not be valid for other types of actions? ToP is concerned with actions within and related to a workpractice. Producers perform actions in the workpractice in order to create products for clients. There ought to be favourable conditions for the

---

[4] We here think of different application situations as e.g. planning, design and evaluation of IT systems.

[5] In Goldkuhl et al (2001) this potential application of ToP is described in more detail.

producers to perform their actions. The ToP model describes different workpractice prerequisites. In ISAT only one of these (the functionality of IT artefacts) is emphasised as actable. As we see it, however, other prerequisites should also have actable features. Other parts of the workpractice ability, such as knowledge and competence of producers and different documented instructions should also be actable. Actable knowledge is knowledge that guides the actor when performing actions, and thus facilitates good quality in results[6]. Base is an important prerequisite for the workpractice. The base ("raw material") should be actable in the sense that it is easily transformable into products with the aid of suitable (i.e. actable) instruments. Assignments can also be characterised as more or less actable. An assignment that is actable informs the producers in a proper way, so they can accomplish what is expected. Diffuse assignments leave producers with uncertainty and do not have the same actability. It is difficult for producers to act properly when trying to follow vague assignments.

This line of reasoning is based on our view and definition of actability. We conceive actability to be a property of something, which *enables* and/or *contributes* to the performance of actions. Actable objects can be *external objects* (as e.g. artefacts or documents) or *internal states* (e.g. an actor's knowledge about something). We designate that actability does not only include *executable* properties which enable the action to be performed, but also *informative* properties, which guide the actor in his choice, performance and assessment of actions[7]. Such informative properties can be applied to questions concerning what to do, why to do something or why not to do something, how to perform, when to perform and where to perform, and how to assess the outcome.

3.4. Relations between BAT and ISAT

We will now focus on relations between Business Action Theory and Information Systems Actability Theory. As described above, BAT contains no references to artefacts. IT systems or other artefacts are not mentioned as categories in BAT. This means that if one describes business processes which include IT systems, there is no conceptual support from BAT for artefact descriptions. On the other hand, ISAT gives a detailed description of different IT artefact functions.

The two theories hold different views regarding actors/performers. In a business-to-business context, BAT is restricted in its actor view to "organizations as actors". The supplier and the customer (as organizations) are viewed as the main actors, which also involves an inter-organizational perspective. In ISAT, the main actors/performers are the IT systems and their human users. This means that BAT focuses on the

---

[6] This view is fully in line with Dewey (1938) and other proponents of American pragmatism.
[7] We are here inspired by Mead's (1938) view on actions with its perceptual, manipulatory and consummatory phases.

organizational level and does not differentiate between different performers (humans or artefacts) in the organization. ISAT has more of an intra-organizational focus, recognising different performers (as IT systems or human users) and their actions. There is no explicit focus on inter-organizational issues in ISAT. One consequence of this implicit intra-organizational focus is that the relations to external actors (customers/suppliers) are weak in ISAT. BAT, as mentioned above, focuses on commercial practices. In ISAT, there is no such delimitation. ISAT can be applied to both commercial practices and non-commercial practices.

One consequence of these differences between the theories is that there is a *categorical distance* between them, which makes it hard to relate the theories. However, the two theories have a common background in the communicative action framework. They both focus on different aspects of communicative actions; in BAT communicative acts are also seen as business acts and in ISAT communicative acts are also seen as IT mediated acts. Both theories keep a close link to the communicative action origin[8]. We think that the theories should be brought closer to each other. BAT should recognise intra-organizational issues; human actors and artefacts and their different roles and functions should be acknowledged. ISAT should recognise the inter-organizational business context more explicitly.

In section 3.3 (ToP vs. ISAT), we discussed the potential of expanding the actability view to the workpractice domain. We think that this is also valid for BAT in a transferred sense. For a supplier to perform its business acts towards a customer there have to be different internal conditions. Such conditions (implicit in BAT, but explicit in ToP) should support the performance of the different acts. These conditions should thus be actable. The same reasoning applies to the customer. This is fully in line with the discussion above concerning ToP (sec 3.3). The discussion can be expanded to the interactional sphere between customer and supplier. What the supplier performs towards the customer should be actable for the customer. E.g. the offer and its product descriptions should be actable for the customer in the sense that he can judge what and how to perform. Should the customer purchase or refuse the offer? The customer's actions should also be actable for the supplier. The customer's product queries should be transformable into offers. This means that what is done by one business partner should be actable for the other one too.

The business contract has a unique position as a joint action of both parties. It is an agreement made as a mutual commitment. The contract should be actable for both parties and their subsequent actions. We can call this reciprocal actability. This conclusion leads us further. A business action performed by one actor should not only be actable for the other partner. Such an action should also be actable for the actor in later actions. For example, a business offer made by a supplier should be actable both

---

[8] This also holds for ToP.

for the customer (e.g. it should be possible to make proper purchase evaluations) and for the supplier (e.g. it should be possible to realise into products according to offered prices).

3.5. Comparing the three theories

In sections 3.2-3.4, we have made a comparison in pairs between the theories. In this section, we will bring our comparison to the level of all three theories.

When comparing the three theories some interesting patterns can be found. In BAT there is a restriction to only two *roles*; customer and supplier. ISAT shows two kind of performers; the IT system and the IT system user[9]. ToP applies a broader differentiation between roles. In the first place, there is a differentiation between roles concerned with 1) creating prerequisites, 2) producing results and 3) receiving results. Especially among the first group, several subroles are distinguished; e.g. assigners, providers, sponsors, ability-makers. Some of these roles are even sub-classified; e.g. different types of assigners are identified.

There is a difference between the theories in how to regard *artefacts*. In BAT there is no recognition of artefacts at all. When reading the BAT columns in figure 3.1, there is no reference to IT systems or other artefacts, as opposed to ISAT, where there is a great focus on IT artefacts and different properties of such artefacts. In ToP, artefacts are recognised as one type of instrument. Both IT and other types of instruments/artefacts can be identified. ToP does not contain the fine sub-categories of IT artefacts that ISAT does.

BAT is a model with a focus on the *dynamics* of business interaction. It describes different phases, which are sequentially ordered from a start to an end. ISAT also contains some dynamics. Three types of usage situations are identified and related. The relations between these situations are not as strictly ordered as in BAT. The interactive usage situation is, however, ordered in three generic phases with a strict order (the Elementary InterAction Loop - EIAL). This interaction loop has a clear circular (recurrent) character in contrast to the BAT model, which lacks such a dynamic feature. The ToP model is not oriented to dynamics. It expresses principal relations between different actor roles and it is in that sense abstracted from such dynamics (as sequences of actions), which are expressed in BAT.

A general comment regarding the comparison of the three theories is that it is obvious that they deal with different subject matters. BAT offers details concerning business logic, which is not covered by the other two theories. ToP offers details concerning workpractice logic, which are not covered by the other two theories. ISAT offers details concerning IT usage, which are not covered by the other two theories. But there are also

---

[9] Ågerfalk (2001) has made a sub-classification of different IT users, but we are not treating this classification here.

similarities between the theories. It is interesting to see that all of them, in principal, cover the described types of action. The action characteristics of the four situations are described with the support of the theories, although in different ways and with different emphasis. The three theories give complementary action views of such organizational situations. They all acknowledge communicative actions. However, different aspects of such acts are emphasised from an organizational perspective. In ToP, communicative acts are conceived as acts of a workpractice (work acts). In BAT, the central concept is business act with recognition of both communicative and material business acts. In ISAT, IT mediated acts are considered as communicative acts.

As a result of our analysis and comparison, we have found *similarities* and *dissimilarities* between the theories. The relations between ToP, BAT and ISAT have been clarified. We have been able to compare the three theories according to some *common categories*, which have emerged through our work. The analysis has proved that our initial assumption about theoretical affinity was correct. The analysis has made the different aspects of the common theoretical ground more explicit. The different theories can be seen as complementary, compatible and coherent. Some unnecessary (conceptual and terminological) differences have been identified. We have formulated some proposals for modification and integration in order to increase the theoretical cohesion. These proposed changes include mutual adaptations in order to arrive at a theoretical convergence.

In figure 3.2 we have summarised our comparisons in this section and the sections above (3.2-3.4). While making our summary, we have also made explicit categories for comparison.

In the following, we will summarise the proposed changes in the three theories:

- BAT should use the concept of organizational ability (from ToP)
- BAT should recognise intra-organizational issues; human actors and artefacts and their different roles and functions should be acknowledged (from ToP and ISAT)
- ToP and BAT should adopt an actability perspective (a broadening of the actability concept from ISAT)
- ToP should include product descriptions as one result of the workpractice (inspiration from BAT)[10]
- ToP should adopt the differentiated view of IT artefacts as it is expressed in ISAT ISAT should inherit the more nuanced role apprehension from ToP
- ISAT should use workpractice categories (from ToP) as a conceptual basis when characterising IS

---

[10] This and other changes have been implemented in a new version of the ToP model (Goldkuhl & Röstlinger, 2002).

- ISAT should recognise the inter-organizational business context more explicitly (as BAT does)

Categories	ToP	BAT	ISAT
Scope	Workpractice and its contextualisation	Business interaction	IT usage
Subject	Commercial and non-commercial practices	Commercial practices	Commercial and non-commercial practices
Business logic	Some principle actions are recognised	Main focus; detailed (especially concerning exchange)	No focus
Organizational focus	Inter-organizational and intra-organizational focus	Inter-organizational focus	Intra-organizational focus
Capabilities	Workpractice ability (encompassing view)	Know-how and capacity	Action repertoire of IT system
Dynamics	Abstracted from dynamics (principal relations)	Dynamic phase model (from start to end)	Dynamic phase model (circular)
Roles	Multi-role model (workpractice and related actors)	Two-role model (reciprocal model of business parties)	IT system, IT users and other IT stakeholders
Role character	Three types: • Creating prerequisites • Producing results • Receiving results (with sub-types)	Two interactors in exchange situations: • Customer • Supplier	Two types: • Humans • IT artefacts
Actor view	Recognising organizations and humans as actors	Organizations as actors (no focus on human actors)	Focus on human actors (as IT users)
Artefact/ instrument recognition	Artefact as one type of instrument	No recognition	Detailed focus on IT artefact
IT artefact role	Instrument	No recognition	Instrument and performer
Emphasis of communicative acts	Work acts	Business acts	IT mediated acts

Figure 3.2 Comparison between the three theories

4. SOCIO-INSTRUMENTAL PRAGMATISM

The three theories described all have their theoretical basis in language action. Yet, they all include more than an LA-orientation. In this section, we will reconstruct and articulate some of the common theoretical thread of the three theories. We call this common ground socio-instrumental pragmatism. Elements of this theory can also be found in some earlier publications (Goldkuhl, 2001; 2002; Goldkuhl et al, 2001; Goldkuhl & Ågerfalk, 2002).

The basic concept is action. We start with a classical view on action: A purposeful and meaningful behaviour of a human being. We acknowledge the intentionality of human action. A human intervenes in the world in order to create some difference. A human performs an act and thereby creates some result. Often, the intention does not lie in the result, but rather in possible subsequent effects of the action and its result. The distinction between an action result (which lies within the range of the actor) and action effects, which may arise as consequences outside the control of the actor, is important (von Wright, 1971). Action effects can be both intended and unintended. An action is always performed in a situation of time and space and with constraining and facilitating factors. An action is performed in the present based on a history and aiming for the future. See figure 4.1 for an illustration of human action.

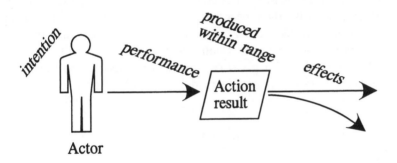

Figure 4.1 A model of human action

This classical action model is expanded into a model of social action. A social action is an action oriented towards other persons (Weber, 1978). It can be a communicative act; e.g. someone saying something to another person. The result of this act is an utterance. Effects of the act are the interpretation and understanding of the listener and his subsequent responses or other actions[11]. The listener is a recipient of the action result. Through such a social action, relations between intervening actor and recipient are established (Habermas, 1984), which is also an effect of the performed action. A communicative action, like a request, gives rise to certain expectations between the actors concerning future actions. A social action is, however, not restricted to communication. Even material actions count as social actions if they are directed towards other persons. A supplier delivering physical goods to customers is an example of a social and material action (Goldkuhl, 2001).

---

[11] Besides the effects directly related to the intended listener, there might be other effects; e.g effects on other persons listening to the communication.

In the discussion above, we have focused on intervening actions. These are actions aiming at changes in the external world. But there are other kinds of actions, which do not have such purposes. When a person reads a book or listens to some conversation, his purpose is to inform himself. He is not making an intervention into the external world. The actor performs such perceptual acts in order to influence (change or sustain) his inner world. His interpretation is based on his prior knowledge including expectations in the face of the actual situation. We distinguish thus between two fundamental types of action: 1) intervening acts aiming at external change and 2) receiving acts aiming at internal change[12]. If we look at communication between two persons, such a situation will consist of an intervening (communicative) act performed by the speaker and a receiving (interpreting) act performed by the listener. The speaker produces an utterance, which is a sign, and the listener interprets this sign. A sign is something produced and something interpreted, and as such it is a link between two acts (a communicative act and an interpretative act) in social interaction. In a typical communication, the roles of speaker and listener shift over time. A listener becomes a speaker when he responds to the initial speaker who then becomes a listener. Different intervening actions are related to each other in patterns of subsequent actions. An initiative gives rise to a response. Such a responsive action will also have the role of an initiative if it gives rise to further responses in the social interaction (Linell, 1998). A simple model of social action is depicted in figure 4.2.

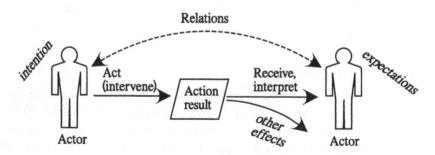

Figure 4.2 A model of social actions

For the performance of most actions, people need instruments of different kinds. When communicating, people need a common language as an instrument. To perform material actions, one often needs external instruments. Such instruments extend the ability of an actor. For example, when transporting and lifting heavy goods one needs certain (external) devices. For some actions, external instruments have a facilitating role. Some other actions are even impossible to perform for a human without

---

[12] These different acts correspond to the distinction of overt and covert actions (Schutz, 1962; Goldkuhl, 2002). Covert actions include, however, also the category of action-through-reflection (ibid).

the aid of certain instruments, which in such cases have the role of enablers.

An external instrument is nearly always artificially made; i.e. an artefact. Artefacts can have different roles in relation to humans, and they can also be more or less advanced. We distinguish between three artefact roles[13] (and their corresponding types of action):

- Static tool (artefact-supported human action)
- Dynamic tool (human-artefact co-operative action)
- Automaton (human-defined artefact action)

One example of the first artefact role is a human wielding an axe when chopping wood. A human manoeuvring a car is an example of the second artefact role. This involves an active use and surveillance by a human. A washing machine is an example of the third artefact role. A human initiates the machine, which then works autonomously. This last category means that an instrument has got the ability to perform actions independent of humans. This independence is however not total. It is conditioned by the action repertoire of the artefact, which has been constructed by humans. As mentioned above, it is also conditioned by human initiation and usually by human interruptance.

Instruments can thus be used for performing material interventions. Instruments can be used to refine and move objects. A human, when performing material acts, works on material objects. Objects are transformed through actions. When baking, different ingredients (the raw material) are used as a *base* for production of the result; e.g. a cake. In transportation an object is moved from one place to another. The object at the original place is a base in this transportation act, and the object at its destination is the result. In figure 4.3 we have refined the action model to a socio-instrumental action model. We have also included some other important action aspects in order to establish a more comprehensive model. All these aspects are not commented in our text here. We refer to earlier publications concerning this model (e.g. Goldkuhl, 2001; Goldkuhl & Ågerfalk, 2002).

Thus, for the performance of many actions, humans use external instruments. There are also many internal preconditions, which can be seen from fig 4.3. People should, of course, utilise their own knowledge for action. People should be knowledgeable in order to act. The world is perceived and conceived by conscious humans. Human abilities are, however, not only developed in fully conscious ways. Learning is often an evolving process, based on reflexive repercussion from intervening actions and effects (Giddens, 1984).

---

[13] The borders between these three categories are not always distinct. These categories have been described earlier by Goldkuhl & Ågerfalk (2002).

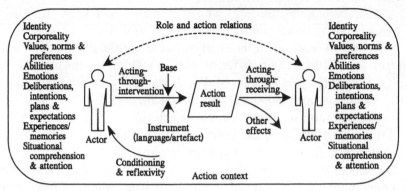

Figure 4.3 A model of socio-instrumental actions (modified from Goldkuhl & Ågerfalk, 2002)

Many actions are performed within organizations. Humans are acting in organizational roles. When a human (as an employee) is performing an action within an organization, he acts on behalf of that organization (Ahrne, 1994; Taylor & Van Every, 2000). This also means that the organization performs this action. A human performing an organizational action is always a dual action; at the same time performed both by a human and by the organization. As mentioned above, actions can be performed by humans and artefacts. This means that even artefacts can perform organizational actions. In this view an organization is considered to be an actor. It can, however, not act by itself. It always has to act via its human and artificial agents.

In order to illustrate some aspects of SIP, we will use a simple example. The example was introduced in sec 3 above. We used it in that section to illustrate the three theories BAT, ToP and ISAT, and the relations between them. Now the time has come to use the same example to illustrate some aspects of socio-instrumental pragmatist theory. In figure 4.4, we will characterise the four action situations (cf. sec 3.1 above) using some categories from SIP. These generic action categories have been used to describe the four different action situations in a comparable way. This example shows the applicability of these generic categories to reveal similarities and dissimilarities between different action situations. The described aspects give a complementary view in relation to the views conveyed by the other three theories. The SIP view is fully congruent with the views of the other theories.

Action examples Action categories	1) Customer searching among available products at the web site	2) Customer registering an order through the web site	3) IT system handling of orders and producing of delivery directives	4) Stock workers picking products from inventory and delivering to customers
Performers	Customer + web site	Customer + web site	IT system	Stock worker
Main interventionist	Web site	Customer	IT system	Stock worker
Character of performers & performance	Cooperative human & artefact action	Cooperative human & artefact action	Artefact action	Human action with artefact support
Character of human action	Inquiring and interpretative action	Communicative action (order)	--	Material action (fulfilment of received order)
Character of artefact action	Guiding and showing (=communicative action; offer)	Guiding & receiving action	Updating & communicative action (directive)	(only support)
Type of artefact	Web-based IT artefact	Web-based IT artefact	IT artefact	Material handling equipment
Role of artefact	Dynamic tool	Dynamic tool	Automaton	Static & dynamic tools
Initiative for action	Customer's purchase need	Customer's discovery of attractive product offer	Registered order	Delivery directive
Base	Product descriptions at web site	Customer's specified purchase need	Registered order	Products in inventory
Other important action prerequisites	Web functionality at customer's place	Understanding of how to purchase through the web	Programmed action repertoire of IT system	Job description for stock workers
Main action result	Customer knowledge about purchase possibilities	Customer's web-registered order	Delivery directive	Delivered products
Action result character	Knowledge	Signs (electronic)	Signs (paper)	Material objects
Recipient of action result	Customer	Web site	Stock workers	Customer
Possible effects	Possibilities for customer to purchase products	Delivery of products to customer	Delivery of products to customer	Customer's utilisation of products

Figure 4.4 Illustration of different action categories (eCompany example)

One question is how to conceive SIP in relation to the three other theories (ToP, BAT, ISAT). Is it a fourth theory on the same level as the others? As a common theoretical thread we would not consider it so. We rather consider SIP to be a *progenitive theory* for the other three theories. This means that ToP, BAT and ISAT are based on and incorporate theoretical constructs of SIP. The SIP theory, as a generic view of socio-instrumental actions, has a *generative power* for development of other more particularised theories; i.e. such theories have a narrower focus and a more dedicated domain, as is the case with ToP, BAT and ISAT.

5. TOWARDS AN INTEGRAL UNDERSTANDING OF ORGANIZATIONS AND INFORMATION SYSTEMS

Our intention with this chapter is to contribute to an integrated understanding of organizations and information systems. This has been pursued mainly through investigating three theories concerned with workpractices, business interaction and information systems. This investigation has led to an articulation of the common theoretical thread of these theories (socio-instrumental pragmatism). We will now *summarise* what has been achieved by formulating some important principles concerning organizations and information systems. What we present here is to be regarded as *important selections* from these four theories. It is a way of *essentializing* what has been said above.

Organizations imply acting – people are performing actions aiming at results and effects. People act in order to make differences in the external world. Humans intervene through communication and through material changes. They use instruments (language, artefacts) for enabling or improving their actions. In order to perform knowledgeable interventions, people have to establish an adequate knowing of the world, which is achieved through covert actions of interpretation and reflection.

Action is thus a central concept and this implies actors. Humans are actors, but not the only kinds of actors. Organizations are also conceived to be actors. Organizations cannot, however, act by themselves. They have to act through their agents. Employees in an organization are agents of that organization. These human agents are acting on behalf of the organization. Humans are, however, not the only agents. Different artefacts, such as e.g. IT systems, can be given roles as agents performing organizational actions. This gives rise to some fundamental questions concerning organizations, humans and IT systems:

- How does an organization become and remain an actor?
- How does a human become and remain an agent for an organization?
- How does an IT artefact become and remain an agent for an organization?

It is possible to give one short answer to all these questions: *This is done through communication, but not only*. This answer will be elaborated below. We will try to elaborate on "how to become" and "how to remain".

Organizations are constituted and established through communication. Without constitutive acts (of a communicative nature) performed by the principals behind the organization and different legal authorities, the organization cannot exist (Searle, 1995; Taylor & Van Every, 2000). An organization exists as an agreement (a communicative fact) between the principals and other parts of the society. Through such constitutive actions, an organization is given a formal authority to act. Hence, communication does play a decisive role, when an organization becomes both an organization and an actor. But communication is not enough. Financial and material resources should also be furnished. If not, an organization will have no capacity to act.

Organizations exist through recurrent patterns of actions. Such patterns (institutions) have to be continuously reproduced through actions performed by different organizational agents (ibid and Boden, 1994). Many organizational communicative actions are performed by IT systems. Nowadays such systems play an important role in the continuous reproduction of the organization.

The existence of many agents within an organization and many performed actions gives rise to a need for coordination. This means that different agents should be adapted to each other and that different actions should be adapted to each other as well. An organization exists through multi-action and multi-agent constellations. Organizational coordination is mainly pursued through communication. But it is also important to acknowledge that different artefact arrangements have coordinative forces in the organization.

An organization interacts with outside actors, which it depends on. It serves clients with products, and it is served by suppliers providing pre-products. An organization ceases to exist if it cannot serve other parts of the society. Communication plays an important role in an organization's interaction with its environment. Business agreements are developed and established through communication. Mutual commitments are created and resolved in interactional patterns. Such commitments have to be forwarded into the organization and remembered for future actions (e.g. for fulfilment of commitments). IT systems play different roles in the organization's communication with outside actors. Important functions of IT systems are to exchange proposals and commitments and to keep a memory of the proposals and commitments made.

Humans become agents of an organization when they are enrolled in that organization. Enrolment is performed through communicative acts (agreements). To appear as an organization agent means to act on behalf of the organization, to act as a representative. As organizational agents, humans are assigned and appointed to organizational roles. In order to exert an organizational role in a competent way, the agent has to learn the rules and routines of the organization. It is necessary to adapt the conduct to other agents of the organization as well as to actors outside the organization. Hence, communication plays important roles when a human becomes and remains an agent of the organization. But communication is not enough. As being an employee there is a need for monetary compensation for the work performed.

IT systems can also be agents of an organization. A system can be purchased or developed in-house. IT systems are established through design actions based on human intentionality. These design actions are of a communicative nature and they have a regulative force for the functioning of the system. These established rules of an IT system (cf figure 2.3 above) govern the actions of that system in its organizational use context and thus maintain organizational patterns. But communication is not enough in this case either. There is a technological base for IT systems providing hardware and software for executing rule-governed artificial behaviour. This rule-governed behaviour implies performance of pre-defined communicative actions. These communicative actions of the IT system have an impact on the actions performed by humans within and outside the organization. Some actions (in interactive use situations) are performed by humans and IT systems together. These actions are co-produced by the human and the artificial agents. The different agents have, of course, distinct roles in such co-operation based on their respective human and artificial character.

In order to create an integrated understanding of organizations and information systems there is a need for the understanding of

* human action and social interaction;
* communication as creation and interpretation of signs;
* usage of technology and artefacts; and
* how these phenomena interplay in organizational settings.

Our brief contribution to such an integrated understanding has mainly been pursued in this section by posing some fundamental questions and giving some answers to these questions. Furthermore, a theory on organizations and information systems should, according to our view, be built on some basic constructs. These constructs are:

* Actions (of different kinds; e.g. of communicative, interpretative or material character)
* Performers (actors/agents) of actions (organizations, humans, artefacts)
* Action objects as preconditions and results (of a signifying or material character)
* Patterns of actions
* Relations between actors established through social actions

Our claim is that these categories form a fundamental basis for the development of a theoretical understanding of

* Organizations
* Information systems
* The relations between organizations and information systems

6. CONCLUSIONS

The base for this chapter has been three existing theories (within a theory family) concerning business interactions (BAT), workpractices (ToP) and information systems (ISAT). The starting point was unclear relations between the theories. This gave rise to our purpose to clarify and integrate the theories.

In this chapter we have pursued the following. We have

- clarified the relations between the theories of ToP, BAT and ISAT
- given a proposal to conceive ISAT and BAT as magnifications of ToP (i.e. ToP has "parent relations" to ISAT and BAT)
- taken steps towards an articulation of the underlying theoretical thread: "Socio-instrumental pragmatism", which serves as a progenetive theory for the other theories
- exemplified and compared the four theories through the use of a common example
- proposed changes in the three theories with the purpose of convergence: They should be more transparent to each other through the borrowing of concepts implying more harmonious concepts and terminology (mutual adaptations)
- sketched essential constructs and principles of an integral theoretical understanding of organizations and information systems

Our change proposals should be seen as improvements of each theory as well as of the theories all together (the theory family). Our work should be considered as steps towards a more integral view on information systems and organizations. We believe that the route towards such an encompassing understanding goes through an enhanced understanding of socio-instrumental actions. However, there is a need for further research in this direction. The future development of the four theories (SIP, ToP, BAT and ISAT) should be pursued concomitantly and with the purpose of providing further contributions to the requested need for integral understanding.

ACKNOWLEDGEMENTS

The authors are grateful to Pär Ågerfalk for his good comments on a draft of this chapter. Part of this research has been financially supported by the Swedish research council VINNOVA.

REFERENCES

Ågerfalk P (2001). Who´s the user in user-centered design? In *Poster sessions: Abridged proceedings. HCI International*, New Orleans
Ågerfalk P (1999). *Pragmatization of information systems - a theoretical and methodological outline*, Licentiate thesis, IDA, Linköpings universitet

Ågerfalk P, Goldkuhl G, & Cronholm C (1999). Information Systems Actability Engineering – Integrating Analysis of Business Processes and Usability Requirements, in proceedings of *the 4ᵗʰ Int Workshop on the Language Action Perspective* (LAP99), Copenhagen

Ahrne G (1994). *Social organizations. Interaction inside, outside and between organization*, Sage, London

Austin JL (1962). *How to do things with words*, Oxford University press

Axelsson K, Goldkuhl G, & Melin U (2000) Using business action theory for dyadic analysis, accepted to *10ᵗʰ Nordic workshop on inter-organisational research*, Trondheim

Boden D (1994). *The business of talk: Organizations in action*, Polity Press, Cambridge

Castells M (1996). *The information age. Economy, society and culture. Vol 1. The rise of the network society*, Blackwell, Massachusetts

Cronholm S, Ågerfalk P J, & Goldkuhl G (1999). From Usability to Actability, In Proceedings of the *8th Intl. Conference on Human-Computer Interaction* (HCI International'99), München

Davenport TH (1993). *Process innovation. Reengineering work through information technology*, Harvard Business School Press, Boston

Dewey J (1938). *Logic: The theory of inquiry*, Henry Holt, New York

Giddens A (1984) *The constitution of society. Outline of the theory of structuration*, Polity Press, Cambridge

Goldkuhl G (1998). The six phases of business processes - business communication and the exchange of value, accepted to the *twelfth biennial ITS conference "Beyond convergence"* (ITS´98), Stockholm

Goldkuhl G (2001). Communicative vs material actions: Instrumentality, sociality and comprehensibility, in Schoop M, Taylor J (Eds.), *Proceedings of the 6ᵗʰ Int Workshop on the Language Action Perspective* (LAP2001), RWTH, Aachen

Goldkuhl G (2002). Anchoring scientific abstractions – ontological and linguistic determination following socio-instrumental pragmatism, in *Proceedings of European Conference on Research Methods in Business*, Reading

Goldkuhl G & Braf E (2002). Organisational Ability - constituents and congruencies, in Coakes E, Willis D, & Clarke S (eds.), *Knowledge Management in the SocioTechnical World*, Springer, London

Goldkuhl G, Lyytinen K (1982). A language action view of information systems, In Ginzberg & Ross (Eds.), *Proceedings of 3rd International Conference on informations systems*, Ann Arbor

Goldkuhl G & Melin U (2001). Relationship Management vs Business Transactions: Business Interaction as Design of Business Interaction, accepted to *the 10th International Annual IPSERA Conference*, Jönköping International Business School

Goldkuhl G & Röstlinger A (1999). Expanding the scope: From language action to generic practice, in Proceedings of *the 4ᵗʰ Int Workshop on the Language Action Perspective* (LAP99), Jönköping International Business School

Goldkuhl G & Röstlinger A (2000). Beyond goods and services - an elaborate product classification on pragmatic grounds, in proc of *Quality in Services* (QUIS 7), Karlstad university

Goldkuhl G & Röstlinger A (2002). The practices of knowledge – investigating functions and sources, accepted to *the 3rd European Conference on Knowledge Management (3ECKM)*, Dublin

Goldkuhl G, Röstlinger A, & Braf E (2001). Organisations as practice systems – integrating knowledge, signs, artefacts and action, in proceedings of *Organisational Semiotics: Evolving a science of information systems*, IFIP 8.1 Conference, Montreal

Goldkuhl G, & Ågerfalk P J (2002). Actability: A way to understand information systems pragmatics. In Liu K et al. (eds.), *Coordination and Communication Using Signs: Studies in Organisational Semiotics – 2*, Kluwer Academic Publishers, Boston

Habermas J (1984). *The theory of communicative action 1. Reason and the rationalization of society*, Polity Press, Cambridge

Holm P (1996). *On the design and usage of information technology and the structuring of communcation and work*, PhD Diss, DSV, Stockholm university

Kuutti K (1996) Activity theory as a potential framework for human-computer interaction research, in Nardi B A (Ed, 1996) *Context and consciousness. Activity theory and human-computer interaction*, MIT Press, Cambridge

Linell P (1998). *Approaching dialogue. Talk, interaction and contexts in dialogical perspectives*, John Benjamins Publ, Amsterdam

Mead G H (1938). *Philosophy of the act*, The university of Chicago Press

Medina-Mora R., Winograd T., Flores R., & Flores F. (1992). The Action Workflow Approach to Workflow Management Technology, In: Turner J., Kraut R. (Eds.), *Proceedings of the Conference on Computer-Supported Cooperative Work*, CSCW'92, ACM Press, New York

Nardi B A (1996). Studying context: A comparison of activity theory, situated action models and distributed cognition, in Nardi B A (Ed.), *Context and consciousness. Activity theory and human-computer interaction*, MIT Press, Cambridge

Nielsen J (1993). *Usability engineering*, Academic Press, San Diego

Nilsson E (2000). A language action perspective on knowledge management, in proceedings of the 5th *Language Action Perspective* (LAP2000), Aachen

Nonaka I & Takeuchi H (1995). *The knowledge-creating company. How Japanese Companies Create the Dynamics of Innovation*, Oxford University Press

Schoop M (1999). An empirical study of multidisciplinary communication in healthcare using a language action perspective, in Proceedings of the 4th *Int Workshop on the Language Action Perspective* (LAP99), Jönköping International Business School

Schutz A (1962). *Collected papers I*, Martinus Nijhoff, Haag

Searle J R (1969). *Speech acts. An essay in the philosophy of language*, Cambridge University Press, London

Searle J R (1995). *The construction of social reality*, Free Press, New York

Stamper RK (2001). Organisational semiotics. Informatics without the computer, in Liu K, Clarke RJ, Andersen PB, & Stamper RK (eds.), *Information, organisation and technology. Studies in organisational semiotics*, Kluwer Academic Press, Boston

Taylor J, Van Every E (2000). *The emergent organization. Communication at its site and surface*, Lawrence Erlbaum, London

Von Wright G H (1971). *Explanation and understanding*, Routledge & Kegan Paul, London

Walsham G (1997). Actor-network theory: Current status and future prospects, in Lee AS, Liebenau J, & DeGross JI (Eds.). *Information systems and qualitative research*, Chapman & Hall, London

Weber M (1978) *Economy and society*, University of California Press, Berkeley

Winograd T, & Flores F (1986). *Understanding computers and cognition: A new foundation for design*, Ablex, Norwood

Part III

Knowledge-oriented approaches

Chapter 8

Multiple Meanings of Norms

Ewa Braf

ABSTRACT

This chapter is about norms – norms in organizations. The chapter explores different theoretical definitions of norms and presents some empirical illustrations of norms that influence organizational performance. The chapter will show that the notion of 'norm' involves many different aspects and interpretations. One suggestion in the literature is that norms, together with attitudes, constitute knowledge. Is this a proper way to conceive of norms? Are there other fruitful explanations? The purpose of this chapter is to contribute to the discourse concerning the meanings of norms. I believe this kind of discourse is important, as norms are part of organizational practices. Therefore, we need to understand what we mean by norms and what functions they have.

1. INTRODUCTION

Norms have an impact on organizations and information systems and their development. This has been emphasised by Stamper in several publications (e.g. Stamper 1996; 2001). I consider this as a very important issue. Unfortunately, this is often disregarded in academia as well as in practice. One reason that triggered me to write this chapter concerned the meanings and functions of 'norms', i.e. *what do we mean by 'norms'?* Stamper argues that norms, together with attitudes, constitute knowledge. He also talks about different categories of norms (i.e. behavioural, evaluative, cognitive and perceptual) and claims that "all knowledge falls into one of these well-established categories" (Stamper 2001:151). This might be one way to understand the meaning of norms, but it also raises some questions that I believe need to be reflected upon. For example, to equate knowledge with norms seems to imply that knowledge is normative. However, *is knowledge always normative?* Another question concerns the creation of norms, i.e. *how are norms established?* Following Stamper (2001), the background of norms includes knowledge of the likely consequences of different behaviour. This implies that first, human actors need knowledge (which, according to Stamper, is 'norms') and then they create norms (which, according to Stamper, is recognised as knowledge). This seems to be a circular definition that needs to be sorted out. A closer investigation of the above questions should not only include Stamper's definitions but also other authors' explanations, which might facilitate interpretation and understanding.

Another condition that triggered me was the woolly terminology that often can be found in the literature (see also Braf, 2001; Stamper, 2001). As humans we use words to express meaning and to communicate. As long as we have the same understanding of words we use, there is no real problem. The problem arises when we put differing meanings into words without being clear about it. For example, the 'knowledge management' literature abounds with vague terminology, where words like 'information' and 'knowledge' are not clearly defined (cf. Braf, 2001). Moreover, the same word can be used in different settings and thus have different meanings. In order to understand each other it is important to understand what we *mean* by the words we use, i.e. to create intersubjective knowledge. This does not imply that I believe there is any final single solution. Quite the reverse, there is seldom any precise essence that explains everything straight and clear. Following Wittgenstein's (1958) 'family conception', I would rather advocate a multifaceted approach to understanding different meanings of a notion – in this case the meanings of 'norm' in organizational contexts. It might also be fruitful not only to consider the word norm but also other related words like the 'normative' and 'regulate'.

The above reasoning concerns theoretical issues that ought to be of interest to carry on a fruitful dialogue concerning the meanings of norms and other related notions. The theoretical problems mentioned have implications on how researchers can study the area of norms. For example, *what do we mean when we use the word 'norms'? In what ways is it meaningful and adequate to talk about norms? What is the relation between knowledge and norms?* It is essential to consider theory in this matter, but we also need to ask if there are any practical problems concerning the meanings of norms? Provided that there is no real practical relevance, there is a risk that a discussion on norms will end up in a pure philosophic exercise.

From a practical point of view, I believe there is a need for understanding the meanings and functions of norms. However, in contrast to the theoretical issues that are very much concerned with a so-called "type level", the practical interest lies on an "instance level". While the type level is concerned with *theoretical meanings* as such, the instance level concerns the *specific content* of norms.

When actors perform different activities they are more or less guided by models and working methods (i.e. kind of norms) that the organization has formulated. One can, however, not take for granted that the actors always comply with those models and methods. The actors might have other, more personal guidelines that do not correspond with the ones of the organization. Still, those individual norms might be the ones that first of all are followed. I do not regard this kind of opposition as strange or wrong. I consider it to be a common phenomenon of organizations as there are, and always will be, different ways of interpretation, understanding and approaching the society around us. Nonetheless, if practitioners would be able to make norms explicit, compare them and acknowledge their inherent differences and possible conflicts, it would be a good step towards reaching a deeper understanding of how organizations work. As I believe norms are part of, and thus influence, practices, they also have a critical role in the change of work. For example, today's many efforts to implement 'knowledge management' in organizations are highly influenced by different interests within different groups. Another example is the development and implementation of an information system (IS), which can be seen as a means to realise, and even create new norms surrounding a specific practice. Gazendam (2001:1) argues that "the definition of the behaviour of information systems in terms of use cases, semiotics and language action theory gives us levels of interaction and patterns of interaction that can be used as norms of behaviour". Gazendam also claims that the behaviour of virtual actors, like IS, has to be specified based on norms and interaction patterns. Similar thoughts concerning the relation between norms and IS can be found in Barjis et al. (2001), who assert the intrinsic need of norm analysis when developing IS. These authors mean that in many cases business rules are not expressed carefully enough. However, "the specification of norms allows recognition of human responsibilities and obligations and yet the ultimate power of decision-making in exceptional cases" (Barjis et al., 2001:244). Thereby, a proper norm analysis can be seen as a powerful modelling approach for IS analysis and design (ibid.). Still, to perform a norm analysis we need to understand what we mean by norms, and this is what this chapter is about. In other words, the *purpose of this chapter is to contribute to the discourse concerning the meanings of norms*.

The next part of this chapter comprises a discussion of some interpretations of norms that are found in the literature. The subsequent part 3 proposes how we can understand the notion of norms. Based on this proposal, part 4 gives some empirical examples of norms in organizations. The examples come from two case studies. One concerns a home care unit (see a further description in Goldkuhl et al., 2001), the other a publishing firm. The case studies are mainly used to illustrate norms in organizational settings. Both organizations are anonymous in this chapter. A summary and some final thoughts are presented in part 5.

2. SOME INTERPRETATIONS OF 'NORMS'

To define the meaning of words is far from simple, and different authors often end up with varying interpretations. A definition should help us to understand how and when a specific word is meaningful to use. It should also be possible to distinguish between different words based on their definitions. One way to clarify the meaning of norms is to start from the use of ordinary language, i.e. what we usually mean by the word 'norm'. This is an issue that I will come back to in part 4, but it will also form the basis of my investigation into how different authors explain the notion of 'norms'.

One point of departure is to look into the etymology of notions. The word 'norm' comes from the Latin word *norma*, which means carpenter's square, pattern, rule (Hoad, 1986). The first explanatory word – *carpenter's square* – implies that norms are something external and non-subjective – it is something to use for judgement. For example, a carpenter's square can be used for measuring the right place to saw off a piece of wood, i.e. to guide the sawing action (c.f. "behavioural norms" Stamper, 2001). It can also be used to control whether the sawn wood has the proper length, i.e. to judge if the action result has the right characteristics (c.f. "evaluative norms" Stamper, 2001). This interpretation is similar to Goldkuhl and Röstlinger (1999) who speak of *action norms* and *quality norms*. Action norms are values and rules directly governing the performance of the actor, while quality norms concern desired features of the action result (ibid). One of the other explanatory words – *rule* – is explained as a principle of procedure (conduct) that originates from someone, i.e. the ruler (ibid). This means that we have someone formulating the rule, which is then supposed to be followed by someone. When complying with a rule, we create a kind of *pattern*. Following the discussion above, a pattern or a rule may refer to how to act, or to the characteristic of the desired outcome. This involves both the *focus* and the *function* of the norms. That is, the focus might concern how to perform an action or how to evaluate the result. The function is, then, to guide the action or to facilitate the judgement of the action result. Goldkuhl and Röstlinger (1999) also claim that norms can be seen as part of an actor's know-how. This implies that there is an affinity between norms and knowledge. Still, speaking of norms and knowledge as different organizational prerequisites, as Goldkuhl and Röstlinger do, indicates that there is also a meaningful difference to maintain. This view seems to contradict Stamper (1996; 2001), who affirms that norms together with attitudes are recognised as knowledge, i.e. knowledge = norms + attitudes[1].

---

[1] Following Stamper (1996; 2001), norms can be found on two levels: simple and universal norms. The first kind consists of individuals' attitudes to particulars, while the latter one is stronger in nature and governs our conduct. Stamper (2001:151f) also maintains that, "attitudes are like norms without conditions" and a "condition may be any state of affairs that may be recognised". I do not really understand the distinction made between attitudes

To further investigate whether there is any meaningful distinction between norms and knowledge, I will look into how norms are created. Stamper (2001:150f) uses the concept of marriage to illustrate the creation of norms and says: "The meaning of marriage depends upon a collection of norms about behaviour evolved over time... Often they [read: norms] develop informally as a part of the culture, sometimes a law-giving body, a government or religious council, will enact the norms... The background to these norms will include a knowledge of the likely consequences of various acts". He also asserts that norms produce a particular attitude (simple norms) and can invoke other norms. "All our knowledge consists of norms and attitudes, their particular, unconditional form. The norms produce attitudes, which may lead to action in the environment or, most often, merely to the expression of those attitudes to others" (Stamper, 2001:153). Further, he argues that a community builds its knowledge regarding what to do, i.e. *behavioural norms*, how things should be judged, i.e. *evaluative norms*, how things happen, i.e. *cognitive norms*, and finally what exists in our world, which is described as *perceptual norms*.

Stamper's view ranges from tacit and personal behaviours to explicit and universal rules of how to think and act. It is a very broad view and presumes that all knowledge is regulative, which I question. I also have difficulty understanding his concept, because when trying to illustrate Stamper's view of norms (and knowledge and attitudes) I end up in a circular definition. Stamper equates knowledge with norms and attitudes; still, he uses 'knowledge' to explain the creation and meaning of 'norms' and 'attitudes', and vice versa, see figure 1.

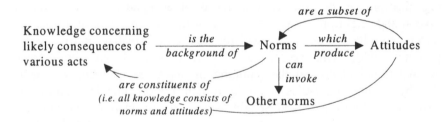

Figure 1: Illustration of Stamper's (2001) relation between knowledge, norms, and attitudes.

In addition to the four types of norms Stamper (2001) presents, Barjis et al. (2001) also speak of *denotative norms*. These are described as norms that direct the choices of signs for signifying, e.g. the choice of a colour to signify happiness or sadness (ibid). Barjis et al. mean that those types of norms influence human behaviour. The authors also stress that norms do

---

and norms. I wonder if we can have an attitude without a condition to have an attitude about? Do we not create attitudes towards something, i.e. a particular condition?

not only prescribe what people *must*, *may* and *must not* do, i.e. regularities of behaviour; norms also define responsibilities and authorities for actors. Thus, an analysis of norms is a means to understand likely behaviour of actors within a specific context and culture.

A similar explanation is presented in the FRISCO Report (Verrijn-Stuart, 2001), where norms are defined as socially agreed rules affecting and to a large extent directing the actions within an organizational system. As an example, one general norm of society is that rules (laws in a legal sense) must be obeyed. Other norms may be formal codes of what constitutes "good" practice. There may also exist norms that are only informally stated or tacitly accepted throughout the organization. Knowledge, on the other hand, is described as a relatively stable and sufficiently consistent set of conceptions possessed by single human actors (ibid)[2]. Although Stamper's semiotic ladder (see e.g. Stamper, 2001) has had a great influence on the FRISCO Report, there seems to be a difference at this point, as the FRISCO Report does not refer to any relation between norms and knowledge.

To regard norms as socially agreed rules, as the FRISCO Report does, is similar to Schön (1983), who talks about the professional-client relationship as a contract constituting a set of shared norms governing the behaviour of each party within the interaction. Some of the norms might have a formal basis in the common legal system, while others constitute informal understandings of what parties can expect from one another (ibid.). Besides the division between informal and formal norms, there might be different significance between norms. For example, Schein (1980) talks about *pivotal norms* and *peripheral norms* (see also Kolb, 1984). The underlying thought is that the adjustment of the actors to the organization can be conceived in terms of acceptance or rejection of pivotal and/or peripheral norms. The actor that accepts pivotal norms but rejects peripheral ones is considered to be a "creative individualist" (Schein, 1980). This person is strongly concerned with both basic organizational goals and the retaining of her sense of identity. She is thereby willing to exercise creativity to help the organization achieve its basic goals. As I understand Schein, norms are considered to be vital for an organization's performance but should not be taken for granted without a conscious reflection on their meaning and consequences.

Regarding norms as essential constituents of organizations is similar to Berger and Luckmann (1966), who talk about patterns (norms) in terms of 'institutional order'. They discuss the creation of institutional order as a process of habitualization and institutionalisation. One difficulty is when a specific institutional order is to be transferred to new actors. As those new actors are not aware of the prevailing order, they do not know how to act and why. Thus, there is a need for legitimation, which is seen as a process of explanation (to ascribe cognitive validity) and justification (to give

---

[2] I do not really agree on this view of knowledge, but that is a discussion that will not be pursued in this chapter.

normative dignity to the practical imperatives). In this way, Berger and Luckmann assert that legitimation is not just a matter of values; it also, and always, implies knowledge. This view is in line with Stamper (2001), but there seems to be one important difference. Berger and Luckmann uphold a distinction between knowledge and norms (values), while Stamper equates knowledge with norms and attitudes.

My interpretation of Berger and Luckmann is that the establishment of norms presumes humans possess knowledge about certain conditions. Then, this knowledge is exposed to evaluation, which as such implies some conception of what is good and bad. The result of the evaluation is a legitimation of right and wrong concerning the known conditions. On the basis of the desired and undesired values, norms are established. Thus, norms concern what *ought to be* or *not ought to be*. Berger and Luckmann maintain that by having knowledge about some specific situation and roles (prerequisite), individuals can perform a value-oriented action and come to the conclusion what the proper norms should be about (see figure 2). The norms will, however, not exist as part of the individual unless the norm has been *internalised* (ibid.; see also Schutz & Luckmann, 1973).

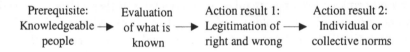

Prerequisite:	Evaluation	Action result 1:	Action result 2:
Knowledgeable →	of what is →	Legitimation of →	Individual or
people	known	right and wrong	collective norms

Figure 2: An illustration of Berger and Luckmann's (1966) view of norm creation.

Closely related to the idea of internalisation is Rolf (1995)[3], who discusses rules and tradition. Rules can be constituted and formalised by the use of language (signs) or exist without any explicit, verbal formulation (c.f. Schön, 1983; Verrijn-Stuart, 2001). We can, for example, talk about etiquette without having it formalised. A tradition can also be seen as a set of socially constructed rules. For example, an organization is a social system that contains rules for how the co-workers should appear in public when representing the organization. According to Rolf, the purpose of tradition is to secure and transfer action patterns and norms that, in turn, create social order (c.f. Berger & Luckmann, 1966). Thereby individuals can predict the acts of others and expectation on themselves (cf. Barjis et al., 2001). The pattern of a tradition specifies how one should behave. In this way, rules can be seen as specific norms that might be part of a greater whole, i.e. a tradition. One important issue, accentuated by both Berger and Luckmann (1966) and Rolf (1995), is that norms are not something that simply exists; humans create norms.

When trying to understand the meanings of norms, the review of different authors' explanations has shown that several aspects are emphasised. For example, some talk about the *creation* of norms and the

---

[3] Rolf (1995) is a study and interpretation of Michael Polanyi's (see for example Polanyi, 1966) theory of the tacit dimension of professional knowledge.

origin in terms of the *actor* establishing a norm, i.e. the creators can be the actors themselves or some external party (e.g. Stamper, 2001; Berger & Luckmann, 1966). Some talk about the *focus* and *function* of norms (e.g. Goldkuhl & Röstlinger, 1999; Verrijn-Stuart, 2001). Some emphasise the *characteristics* of norms in terms of informal or formal (e.g. Schön, 1983; Rolf, 1995; Verrijn-Stuart, 2001) or in terms of significance and weight (Schein, 1980). On the basis of the review, the next part aims to further investigate and propose how to grasp the notion of norms.

3. A PROPOSAL OF HOW TO UNDERSTAND 'NORMS'

To further investigate how we can understand the word 'norms', I believe it is important to clarify its ontological as well as its linguistic status (see e.g. Goldkuhl, 2002). Concerning ontological determination, we need to ask ourselves *in what ontological realms does the phenomenon of norms exist?* Is it a thought, something said, or something written? I would say that norms can exist in an *intersubjective realm* in the sense of being socially shared among actors (cf. Chong & Liu, 2001; Stamper, 2001). In an organizational context, I also believe it is relevant to talk about norms in an *intrasubjective realm*. For example, if one actor has developed certain norms within one organizational context and then starts to work in another organizational context, her established norms will prevail (at least for some time) even if they do not correspond to the norms in the new context. Norms can also exist in a *sign realm*, e.g. a written law or rule that aims to communicate the content of the formalised norm. Following Gazendam et al. (2001), norms, as signs, can also be manifested in the function of IS. This is a kind of *artefact-related realm*, which is essential since many organizations are dependent on their support on and use of technology.

Continuing with the linguistic determination, words can have different forms in terms of being a noun, a verb, or an attribute. The etymology of 'norm' is the *noun*, i.e. a carpenter square, rule or pattern. From this original form we created the *verb* 'to regulate' (which concerns the creation of a norm) and the *attribute* 'normative'. Except for the noun carpenter square, the other nouns, the verb and the attribute do not signify anything particular standing alone. I mean that a rule or a pattern concerns something else; this is also valid for the verb and the attribute. For example, to *regulate* is to make the behaviour comply with a desired and *normative pattern* of behaviour.

The idea that norms govern human behaviour is emphasised by several authors (e.g. Schön, 1983; Verrijn-Stuart, 2001). A principle of conduct does, however, not arise by itself. Someone needs to, more or less consciously, valuate different conditions and then establish what is believed to be the proper way to act and behave in the specific situation. Following Berger and Luckmann (1966), this can occur through habitualization, i.e. a tacit development of norms, or through a transfer of norms to new actors, which often requires explicit legitimation.

Then, what does it mean to 'valuate different conditions'? Following Stamper (1996; 2001), this concerns knowledge of the likely consequences of various acts. In other words, to develop norms we need to have a certain amount of knowledge about the situation in question. This is also in line with Berger and Luckmann (1966), who emphasise the need for knowledge to create norms. Still, in contrast to Stamper, Berger and Luckmann do not equal norms with knowledge. Following Stamper's definition, it is not really meaningful to speak of knowledge as one issue and norms as another. There is no meaningful difference to maintain, as each of the notions is used to explain the other. I do, however, question if this view is a proper way to understand the tenor, or tenors, of norms. I believe, for example, that there are other kinds of knowledge than regulative ones. Thus, we need a better model for explanation. Nevertheless, as several authors imply, there is an important relation between the notion of 'norms' and 'knowledge'. The challenge is how to identify this relation, together with the similarities and differences.

Here, we might get some guidance using Wittgenstein's (1958) ideas about "family similarities" (see also Monk, 1991). The words "norm" and "knowledge" are both examples of "family concepts" in the sense that they can have different meanings depending on the context where they are used. As Wittgenstein (1958) shows, the same notion can be used in different "language-games", and thereby they can represent different meanings. Following the assumption that the words 'norm' and 'knowledge' can have different meanings in different situations, there might be situations where their respective meaning does not differ to any appreciable extent. On the other hand, there might be situations in which there is a difference meaningful enough to talk about[4].

This discussion calls for an explanation of my view of knowledge. I regard knowledge as something known by a subjective holder. In this way it is more appropriate to talk about 'knowledgeable people' or 'knowing individuals'. With this I do not mean that, for example, books and databases contain knowledge as such; they contain representations of someone's knowing. Following Walsham (2001), I argue against the view of knowledge as a commodity or a quantifiable tradable asset. Instead, I advocate a more human-centred view of knowledge, with a focus on how people develop, use, and share what they know.

I would say, as Berger and Luckmann (1996), that norms are created on the basis of knowledge, about a certain context in terms of understanding and conceptions (see also Stamper, 2001). Hereby, knowledge is a prerequisite for the establishment of norms. Knowledge is also a basis (as a kind of value director) for formulating a specific norm. However, knowledge is not always normative. Knowledge can also be explanatory, illustrative, categorical, predictable, etc. (see illustration in

---

[4] I have earlier made this kind of "language game" analysis of different meanings (similarities and differences) concerning the concepts of knowledge and information, cf. Braf (2001).

figure 3). This is a matter of different *functions* of knowledge. As human beings we can know different things without having that knowledge governing our actions. Norms, on the other hand, are directed at functioning as a value standard for action. In order for norms to get and have the intended effects, individuals need to be aware of the norms and their meaning, that is, they need to be internalised (c.f. Berger & Luckmann, 1966). In this way, individuals need to have knowledge about different norms and their application. I would say that norms are one possible part of knowledge, and this knowledge is of a governing nature. I would also say that institutionalised, normative knowledge (i.e. norms) might have greater durability than other kinds of knowledge.

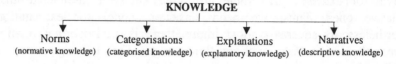

Figure 3: Knowledge and some of its subclasses.

On the basis of the discussion above, I propose the following explanation of norms: *A norm is knowledge concerning value standard for action and action result and governs human behaviour.* Then, how does this correspond to Stamper's categorisation of norms? As mentioned earlier, a norm can function as a guideline concerning how to act, which can be compared with Stamper's *behavioural norms* (c.f. 'action norms' Goldkuhl & Röstlinger 1999). A norm can also be used to measure the action result, which seems to be similar to Stamper's *evaluative norms* (c.f. 'quality norms' Goldkuhl & Röstlinger, 1999). I also believe that norms can influence human cognition and perception. But the cognition and the perception as such fall into other subclasses of knowledge, e.g. explanation and categorisation. I would say that those subclasses are examples of knowledge that we need to have as a prerequisite in order to make evaluations and create norms.

I have now discussed the ontological and linguistic determination, the relation to knowledge, and the focus and function of norms. Another aspect concerns the *creation of norms*. It could be the result of a habitualization process where actors more or less consciously establish norms within a given context, e.g. a group of actors who establish some common working norms. Some actors can also establish norms that, in turn, are transferred to other actors (c.f. 'legitimation' Berger & Luckmann, 1966). One example is the legal system that is defined by the government and transferred to the citizens, or the business management defining some quality norms that should govern the performance of the operative actors. The distinction between those two ways is whether the norms are internally or externally established. In this connection we can also talk about the level of formalisation. If a norm is made explicit and formalised, it might have a more obvious influence on actors. Otherwise, the norm would be manifested in the actions of the individuals who know about and obey the norm, but it might not be apparent to others that are not familiar with the specific norm. In this way, when talking about norms, it is not only a matter of their creation and creator(s). It is also most important to consider how established norms are transferred and conformed to by other individuals than the originator.

Another aspect concerns the significance of norms imputed by the original creator and the other concerned parties. As said above, Schein (1980) mentions pivotal and peripheral norms. In this connection, it is important to clarify the significance to whom and in relation to what. For example, the original creator of a norm might regard the norm as pivotal while another actor considers it to be peripheral. The significance might also vary depending on the situation in question, i.e. sometimes a norm might be in the foreground, sometimes in the background. These kinds of divergences have consequences on whether the creator can expect a norm to be followed or not. The creator can, of course, emphasise the significance of a norm by formulating some kind of penalty if the norm is not complied to. For example, if one does not obey an, according to the creator, peripheral norm, the consequences might not be that severe. However, if a pivotal norm (e.g. a law) is disobeyed, the consequences might be both obvious and rigid. The legal system is an example of this. Still, the particular situation and the judgement of the actors supposed to be governed by the norm will decide whether the norm should be followed or not.

As shown, there are different aspects, or characteristics, that can be used to clarify the meaning of norms, and (at least some of) those are summarised below.

1. Ontological determination
   - Intrasubjective (an individual thought)
   - Intersubjective (a shared thought)
   - Linguistic (signs)
     a. Oral utterances
     b. Written utterances
   - Artefact-related (norms manifested in the artefact functionality)
2. Relation to knowledge
   - One subclass of knowledge that aims at governing human behaviour
3. Primary focus and function
   - Action (behaviour) norms – guide what to do and how
   - Quality (evaluative) norms – guide how to evaluate the action and action result
4. The creation

- Via internal habitualization – might be a tacit or explicit establishment
- Via external formulation and transfer – requires explicit legitimation

5. Significance
    - Pivotal versus peripheral - depends on
      - o to whom,
      - o the situation in question
      - o the possible sanctions when not complying with a norm

I believe those aspects and characteristics of norms are important to understand norms and their effect on human conduct. Norms influence how actors behave and how to evaluate the quality of action results. Comparing the notion of 'norms' with the notion of 'knowledge', there are both differences and similarities (see illustration in figure 4). One important similarity is that norms are a subclass of knowledge that individuals act upon. However, there is also a difference, as all knowledge is not normative in the same way as norms are supposed to be. There is knowledge about the world that does not directly influence our behaviour. I believe that this is a difference that is important to preserve, and we should not try to blur this boundary. Following Berger and Luckmann (1966), I wish to stress that knowledge about the world is a prerequisite to create norms; without such knowledge there will not be any norms.

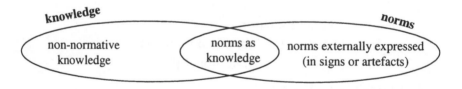

Figure 4: The relations between norms and knowledge

4. NORMS IN ORGANIZATIONS – EMPIRICAL EXAMPLES

In this section I will use some empirical examples to illustrate some of the different aspects and characteristics of norms as presented above. One case concerns a *home care unit*, whose practice is partially controlled by the social welfare administration and the state. The social welfare administration makes the decisions about who should have elder care and what kind of care a specific person needs. The state, together with the welfare board of the local government, defines the services which should be included in personal care. In this way, these parties represent some of the care unit's assigners, but they are also an *external creator* of norms that govern the home care unit. Those norms are partly about *action norms* but foremost about *quality norms* concerning the services.

For example, the state (*external part*) promulgates certain laws and regulations (*written norms*) that affect the home care practice, both in terms of *action* and *quality norms*. There are, for example, specific laws concerning social insurance, social services, and nursing that need to be considered in the performance of the nurses. There are also laws that govern the administration of personal information, e.g. the Official Secrets Act and the Personal Data Law. The social welfare board (*external part*) is another formulator who requires certain economic frames, quality levels, and business goals. These are *quality norms* concerning the *actions and action result, and s*ome are *orally articulated*, some *written*. The production management is more of an *internal norm creator* which formulates guiding principles concerning how to perform nursing services (*action norms*) and how to pursue quality and development work (*quality norms*). One *articulated, intersubjective action norm* that is internalised in the work of the nursing staff is that they want to give "personal service" to each person receiving care (client). This norm is in line with the social welfare board that wants the care to be tailor-made for the specific needs of the client. In this way, the staff together with the social welfare board consider this norm to be *pivotal* and therefore it is as such complied with.

The norms, issued by the social welfare board and the state, are evaluated once a year through interviews, observations and a written report. If the laws promulgated by the state are not followed, the client reacts, or more likely some of her relatives. This has happened within another care unit where the quality was not good enough, i.e. the *formulated action* and the *quality norms* were not complied with. As a consequence, some clients were ill treated, and one could read about some of these cases in newspapers. This kind of publicity only had negative effects on that unit, i.e. the consequence of disobeying the norm was strong in a negative sense. If someone were to be found guilty, it might also result in other sanctions than bad publicity. Even if this would not happen to the unit care in question, the workers and other interested parties had witnessed the story, which made them even more aware of securing and striving for the action and quality norms in question.

One similarity between the home care unit and the publishing firm is that they both are subject to externally formulated and internally created norms. The characteristics do, however, differ even if the roles of some of the creators are similar. The state, specific public authorities and different interest groups *formulate external, written norms* as laws and regulations. One norm is the school system, which prescribes the content (subjects), structure and quality the schools should represent. In turn, this requires certain products and quality of the publishing firm, as its major client is the school market. In this way, they represent both *action and quality norms* for the publishing firm, as the firm needs to comply with the regulations in order to be able to sell its books. As times goes by, politicians change the school system, which might affect the publishing firm's product repertoire. Copyright is another regulation that has effects on the firm's practice. Examples of different interest groups are the society of authors and the society of illustrators. Those societies handle the interest of their members in terms of their rights, working situation and compensation. These are all examples of *written, pivotal norms* that are externally formulated. Nevertheless, this does not mean that all employees comply with these norms or consider them being equally valuable.

Internally formulated norms derive from the owner, the management and from the employees themselves (*internal creators*). The owner demands certain profitability; otherwise the units risk being sold or liquidated. Other internal norms are formulated in the environmental (ecological) and quality policy that the firm has *written* down (i.e. *quality norms*). The environmental policy is especially important regarding the purchasing of printing with external printing offices. The quality policy permeates the whole development and production of books. In this way, the *quality norms* evoke and call for certain *action norms* (c.f. figure 1 above). The firm's trademark represents a high quality and goodwill (also a competitive means), which is in line with the norms of the management and the employees.

One interesting norm concerns the level of quality. There is a tendency that the editors, in comparison with the management, want to reach a higher quality level and thereby work for a very long time with formulations and structures of the book. This is, in turn, due to other internalised norms (and professional pride) like the feeling of the editors that each of their books "like a baby", and should be perfect. The management, on the other hand, argues that this causes the production to take too long, as a result of which the cost and time budget is often exceeded. Thus, even if all internal parties consider quality to be a pivotal norm, it is sometimes put in the background by the management in favour of other values. This is an example of conflicting norms. One challenge for the firm is to reach a quality level (*quality norm*) that is sufficiently high without jeopardising the reputation of the firm's products and trademark. The quality norm also needs to be balanced with another norm concerning a "good flair for business". The management means that the focus should not be so much on the production and the books themselves but more on the potential needs of the clients.

Another *quality norm* that is not formalised, but still internalised within many of the editors, is a proper use of language including a correct use of different words and notions. The editors also value respect and humbleness in their relation to the author, which could be seen as both *action norms* and *quality norms* in the working relationships. These are norms that are so strong with some of the editors that they tend to be more loyal to the authors than to the firm.

5. CONCLUSION

The purpose of this chapter is to contribute to the discourse concerning how we can understand the meanings and functions of 'norms'. I have tried to do that by presenting different aspects of norms that I believe are important. One of those aspect concerns the relation between norms and knowledge. I regard norms as one subclass of knowledge, i.e. it is knowledge that has been made normative. There are, however, also other kinds of knowledge that do not directly govern how to act in different situations or what quality result to reach. Those other subclasses of knowledge are needed as a prerequisite in order to evaluate different situations on the basis of which one is able to create norms.

I have also emphasised that the notion of norms must be understood in a multi-existential context with different ontological realms. This means that we need to understand the intrasubjective, the intersubjective, the linguistic, as well as the artefact-related realms of norms. Other aspects of norms are their focus and function, their creation and their significance, which all may vary depending on the situation in question. To use Wittgenstein's (1958) expression, the word 'norm' has different meanings in different "language games".

Then, so what? Why bother about different aspects or characteristics of norms? Why bother to define what we mean by the word 'norm'? I would start by saying that norms are part of, and influence, practices. Thus, in order to understand how an organization works, who, and what governs the activities performed, what quality to strive for, etc., we need to consider the norms that influence the practice and its actors. We also need to understand what possible norm conflicts exist in an organization and between different groups or workers. We need to understand how those conflicts might affect the practice. This kind of understanding is particularly important when working with changes.

For example, if an organization (as the home care unit) is to implement a new IS, then, at least, some norms need to be manifested in the systems. Otherwise, the IS will live its own life at the side of the rest of the practice instead of being an integrated part of the organization. Another example concerns the publishing firm who tried to make the editors proofread and make their corrections directly on the screen instead of printing paper copies. The management considered this new working norm to be more efficient, but lacked the ability to convince the editors to change their traditional working norm. Thus, even if the technical functions were in place, they were not utilised as the editors wanted to preserve their prevailing norm. This shows that norms are not always easy to change.

Still, as Berger and Luckmann (1966) argue, we continuously make knowledge normative as we acquire new knowledge and experiences about reality. In this way, the creation of norms is an ongoing practical process – this we must know in order to understand organizations and how they evolve. One practical problem is that different norms are internalised within different interest groups, which, in turn, results in norm conflicts due to different individuals' values and priorities. I do not believe that we neither can nor should try to erase all such conflicts, but we should focus on the understanding of existing norms, why they exist and what effect and consequences that has in actual practice.

To articulate norms, make comparisons possible, acknowledge varying norms and admit norm conflicts is a good step towards reaching an enhanced understanding of how organizations work. The understanding of norms is especially critical because norms have a kind of permanence. They are not just occasional but have a force to constitute practices. In other words, norms represent a kind of organizational regularity. Hereby, the creation of norms should not be considered as happenings but as a force of tradition. As norms have permanence, they also have power. Written norms can also have power but not if they end up as "dead texts". Written norms only then have power, when their meaning is, and continues to be, internalised within humans or is manifested in the functions of information systems.

I wish to conclude this chapter with the following reasoning: *Knowledge about the world is a primary human ability. Other abilities are secondary as they derive from the knowing of individuals. All knowing is not normative, but some is, and that we can call norms.*

REFERENCES

Barjis, J., Dietz, J., & Liu, K. (2001). Combining the DEMO Methodology with Semiotic Methods in Business Process Modelling. In Liu, K., Clarke, R.J., Andersen, P.B., & Stamper, R. K. (Eds.), *Information, organisation and technology: Studies in organisational semiotics*. Boston, MA: Kluwer Academic Publisher.

Berger, P. & Luckmann, T. (1966). *The social construction of reality. A treatise in the sociology of knowledge*. London: Penguin Books.

Braf, E. (2001). Knowledge or Information - what makes the difference? In *Proceedings of IFIP WG8.1 Working conference organisational semiotics: evolving a science of information systems, 24-26 July, Montreal, Canada*.

Chong, S. & Liu, K. (2001). A Semiotic Approach for Distinguishing Responsibilities in Agent-Based Systems. In Liu, K., Clarke, R.J., Andersen, P.B., & Stamper, R. K. (Eds.), *Information, organisation and technology: Studies in organisational semiotics*. Boston, MA: Kluwer Academic Publisher.

Gazendam, H. (2001). Semiotics, Virtual Organisations, and Information Systems. In Liu, K., Clarke, R.J., Andersen, P.B., & Stamper, R. K. (Eds.), *Information, organisation and technology: Studies in organisational semiotics*. Boston, MA: Kluwer Academic Publisher.

Goldkuhl, G. & Röstlinger, A. (1999). Expanding the Scope – From Language Action to Generic Practice. In *Proceedings of the fourth international workshop on the language action perspective on communication modelling, Copenhagen, Denmark, September 12-13, 1999*.

Goldkuhl, G., Röstlinger, A., & Braf, E. (2001). Organisations as Practice Systems – Integrating knowledge, signs, artefacts and action. In *Proceedings of IFIP WG8.1 working conference on organizational semiotics, Montreal, QC, July 23-25, 2001*.

Goldkuhl, G. (2002). Anchoring scientific abstractions – ontological and linguistic determination following socio-instrumental pragmatism. In *Proceedings of European conference on research methods in business and management (ECRM 2002), Reading, 29-30 April 2002*.

Hoad, T. F. (1986). *The concise Oxford dictionary of English etymology*. Oxford: Oxford University Press.

Kolb, D. A. (1984). *Experiential learning. Experience as The Source of Learning and Development*. New Jersey: Prentice Hall.

Monk, R. (1991). *Ludwig Wittgenstein: The Duty of Genius*. UK: Vintage.

Polanyi, M. (1966). *The tacit dimension*. London: Routledge & Kegan Paul.

Rolf, B. (1995). *Profession, tradition och tyst kunskap*. Nora: Nya Doxa.

Schutz, A. & Luckmann, T. (1973). *The structures of the life-world*. Evanston: Northwestern University Press.

Schein, E. H. (1980). *Organizational psychology*. 3rd edition. London: Prentice-Hall.

Schön, D. A. (1983). *The reflective practitioner. How professionals think in action*. Great Britain: Basic Books.

Stamper, R. (1996). Signs, information, norms and systems. In Holmqvist, B., Andersen, P. B., Klein, H. & Posner, R. (eds.), *Signs at Work*. UK: De Gruyter.

Stamper, R. (2001). Organisational Semiotics: Informatics without the Computer? in Liu, K., Clarke, R.J., Andersen, P.B., & Stamper, R. K. (eds.), *Information, organisation and technology: Studies in organisational semiotics*. Boston, MA: Kluwer Academic Publisher.

Verrijn-Stuart, A. A. (ed.) (2001). *A framework of information system concepts*. The Revised FRISCO Report (Draft January 2001). Netherlands: IFIP.

Walsham, G. (2001) Knowledge management: The benefits and limitations of computer systems, *European Management Journal, 19(6)*, 599-608.

Wittgenstein, L. (1958) *Philosophical investigations*. Oxford: Basil Blackwell.

Chapter 9

Models as coherent sign structures

Henk W. M. Gazendam

ABSTRACT

This chapter explains how models function as the glue that keeps organizations together. In an analysis of models from a semiotic and cognitive point of view, assumptions about evolutionary dynamics and bounded rationality are used. It is concluded that a model is a coherent sign structure, consisting of a network of a diversity of signs, and used by an actor for understanding or constructing a system of application. People use models because they are coherent, cognitively manageable units of knowledge. By their efficient organization, these knowledge units enable the development of flexible and adequate habits of action.

In an investigation into the complexity, coherence, boundaries, and components of models, assumptions about construction, emergence, and the coherence mechanism are used. Based on their use, models develop semiotic shortcuts in the form of new sign layers to the representation, namely iconic representations, language representations, and conceptual representations. Models change and find their boundaries based on a dynamics of coherence. The coherence mechanism must be seen as an alternative for foundational reasoning and fits well into an open, constructivist world view.

In an explanation of the role of models in organizations, assumptions about methodological individualism and distribution of knowledge are used. An organization is seen as a multi-actor system based on habits of action aimed at cooperation and coordination of work. These habits of action are supported by organizational knowledge in the form of shared artefacts, stories, institutions, designs and plans. Shared institutions, designs and plans can be seen as shared normative models that make up for the difference between the organization as a whole and 'the sum of' the individual actors. They are the glue that keeps the system together. Shared normative models are created by actors and, in turn, influence actor behaviour by forming habits, thus creating a cycle of selection and reinforcement, where some models and norms are reinforced and other models and norms disappear.

1. INTRODUCTION

In earlier publications, the modelling of organizations and information systems has been explored (Gazendam, 2001, 2002). The modelling methods explained were the use of metaphors in modelling virtual organizations, interaction analysis in use case modelling, category-based abstraction in object modelling, and a method for the conceptual specification and analysis of organization theories. All these methods explain how to construct the appropriate model elements and their relationships, however an investigation of the functioning of a model as a whole is lacking. Questions arise about how models can be seen from a semiotic point of view, how people use models, how the coherence and boundaries of a model are established, and what role models play in organizations.

In trying to answer these questions, the following *basic assumptions* will be used:
(i) the view that an *evolutionary dynamics* drives living beings, leading to optimized behaviour based on semiotic adaptive shortcuts (Bouissac, this volume),
(ii) the view that all artefacts and sign structures have to be *constructed* within boundaries of reasonable computational costs (*bounded rationality*) (Simon, 1945/1976; Gigerenzer & Selten, 2001),
(iii) the rejection of a closed and static world view that is predominant in mainstream mathematics and logic, and the adoption of *construction and emergence* as basic mechanisms (Wolfram, 2002),
(iv) the use of the *coherence mechanism* as an alternative for foundational reasoning (Thagard, 2000),
(v) the view that an organization only exists as a collection of cooperating actors, the material structures they use, and the organizational knowledge of these actors, and that there are no other carriers for organizational knowledge than actors and documents (*methodological individualism*) (Franssen, 1997), and
(vi) the insight that *all knowledge is distributed*, and that socially shared knowledge has to be negotiated.

First, models will be explained from a semiotic and cognitive point of view, using assumptions about evolutionary dynamics (i) and bounded rationality (ii) (section 2). Next, the complexity, coherence, boundaries, and components of models will be discussed. Here, assumptions about construction and emergence (iii) and about the coherence mechanism (iv) play an important role (section 3). Finally, using in particular the assumptions about methodological individualism (v) and distribution of knowledge (vi) (section 4), we will turn to the role of models in organizations.

2. A SEMIOTIC APPROACH TO MODELS

2.1. The use of models

The word 'model' stems from Latin, where it means measure. It is the diminutive form of the word 'modus', meaning measure, standard, regulation, or rule. In medieval times, the word 'model' was especially used for physical models in building, especially church building, and bell-foundry (Meyers Konversations-Lexicon: Fünfte Auflage, 1897, Vol. 12, p. 409). From medieval times on, the use of 'model' for a variety of physical models became widespread. Craftsmen used models to show what they could make, using them as examples, specimen, samples, patterns or prototypes.

"A *model* is a physical representation that shows what an object looks like or how it works." (Collins COBUILD English language dictionary, 1987).

Such a *physical model* is a physical system representing another physical system (Nauta, 1970, p. 46, p. 184). Peirce would classify physical models as iconic representations, based on some kind of resemblance between model and modelled entity.

Later on, the 'model' concept was used for non-physical representations as well, for instance for economic models, and for diagrams used in the design of information systems. This more abstract use of models is connected to the rise of the 'system' concept from (approximately) 1930 to 1960 (Emery, 1969). According to systems theory, a model is a representation of a system.

"A *model* of a system or process is a theoretical description that can help you understand how the system or process works, or how it might work" (Collins COBUILD English language dictionary, 1987).

In 1943, Craik introduced the model concept in cognitive psychology. Knowledge does not consist of an unordered collection of rules, productions, or behavioural functions, but is organized in the form of mental models (Craik, 1943; Johnson-Laird, 1983; Thagard, 2000). People think using mental models (Craik, 1943).

"By a model we thus mean any physical or chemical system which has a similar relation-structure to that of the processes it imitates. . .

My hypothesis then is that thought models, or parallels, reality – that its essential feature is not 'the mind', 'the self', 'sense-data', nor propositions but symbolism, and that this symbolism is largely of the same kind as that which is familiar to us in mechanical devices which aid thought and calculation . . .

If the organism carries a 'small-scale model' of external reality and of its own possible actions within its head, it is able to try out various alternatives, conclude which is the best of them, react to future situations before they arise, utilize the knowledge of past events in dealing with the present and the future, and in every way to react in a much fuller, safer, and more competent manner to the emergencies which face it."

Johnson-Laird (1983) has elaborated this hypothesis:

"The psychological core of understanding, I shall assume, consists in your having a 'working model' of the phenomenon in your mind." (Johnson-Laird, 1983, p. 2)

Boden (1977) discusses the claim of Johnson-Laird by saying:

"[Johnson Laird's] central claim is that people solving problems (even problems that are amenable to the methods of logic) typically do not use logic, although occasionally some individuals do. Rather, they reason by constructing and transforming a class of representations of a more natural kind than lists of logical rules. He argues that mental models can support valid reasoning (although some lead to error), and that computational efficiency favours them over formal rules of inference. In short, whereas formal logic is a culture-specific cognitive resource (which even professors of logic often ignore), the ability to construct and reason with mental models is a general feature of the human mind." (Boden, 1988, p. 177)

Nowadays, models can use a diversity of representational elements, linguistic (symbolic) as well as non-linguistic (iconic). A model may be based on an analogy or metaphor (symbolic elements), may contain data structures and formulas (symbolic elements) as well as diagrams, map-like pictures or even physical scale models (iconic elements). For instance, a scale model of a ship depicts the ship in three dimensions, reproducing the ship's spatial proportions but not its size. It may or may not have a motor reproducing the motor capabilities of the ship at a scale that is compatible with the other parts of the model. Therefore, we can say that a model is a relatively complex sign structure consisting of a network of a diversity of signs.

Actors use models to understand or construct systems. A *system* can be seen as a complex, interacting, whole of objects, aspects and processes selected for investigation or design. For instance, one can investigate the weather in the northern hemisphere, or the adoption of innovations in multinational firms, or design a house, or an organizational workflow. The weather in the northern hemisphere, a multinational firm, a house, and an organizational workflow are phenomena complex enough to see them as systems. For investigating or designing them, you need models.

A model must be a *coherent network* of representational elements in order to form an instrument that actors can use for understanding or designing systems. The power of models often stems from the novelty that emerges from the combination of the model parts in a coherent structure. To be useful in practice, a model has to contain *knowledge* about the modelled system, and make it possible to deduct properties of the modelled system without actually measuring these properties at the modelled system. For instance, a scale model of a ship can be used to deduct the speed and manoeuvrability of actual, large ships that have the proportions of the scale model. In deducting these properties, a method for measuring properties of the model, of calculating the unknown properties, and so on, has to be applied, the so-called *calculus*.

Actors use models for a variety of purposes, such as, for instance, describing something, explaining what has happened, suggesting a course of action, or designing something. A model can be used for creating new objects or systems in the world. In this role, models are more *pre*presentations than representations. These new objects or systems may be signs or models themselves. For instance, the model embedded in the computer program of the university causes the monthly payment of our salaries, something that is of some importance in daily life. Another example is a scale model of a ship that has been made for testing a ship design. The scale model helps in creating 'real', large ships.

The process of designing and of application of designs is generally a chain of designing a model, translating this model into a new model of another type, elaborating this new model, translating this again into the next model type, and so on. For instance, in creating a computer program there may be a chain of designs consisting of use case model, object model, interaction models, and Java program.

Many models describe man-made artefacts, man-made conventions, or even mental models of people. One could say that models surround each object, process, or system in this man-made furniture of the world: models that have helped create it, models that explain it, mental models for handling it, and so on.

Models will always see its systems of application from a specific point of view, and will highlight specific aspects of these systems accordingly. Based on different aspects that are highlighted, many different models can be made for a specific system. The other way round, a specific model may be applicable to a variety of systems in the task environment of an actor.

Resuming, we can now define a model. From a semiotic point of view, a *model* is a *coherent sign structure*, consisting of a network of a *diversity of signs*, and used by an actor for understanding or constructing a *system of application*[1]. As a cognitively manageable island of coherence, a model enables coherent reasoning of an actor about systems of application.

2.2. The sign nature of models

According to the semiotic approach (Peirce, 1878/ 1958a, p. 113, 1904/ 1958b, p. 381; Goodman, 1976; Jorna, 1990), a model is a sign. Semiotics studies communication with signs, symbols, and texts in a central role based on the concepts of semiosis and sign. *Semiosis* is the process of interpretation and development of signs (thoughts). A *sign* represents an object in a certain respect (ground), and determines a resulting idea (interpretant). In semiotics the sign is part of a representation, or a representation itself. Because of its definition in the context of semiosis, the sign concept in semiotics is a dynamic concept. In the context of this semiotic approach, we can now say in a more precise manner that a *model* is a *sign structure* that functions in a *triadic sign system* consisting of sign (model), *object* (system of application) and *interpretant* (resulting idea in the mind of the interpreting actor). Generally, a model is intended for use as a tool in the study or construction of something else: the *system of application*. There will be a class of systems to which the model may be applied: the *compliance class* (Goodman, 1976, p. 144) of the model.

Not all triadic sign systems are complete. Signs may wait for actors that interpret them, like paintings that have been stored in museum cellars where nobody sees them, while other signs may be waiting to be applied to a system for application, like a design for a house waiting for realization.

Models may be represented within actors, like *mental models* in humans and animals, and *computer models* in computers or robots. Mental models are not observable in a direct manner because you cannot read signs in the mind. Models may also reside outside actors in the ecological environment as *document models*. Any passive carrier of signs other than an actor can be seen as a *document*, and models carried by a document are document models. Document models are signs in motion or persistent document models. *Signs in motion* are signs carried by a transient medium like sound waves. Although signs in motion are carried by a transient medium, the sign structures that are carried may escape a transient existence because they are stored in the minds of actors that perceive them, or recorded on a persistent medium. *Persistent document models* are carried by a relatively persistent medium, such as printed paper or a

---

[1] This definition of 'model' is more general than the use of 'model' in mathematical models or programming modules in DSS theory, and differs also from the use of 'model' in logic, where a model is a situation or world in which all statements of a theory are true.

compact disc. Document models can be observed an interpreted in a more or less direct manner.

In the semiotic approach, it is assumed that the actor has to construct and apply the model actively. Construction of models in real time, and emergence of sign structures acting as semiotic adaptive shortcuts in evolutionary time are part of this semiotic approach. This differs from the *traditional systems theoretical approach*, where the process of constructing and applying a model is not a topic to be studied. In the systems theoretical approach, a model is a system representing selected characteristics of another system (In 't Veld, 1988, p. 101), often interpreted as a carrier of facts about the real world, a mirror of nature (Rorty, 1979)[2]. In the *semiotic approach*, however, models generally are no longer passive representations of a given system (although, in some cases, the wish to understand a given system of application may trigger model building). Models are sign structures that have to be constructed and adapted by an actor based on examples, data about the system of application, theories and metaphors. They can be used by an actor for actively selecting, naming, interpreting, or even creating systems of application.

2.3. Sign layers

People use models because they are coherent, cognitively manageable units of knowledge organized by using semiotic adaptive shortcuts and sign layers. By their efficient organization, these knowledge units enable the development of flexible and adequate habits of action despite the physical limitations of the human and animal cognitive system and the necessity to react in a timely way.

Living beings are driven by an evolutionary dynamics, leading to a species-specific optimized behaviour. The use of sign structures by animals and humans is part of such behaviour that emerges in evolutionary time. Sign structures act as semiotic adaptive shortcuts that help a timely determination of adequate behaviour (Bouissac, this volume). Internal sign structures, organized as mental models, can be seen as a world model that helps in orientation and in the flexible determination of optimal behaviour. External sign structures, such as signs in motion and document models help in remembering and communicating, thereby helping optimal behaviour and survival. Building and adjusting a world model is based on the active exploration by the actor of its ecological environment, its semiotic Umwelt (Von Uexküll & Kriszat, 1936/ 1970; Von Uexküll, 1998).

The affordance mechanism is a basic mechanism in the creation of a world model and the connected repertoires of behaviour. An *affordance* is

---

[2] Strangely enough, in logic, the system of formulas –what we would call a formal model– comes first and the so-called model, a situation or world where these formulas are true, has a derived role.

a set of properties of the environment that makes possible or inhibits activity (Gibson, 1979). According to Gibson (1979, p. 127)

"The affordances of the environment are what it offers the animal, what it provides or furnishes, either for good or ill. . . . As an affordance of support for the animal . . . they have to be measured relative to the animal. They are unique for that animal. They are not just abstract properties. They have unity relative to the posture and behavior of the animal being considered.". "The affordance of something does not change as the need of the observer changes." (Gibson, 1979, p. 138). "The medium, substances, surfaces, objects, places, and other animals have affordances for a given animal. They offer benefit or injury, life or death. This is why they need to be perceived."(Gibson, 1979, p. 143). "[Affordances] . . . have been strikingly constant throughout the whole evolution of animal life." (Gibson, 1979, p. 19)

Objects are discriminated because of what they afford, not as belonging to a fixed class of objects defined by its common characteristics. The same object may correspond to several affordances. For instance, a stone may be a missile, a paperweight, a hammer or a pendulum bob (Gibson, 1979, p. 134). According to Stamper (2001, p. 140), animals and humans develop repertoires of behaviour tuned to affordances in order to survive[3]. If information is available in ambient light for perceiving, then affordances will be perceived. This means that affordances, being Gestalts, will be perceived rather than function as raw sense data (Gibson, 1979, p. 140). This means that perception ". . . has to be a process of construction." (Gibson, 1979, p. 304)

From a semiotic point of view, one could say that the perception of affordances is a process of construction of signs in the animal (or human) mind. This fits in the view that all artefacts and sign structures have to be *constructed* within boundaries of reasonable computational costs (Simon, 1945/1976; Gigerenzer & Selten, 2001).

The status of these signs is a subject of discussion. According to Peirce (1904/ 1958b, p. 391), signs are indexes if they are caused by their object. Because these processes occur automatically and subconscious, we could say that these signs are indexes. On the other hand, there is an interaction of the animal mind with the raw data that enter the senses, organizing the perception in terms of affordances, which interferes with a pure causation by the object. Maybe it is best to speak of *semi-indexical sign structures*[4]. So, affordances are represented as semi-indexical sign structures. These semi-indexical sign structures are connected to their interpretants in the human or animal mind. These interpretants can be feelings, or efforts to

---

[3] I do not follow Stamper in his statement that affordances *are* invariant repertoires of behaviour (Stamper, 2001, p. 141), but distinguish between affordances as properties of the environment and the repertoires of behaviour tuned to those affordances as properties of the human or animal actor.

[4] A semi-indexical sign structure results from a process where raw data resulting from the interaction between actor and environment are unconsciously filtered, transformed, and matched to patterns (e.g., Marr, 1982; Jorna, 1990, p. 57).

act, or goal-oriented repertoires of behaviour that Peirce calls *habits of action* (Peirce, 1907/ 1998, p.430). A habit of action consists of a commitment to act and a connected action program that governs the actual acting. Habits of action are mostly unconscious (Peirce, 1905/1958c, p. 189), and can also be considered as semi-indexical sign structure. A unit consisting of a semi-indexical representation of an affordance and its associated habit of action can be seen as a *unit of tacit knowledge*. Because affordances are specific for an animal species, tacit knowledge will be specific for an animal species as well. In this way, the affordance theory explains the formation of tacit knowledge.

The world model of an actor consists of smaller knowledge units, islands of coherence, in other words, models. The world model expands and reorganizes aimed at supporting an actor in typical behaviour patterns, such as orientation while wandering around in the environment, communication and reasoning. Based on their use, models perform processes of *self-organization* (Port & Van Gelder, 1995) in which structures are created allowing semiotic adaptive shortcuts (Bouissac, this volume) that are useful for survival. Forming shortcuts means that sign structures are added that act as access paths to sign structures already present. These new sign structures act as higher level concepts, tuned to a specific type of use. For instance, a two- or three-dimensional spatial mapping structure is added to the layer of tacit knowledge, thereby forming an efficient map of the environment.

> "We begin by presenting a model of mature spatial coding as involving the coding of information with respect to two different possible frames of reference, the viewer and the external environment, as well as the hierarchical combination of information coded at various grains of resolution."
> (Newcombe & Huttenlocher, 2000, p.10)

The addition of such a new organizing sign structure can be seen as the addition of a new sign layer (Gazendam, 2001), or the addition of a dimension giving access to knowledge already present (Cijsouw & Jorna, this volume).

In the processes of reorganization and enrichment of the models that make up the actor's world model, three steps can be distinguished. The first step in these processes is the creation of efficient maps of the environment, which are iconic representations. Simple iconic signs for use in communication also emerge. The second step involves the use of language for efficient communication, and the associated language representations. The third step is the creation of notations for the support of efficient reasoning and the associated use of conceptual representations. For these three steps of self-organization of sign structures, Sebeok (1994) distinguishes three modelling systems:

- the Primary Modelling System (PMS): Simulative forms of semiosis that use iconic and indexical representations;
- the Secondary Modelling System (SMS): Verbal forms of semiosis that use linguistic symbolic representations;
- the Tertiary Modelling System (TMS): Abstract forms of semiosis that use conceptual symbolic representations.

In each structure, elements that enable shortcuts are added, thus adding a new 'dimension' to the representation. These processes of creation and reorganization of signs in interaction with the environment lead to a diversity of sign structures that are organized in layers.

Tacit knowledge (Sign Layer 1) is based on an optimal efficiency of perception and action. It is processed by Sebeok's Primary Modelling System. It consists of semi-indexical sign structures. A unit of tacit knowledge consists of a habit of action connected to a representation of an affordance.

Iconic representations (Sign Layer 2) are based on an optimal efficiency of world map building. They are processed by Sebeok's Primary Modelling System. They consist of iconic sign structures. Iconic representations attach affordances, such as substances, surfaces, objects, places, and other animals to a representation of the (spatial-temporal) structure of the environment. These iconic representations are organized based on the resolution mechanism (Gazendam, 2001, p. 39), leading to a coherent representation of objects, places, situations, events, and processes. Tacit knowledge and iconic representations together form the layer of direct representations (Gazendam, 2001, p. 37).

Language representations (Sign Layer 3) are based on an optimal efficiency of communication. They are processed by Sebeok's Secondary Modelling System. They consist of symbol structures in natural language. The narration mechanism organizes language representations, amongst others using levels of semiotic granularity (Peirce's determinant types) (Gazendam, 2001, p. 39).

Conceptual representations (Sign Layer 4) are based on an optimal efficiency of reasoning. They are processed by Sebeok's Tertiary Modelling System. They consist of symbol structures in a formal language[5]. You can also call them abstract symbolic representations. The abstraction mechanism organizes conceptual representations, amongst others based on types, individuals, and habits (Peirce, 1904/ 1958b, p. 391; Gazendam, 2001, p. 40).

Cijsouw and Jorna (this volume) distinguish sensory, coded, and theoretical knowledge. *Sensory knowledge* consists of tacit knowledge and iconic representations. *Coded knowledge* consists of sensory knowledge with an extra dimension of language representations. *Theoretical*

---

[5] Formal languages may also have graphical components. An example is the modelling language UML.

knowledge consists of codified knowledge with an extra dimension of conceptual representations. Models that are used in studying organizations and designing information systems belong to the theoretical knowledge type. Therefore, they may contain elements and structures taken from all sign layers. In the next section, we will deal with the complexity, coherence, boundaries, and components of these models at different sign layers.

3. MODEL STRUCTURE

3.1. Model complexity

People make models because they enable coherent reasoning about systems of application (amongst others complex situations, systems and processes). This requirement of coherence means that a model is a sign structure of a certain degree of *complexity*. Bounded rationality puts restrictions on the size and complexity of models that have to be handled by the human cognitive system. Therefore, models are generally *less complex* than their system of application. In order to be more easily handled, a model always contains less information than the system of application, it contains conceptual structures to compensate for this information loss (Gazendam, 2001), and it contains semiotic adaptive shortcuts for efficient processing by the cognitive system.

Therefore, the mapping between the model and the system of application has to be a selective one, a simplification and interpretation of the modelled system. For instance, if we make a model of the universe, we have to be very selective and use a lot of abstractions and simplifications in order to go from the size and complexity of the universe to a model that is manageable by human actors.

Because of the selective character of models, it is important which type of 'information compression' a model uses: *selection* or *abstraction*, or both. One can observe that scientific theories and scientific models have limited information content (Barrow, 1998). They describe a small part of the world in detail, for instance a model of the ecological system in a specific Dutch canal, the Wijmers at Loppersum, or the whole universe in a very abstract way, for instance Einstein's relativity theory, or do something in-between.

The observation that models have limited information content means that it is more plausible that there is no single mental model in the human or animal mind, but that there are many mental models, which may be mutually incompatible. In other words, because of the limits to the cognitive system, there will be strong *local coherence* in models as islands of coherence, but no strong global coherence. These islands of coherence will be related to each other in a loosely connected network.

To be able to cope with the complexity of the system of application, *computer models* often generate an appropriate *complexity* itself. Generating complexity is often based on the *emergence* of novelty by combination (Georgescu-Roegen, 1971, p. 13; Pagels, 1989; Wolfram, 2002). The insight that complex phenomena can be constructed or simulated based on a few simple computational rules, and that properties can emerge based on these computational mechanisms, means a step forward compared to the relatively closed and static world view of equation models and traditional logic (Holland, 1995, 1998; Wolfram, 2002).

> "Usually in computer modeling scientists are trying to model a rather complex system (otherwise why bother to use a computer). The fundamental hypothesis behind simulating complex systems is that the apparent complexity of the system one is trying to model is due to few simple components interacting according to simple rules that are then incorporated in the program." (Pagels, 1989, p. 89)
>
> "To be effective, computer modeling must use a program that is simpler than the system one is modeling. Otherwise one is trying to blindly mimic the system on a computer, without any understanding." (Pagels, 1989, p. 89)

The observation that a model is a coherent sign structure of a certain degree of complexity means that a model *functions as a whole*, which means that leaving out a part generally damages the model as a whole and may render it useless. For instance, leaving out an equation out of an economic model may make the model unsolvable. In this sense, the model is a whole that is more than the sum of its parts. One could also say that a network of vital interrelations connects the components of the model, or that that the model contains descriptions from an irreducible set of different, complementary dimensions.

3.2. Model coherence

Models change and find their boundaries based on a dynamics of coherence. Thagard's *coherence theory* (2000) accounts for the mechanisms of formation and adaptation of models as islands of coherence. The coherence mechanism works by mutual adjustment of the model elements, and of model elements and elements in the system of application. The coherence mechanism goes back and forth between the beginning and the end of reasoning paths, adjusting wherever necessary, until an acceptable equilibrium has been reached. The formation of islands of coherence can be described by computational mechanisms, and can be computationally simulated.

The coherence mechanism must be seen as an alternative for *foundational reasoning*. Thagard (2000, p. 4) argues that foundationalists are wrong. Foundationalists are philosophers and scientists who think that people should reason based on a foundation of indubitable beliefs, for instance axioms or empirical data, and derive conclusions based on logical inference from these beliefs. Thagard argues that it is psychologically more plausible, and philosophically more elegant, to take a coherentist point of view. According to his point of view, people make sense of the world they live in by:

> "fitting something puzzling into a coherent pattern of mental representations that include concepts, beliefs, goals, and actions." (Thagard, 2000, p. 1)
> "A belief is justified not because it is indubitable or is derived from some other indubitable beliefs, but because it coheres with other beliefs that jointly support each other." (Thagard, 2000, p. 5).

The coherence concept fits well into an open, constructivist world view, while foundational reasoning uses a closed world assumption.

Foundational reasoning becomes very complicated when *normative models* are concerned. Reasoning about normative models is reasoning in deontic logic, or reasoning about possible worlds needing nonmonotonic and modal logics (Shoham, 1988). For a coherentist, the use of logic has a more modest place in the wider context of maintaining coherence. Logic is a costly mechanism that is only used sparsely. Logical inference may be used to determine whether two propositions cohere in deductive coherence (Thagard, 2000, p. 53).

Because empirical data have no longer a privileged position of indubitable beliefs, the question of *correspondence* of a model with empirical data becomes a question of coherence between model and empirical data:

> ". . . the relation between a model and the world . . . [is] . . a mapping from the model to some parts of the world in which the model preserves many but not all of the structures and behaviors in the world. Assessing the relation between a model and what it represents can be viewed as a coherence problem . . . Models, like maps, can provide more or less coherent representations of the world. (Thagard, 2000, p. 91)"

In the computational theory of coherence, explanatory, conceptual, and analogical coherence all use the parameter of acceptability of representational elements:

> ". . . accept a representation if and only if it coheres maximally with the rest of your representations." (Thagard, 2000, p. 169)

Important psychological phenomena, however, involve inference as well as emotion. Examples are norms and trust. Coherence theory can integrate cognitive and emotional aspects. Emotion can easily be incorporated as a second dimension using the parameter of emotional valence of representational elements (Thagard, 2000, p. 172). The emotional dimension can be seen as an efficient semiotic adaptive shortcut, a mechanism shortening information processing time (Bouissac, this volume; Gigerenzer & Selten, 2001).

3.3. The boundaries of a model

In reasoning about the boundaries of a model, we need to distinguish the model core, the hidden layer connected to a model, and the support structure of a model. The *model core* consists of sign structures representing the system of application in iconic representations (SL2), language representations (SL3), and conceptual representations (SL4). The *hidden layer* connected to a model consists of sign structures that are hidden as tacit knowledge (SL1) or as an emotional dimension. The *support structure* of a model consists of theories, data models, metaphors[6], and other sign structures coherent with the model core.

Dependent on the type of model (mental model or document model) and the theoretical point of view taken, the boundaries of what belongs to a model are drawn differently.

According to cognitive psychology, hidden or tacit signs in the human or animal mind are relevant for explaining cognition and can be part of a model as a coherent sign structure. Therefore, the *mental model* of an actor according to cognitive psychology (model$_A$) includes the model core and the hidden layer of tacit knowledge and emotions.

According to semiotics, signs used in communication (or intended for use in communication) are subject of study. As a result of this, according to semiotics a model is a *document model* (model$_D$) that includes the model core, but has no hidden layer of tacit knowledge and emotions.

According to coherence theory, what counts is the model as an island of coherence. Because of this, a model according to coherence theory includes a model and the support structure coherent with it. We will call this unit of coherence a *knowledge unit*. A knowledge unit in the human or animal mind includes a mental model (model$_A$) and the connected support structure, and will be called a *mental knowledge unit* (model$_{AK}$). A knowledge unit that is carried by a document consists of a document

---

[6] The root metaphor of a model expresses the basic analogy on which the model is based. For instance you can see, like Bohr did, an atom as a kind of solar system with the kernel in the role of the sun and the electrons in the role of planets circling the sun. A somewhat more modern metaphor for the atom is a kernel with electron clouds around it. Another example is that you can see an organizational workflow as a flow of water through channels, and mills or machines, while at some places leakage occurs (Gazendam, 1993, p. 282). An alternative view on organizational workflows sees them as the collection of transactions generated by traders on a marketplace. Such a root metaphor functions as a qualitative theory that determines the way the iconic representation will sketch the structure of the system of application, and also helps in choosing the theories that will supply the calculus of the model.

model (model$_D$) and the connected support structure, and will be called a *documented knowledge unit* (model$_{DK}$).

We support the view that knowledge in the human mind or animal mind is always organized by means of models. To be more precise, this knowledge encompasses the model core, the support structure of theories, metaphors, and data models, and the hidden layer of tacit knowledge and emotions. This means that knowledge in the human mind (and animal mind) is organized as a network of mental knowledge units (model$_{AK}$) consisting of mental models (model$_A$) and their connected support structures of theories, metaphors, and data models. Knowledge that has been expressed and is carried by documents can be seen as a network of units of documented knowledge (model$_{DK}$) consisting of document models (model$_D$) and the connected support structure of theories, metaphors, and data models.

In knowledge management, one distinguishes the *degree of resolution* of (the iconic part of) knowledge, the *degree of codification* of knowledge and the *degree of abstraction* of knowledge (Boisot, 1995; Van Heusden and Jorna, 2001, p. 100). Because we see knowledge as consisting of knowledge units that are networks of heterogeneous sign structures, some of which are iconic, some of which are symbolic, and some of which are abstract or formal, we are able to operationalize these concepts.

3.4. Sign layers in the model core

We can see the model core as a network of signs taken from all sign layers. Models may contain (Nagel, 1961; Giere, 1999) *iconic representations,* such as diagrams, map-like pictures or even physical scale models (section 3.4.1.), *texts* referring to the system of application (section 3.4.2.), and *conceptual structures,* such as data structures, object models, and calculi that facilitate reasoning (section 3.4.3.). Norms play a role at all sign levels (see section 4.1.).

3.4.1. Iconic Representations

The *iconic representation* in a model is a spatial-temporal representation of the system of application. Iconic representations can be:

- 2-dimensional (e.g., maps, drawings),
- 3-dimensional (e.g., molecule models), or
- 4-dimensional (3dimensional plus time, e.g., a scale model of a ship in a hydrodynamic laboratory, or a scale model of a railway with model trains).

The iconic representation is based on the resemblance to the system of application, especially where its structure is concerned[7]. This

---

[7] Icons that are used in graphical computer software, for instance Microsoft Windows, are not icons in the sense of iconic representations as used here. The meaning is largely

resemblance, of course, only holds for the chosen point of view and for the chosen aspects. Elements in the iconic representation will generally represent elements in the system of application. Mathematically, you can describe this as a mapping relation (Nauta, 1970). There may be some kind of code or legend for distinguishing the several types of elements in the iconic representation.

3.4.2. Texts

The *texts* or language representations in a model consist of symbol structures in a natural language referring to the system of application (e.g., by describing it). Text has a linear structure based on levels of semiotic granularity (Gazendam, 1993, p. 64, 2001, p. 40):

- *symbol* (smallest unit of information transfer), where conventions are described in a code table;
- *word* (smallest unit corresponding to a signified entity, e.g., an object), where conventions are described in a lexicon;
- *sentence* (smallest unit representing a situation or state), where conventions are described in a grammar;
- *story* (larger units referring to e.g. chains of situations or processes), where conventions are described in a narrative grammar of genres or in a system of logic.

Text does not only refer to a signified object, but also expresses intentions of the speaker, and influences the hearer. Because of this, Austin (1962, p. 108) distinguishes locutionary acts, illocutionary acts, and perlocutionary acts:

"Performing a *locutionary act* . . . is roughly equivalent to uttering a certain sentence with a certain sense and reference, which is again equivalent to meaning in the traditional sense. Second, we said that we also perform *illocutionary acts* such as informing, ordering, warning, undertaking, etc., i.e. utterances which have a certain conventional force. Thirdly, we may also perform *perlocutionary acts*: what we bring about or achieve by saying something, such as convincing, persuading, deterring and even, say, surprising or misleading."

Based on this distinction, a text can have a locutionary content and an illocutionary content. We cannot speak of perlocutionary content, because the perlocutionary act is an effect on the hearer of the text that is not

---

determined by convention, and therefore they should be classified as symbols. For instance, you cannot know that the symbol for 'paste' means 'paste' purely on the basis of resemblance or pictorial value. Even if you know that the 'paste icon' means 'paste', this is not easier to remember because of the characteristics of the 'paste icon' as picture. These 'icons' have a status as symbols with some traces of a 'pictorial reference' much like the status of Chinese ideographic characters. The icons found in Russian-Orthodox churches are iconic representations, because their meaning is largely determined by their pictorial value; some parts of these icons, however, have a symbolic meaning that you only can know on the basis of a learned convention.

inherent in the text, but depending on the interaction of text and hearer. The illocutionary content can sometimes be interpreted as related to norms that are communicated.

Searle and Vanderveken (1985) distinguish five types of illocutionary acts: we can say something about the world (assertives), we can tell people to do something (directives), we can commit ourselves to doing something (commissives), we can express our psychological state (expressives), or we can bring about changes in the world through our saying something (declaratives).

The model text can be processed to provide a data structure in a formal language.

3.4.3. Conceptual Structures

With regard to the reasoning about systems of applications, *conceptual structures* or conceptual representations use concepts and rules. Often, they use a formal language. Formal models are conceptual structures expressed in a formal language. Formal models can be handled by humans using their mental calculus engine, which can, once trained, solve equation models or do logical derivations. However, having computers work on formal models is often more convenient. Several types of formal models (equation models, simulation models, rule-based models, connectionist models) can be executed by computer calculus engines creating new symbol structures. Running simulation models (including multi-actor simulations) can easily be done by computers, but is a task that is virtually impossible for humans to do. However, multi-actor systems can be simulated in a non-formal way by humans through playing drama.

The main types of conceptual structures are data structures, object models, and calculi. While the data structure describes a system of application in a specific (instance level) way, the object model and the calculus describe a class of systems of application in a generic (type level) way.

The *data structure* in a model describes the properties of the system of application at the instance level as an ordered collection of data. The data structure generally uses a formal structure or a formal language for description. The data structure is needed to complement the object model or the calculus formulas with specific information about a system of application. For instance, data about persons and their jobs form a data structure that makes it possible to derive the parameters of the flexibility of organizations in an equation model. These data fill the tables in a data base defined by an object model. The object model has the generic role here, defining the form of the data container, while the contents of the container, the data about individuals, form the data structure.

There are two main types of data structure: *black box structures*, in which the system of application is seen as a whole with certain attributes, and *white-box structures* in which the system of application is opened and its internal structure in terms of objects, object attributes, relationships between objects, processes, and attributes of relationships and processes, is represented.

An *object model* is a conceptual structure enabling the perception of, reasoning about, design of, simulation of, and ordering of data about a system of application. It can be seen as a kind of theory about the structure of a class of systems or processes. An object model describes the generic structure of a system of application in terms of objects, classes, their relationships, and their properties. Objects can be/ represent actors, for instance, in a computer-based simulation model of an organization, or affordances in a model according to the Stamper school of organizational semiotics. Properties of objects or classes can be attributes (descriptors), norms, scenarios or methods. A method can be seen as a, generally relatively simple, calculus attached to classes or objects (Goldberg & Robson, 1983). The use of object models is compatible with a bottom-up approach to modelling where construction and emergence play an important part. Typical uses for object models are in the design of information systems and the construction of simulation models of organizations. An object model can be described using several views, for instance a static view, a use case view, an interaction view, and a state machine view (Rumbaugh, Jacobson, & Booch, 1999, p. 24).

The *calculus* of a model is a set of formulas in a formal language enabling the derivation of statements or operations. An example is an equation model of an economic system. Many calculi use a system perspective; they see the system of application as a whole with certain attributes, behaviour rules, and a time evolution that happens in a state space. This is a black box view, contrasting with the white box view of object models. The ability of the actor to handle the calculus is called the *calculus engine*. For instance, if the calculus formulas are equations, you need an equation solver as a calculus engine, whereas when inference rules are involved the appropriate calculus engine would have to be an inference engine.

The function of many models is to connect theories, often written down as collections of mathematical statements, with systems in the world (Thagard, 2000, p. 90; Giere, 1999, p. 73). The calculus in models is based on theories, while the data structure and the iconic representation relate to the system of application. Much in the same way, Nagel (1961, p. 90) thinks that the calculus formulas are the heart of a theoretical complex, while the iconic representation (called interpretation or model by Nagel) supports it by making the link to specific situations. He distinguishes three major components in theoretical complexes:

> "For the purpose of analysis, it will be useful to distinguish three components in a theory: (1) an abstract calculus that is the logical skeleton of the explanatory system, and that 'implicitly defines' the basic notions of the system; (2) a set of rules [of correspondence] that in effect assign an empirical

content to the abstract calculus by relating it to the concrete materials of observation and experiment; and (3) an interpretation or model for the abstract calculus, which supplies some flesh for the skeletal structure in terms of more or less familiar conceptual or visualizable materials."

Each of the rules of correspondence connects an element in the data structure with an element in the system of application.

A model often needs some kind of interpretation procedure to be useful in practice. For instance, to use a map you need a procedure for measuring distances on the map and for calculating the corresponding distances of the terrain. You also need to know the meaning of the symbols on the map (as stated in the legend). Likewise, you need a procedure for interpreting an entity-relationship model in order to be able to program a database table structure in Oracle or Access. In formal models, this interpretation procedure takes the form of calculus formulas that are interpreted by a calculus engine.

On the other hand, a calculus alone cannot be interpreted without an iconic representation or a data structure linking it to a system of application. For instance, you cannot use the formula $E = mc^2$ without a specific iconic representation of, let us say, the 3D structure of a molecule. The iconic representation, and the resulting data structure, is needed to arrange the facts about a specific modelled domain in a way that the calculus, taken from a theory, can use.

Calculus engine types can be distinguished (Bosman, 1996, p. 101) for equation models, simulation models, rule-base models, and connectionist models. Combinations of data structures, object models, and calculi are possible. For instance, a rule based system can be seen as a combination of calculus (the inference engine) with a data structure (the rule base). Another example is agent simulation, where an object model representing the framework of interacting actors is combined with calculi for the simulation of cognition in each simulated actor. Connectionist models can be seen as a combination of an object model consisting of nodes and edges with calculi representing the transformation of signal in each node.

4. ORGANIZATIONAL KNOWLEDGE

4.1. Organizations and organizational knowledge

An *organization* can be seen as a multi-actor system based on habits of action aimed at cooperation and coordination of work. These habits of action are supported by *organizational knowledge* in the form of shared artefacts, shared stories, shared institutions, shared designs and shared plans. Each habit of action consists of a commitment to act in a certain way, and a more or less flexible action program that governs the actual acting.

An organization exists only as a collection of cooperating actors (people , animals, or computer actors), the material structures they use, and the organizational knowledge of these actors. There are no other carriers for organizational knowledge than actors and documents. This point of view is a kind of *methodological individualism* (Franssen, 1997; Van den Broek, 2001, p. 25).

Not all organizational knowledge is expressed as documented knowledge, so that it can easily be directly observed. As a result, when trying to observe an organization, one can discern:

- material structures (generally artefacts), not as signs (fences, buildings, machines, chairs, tables);
- actors as physical objects, not as signs;
- what actors do, not as signs (indicating tacit knowledge);
- what actors express in signs (iconic, language, and conceptual representations);
- documents as signs (iconic, language, and conceptual representations).

Organizational knowledge includes (Jorna, Gazendam, Heesen, & Van Wezel, 1996; Gazendam, 2001, p. 22):

1. *cooperation agreements:* a set of commitments to cooperate;
2. a *work organization:* organizational knowledge about the coordination of work;
3. a *formal organization:* a collection of shared formal agreements and rules expressed in authoritative formal documents;
4. an *organization culture:* a collection of shared beliefs supported by artefacts and stories that guide cooperative behaviour.

Before you can speak of an organization, actors have to constitute an organization by reaching an agreement about their commitments to cooperate, their rights and duties in the cooperation, and the distribution of costs and benefits of the cooperation (Williamson, 1975, 1985; Homburg, 1999). In order to reach these agreements a basis of mutual trust is needed. The work organization is the main topic of one of the founders of organization theory, Henri Fayol (1916/1956, 1916/1984; see also Gazendam, 2002). The distinction between work organization and formal organization has been proposed by Schmidt (1991). According to Schmidt, formal organization is a - not always congruent - layer on top of the work organization safeguarding the interests of the owner and the regulatory bodies (Schmidt, 1991, p. 103). The formal organization can be expressed in for instance, property rights, employment contracts, organization structure descriptions, and business process descriptions. We can see organization culture as a collection of shared beliefs supported by artefacts and stories that guide cooperative behaviour of actors (Jorna, Gazendam, Heesen, & Van Wezel, 1996; Gazendam, 2001, p. 22). Organizational culture can be expressed in, for instance, a company logo, buildings and interior spaces with a symbolic value, sculptures, paintings and other art, clothing, rituals, the company vocabulary, and stories about heroes and important events (Sanders and Neuijen, 1987).

4.2. Norms and normative models

In the history of the model concept, we see that cognitive and normative aspects always have been present. The function of social norms is to restrict individual behaviour to socially acceptable behaviour.

> "A norm is a way of behaving that is considered normal and usual and that people expect from you, for example in society or in a particular situation." (Collins COBUILD English language dictionary, 1987, p. 977)

> "[Norms] . . . specify what actions are regarded by a set of persons as proper or correct, or improper or incorrect. They are purposively generated, in that those persons who initiate or help maintain a norm see themselves as benefiting from its being observed or harmed by its being violated. Norms are ordinarily enforced by sanctions, which are either rewards for carrying out those actions regarded as correct or punishments for carrying out those actions regarded as incorrect. Those subscribing to a norm, or, as I will say, those holding a norm, claim a right to apply sanctions and recognize the right of others holding the norm to do so. Persons whose actions are subject to norms (who themselves may or may not hold the norm) take into account the norms, and the accompanying potential rewards or punishments, not as absolute determinants of their actions, but as elements which affect their decisions about what their actions it will be in their interest to carry out." (Coleman, 1990, p. 242)

According to Peirce, norms are habits of self-preparation and self-control. Norms, being habits of action, develop themselves based on experience (Peirce, 1905/1958c, p. 199; De Jong, 1992; Gazendam, 1997).

Norms as isolated elements cannot account for coherent normative behaviour. They have to be integrated in the models an actor has of other actors and of himself. An important characteristic of norms is that they are reciprocal. *Reciprocity* is typically bound to models you have of yourself, of other actors, and of the models other actors have of yourself. Reciprocity of norms means that a norm works because there will be a beneficial effect for everyone if everyone behaves according to that norm.

A norm tells you how you ought to behave, and you trust that other actors will behave in that way as well.

Reciprocity is also the basis for Kant's categorical imperative:

> "Handle nur nach derjenigen Maxime, durch die du zugleich wollen kannst, daß sie ein allgemeines Gesetz werde."[8] (Kant, 1785/ 1984, p. 68)

Norms have a cognitive as well as an emotional dimension. According to coherence theory, these can be integrated in models. Mental models can integrate norms based on a combination of cognitive and emotive dimensions (Thagard, 2000, p. 165). Document models can integrate norms as illocutionary content.

Depending on the intention with which an actor uses a model the following typology can be made. *Descriptive models* describe an entity in the present (or at some point of time in the past), whereas *normative models* describe the desired or designed state of an entity. Normative models stress the design role, example role, and *pre*presentation role of models.

There are three types of normative models that humans use *from a pragmatic point of view* Gazendam (1986). People make *designs* for a future (possibly desired) object or situation. In order to live from the present to the future, they make *behaviour rule systems* and *plans* for guiding behaviour. The use of normative models may result in internalization. This internalization takes the form of the formation of habits (consisting of objectives and patterns of behaviour) directing activity.

Designs sketch the future systems that one wants to construct or future situations that one wants to realize. Design knowledge can be transferred by using design patterns. A *design pattern* is an abstract framework of a design representing a solution to a problematic set of requirements. Design patterns have first emerged in the architecture of physical buildings and cities (Alexander, 1977, 1979).

Plans tell you what to do, rule systems tell you what the boundaries are for your behaviour as a result of social restrictions. A *plan* states what you have to do to reach a certain goal. A *behaviour rule system* states how to act in certain circumstances. Behaviour rule systems may consist of conventions, legal rules, norms, contracts, and so on. According to Rawls (1971/2000, p. 47), an *institution* is a system of behaviour rules:

> "Now by institution I shall understand a public system of rules which defines offices and positions with their rights and duties, powers and immunities, and the like. These rules specify certain forms of action as permissible, others as

---

[8] "Act only on that maxim whereby thou canst at the same time will that it should become a universal law."(Kant, as translated by Ayer & O'Grady, 1992, p. 229)

forbidden; and they provide for certain penalties and defenses, and so on, when violations occur. As examples of institutions, or more generally social practices, we may think of games and rituals, trials and parliaments, markets and systems of property. An institution may be thought of in two ways: first as an abstract object, that is, as a possible form of conduct expressed by a system of rules; and second, as the realization in the thought and conduct of certain persons at a certain time and place of the actions specified by these rules."

This definition of 'institution' by Rawls distinguishes the institution as an abstract object from the institution as a pattern of behaviour realized in persons. Institutions as abstract objects correspond to systems of social constructs. Each social construct is a socially negotiated concept (for instance, 'order', or 'money owing') to which attributes such as norms and default behaviour scenarios are attached. Social constructs correspond to the social affordances of the Stamper school of organizational semiotics, institutions to a system of social affordances depicted on an ontology chart. Institutions as behaviour patterns correspond to habits. The concept of affordances in organizational semiotics is similar to Rawls' institution concept in the sense that it is used at the level of social constructs as well as that of individual behaviour patterns.

Behaviour according to norms creates social trust.

> "Social trust in complex modern settings can arise from two related source −norms of reciprocity and networks of civic engagement. . . . Norms are inculcated and sustained by modeling and socialization (including civic education) and by sanctions." (Putnam, 1993, p. 171)

> "Norms such as those that undergird social trust evolve because they lower transaction costs and facilitate cooperation. The most important of these norms is reciprocity." (Putnam, 1993, p. 172)

Social systems can exist because of shared normative models, such as institutions, and the trust they create[9]. Shared normative models, especially when they are confirmed by authoritative rituals or externalized in authoritative documents (e.g., sources of law), can be said to exist as systems of social constructs that are more or less independent of the individual actor. Shared normative models are created by actors and, in turn, influence actor behaviour by forming habits, thereby creating a *cycle*

---

[9] Shared normative models do not have to be shared by all participating actors to become the basis of a social system. There has to be a sufficient majority of actors holding the shared normative models that see it as their duty to prevent and correct actions that are regarded as incorrect.

of selection and reinforcement, where some models and norms are reinforced and other models and norms disappear.

> "The emergence of norms is in some respects a prototypical micro-to-macro transition, because the process must arise from individual actions yet a norm itself is a system-level property which affects the further actions of individuals, both the sanctions applied by individuals who hold the norm and the actions in conformity with the norm." (Coleman, 1990, p. 244)

Organizations exist because:

> ". . . as soon as a task grows to the point where the efforts of several persons are required to accomplish it, . . . , it becomes necessary to develop processes for the application of organized effort to the group task." (Simon, 1945/ 1976, p.8)

One of the reasons why the task to be performed cannot be done by one person could be the diversity and depth of knowledge necessary to perform it. In other words, administrative organizations exist because of the boundedness of rationality resulting from the limits of the human cognitive system, *and* because of the *boundedness of knowledge* a person can have. Because of this, all knowledge in organizations is distributed among the persons belonging to the organization. So, the knowledge about normative models, such as institutions, plans and designs is distributed (a micro phenomenon), and the associated habits are distributed as well. The shared knowledge about normative models that we can distinguish as an emergent phenomenon at the level of the social system (macro level) is a result of a process of negotiation, reinforcement and selection. Because of this, we can say (in a metaphorical way) that shared normative models make up for the difference between the organization or social system as a whole and 'the sum of' the individual actors because these models act as *the glue that keeps the system* together.

4.3. Organizational change

Organizations change because (1) actors join or leave the organization, (2) actors change products, markets, and technology, (3) actors change formal structures and power structures, (4) actors create artefacts and tell stories, and (5) actors change their knowledge (Gazendam, 1997). In other words, organizations change because of the actions of actors. These actors use their organizational knowledge organized in models.

When actors join or leave the organization, they modify the pattern of cooperation agreements and the formal organization. When actors change products, markets, and technology, they modify the pattern of work organization. When actors change formal structures and power structures, they change the pattern of formal organization. When actors create artefacts and tell stories, they change the pattern of organization culture. When actors decisively change their knowledge, this can lead to one of the changes described above. For instance, when the technological knowledge of an actor changes, this may lead to the introduction of new technology in the work processes, and cause the work organization to change accordingly.

The mental models of an actor are not necessarily compatible (having competing models at your disposal may be advantageous from an evolutionary point of view). Likewise, there may be differences or conflicts between actors within an organization based on incompatible models. Organizational knowledge is typically distributed among actors, and actors have to negotiate a common world view. The coherence mechanism, in a multi-actor form, ensures that this negotiated world view is sufficiently coherent.

Organizational knowledge in the form of models can change because models are adapted, they are structurally changed, they spread over a population of actors, and eventually they become extinct. Models are adapted by adjusting them to, for instance, new data about application and new theoretical insights. Because models are linked to existing theories, metaphors, insights and empirical data, they tend to be reluctant to integrate contradictory evidence or insights. However, as soon as contradictory evidence and insights have gained enough weight as a counter-model, a revolution in the structure of the original model can occur (Thagard, 2000, p. 75). Within a population of actors, models are transferred through speaking and listening, writing and reading, discussion, application, and so on. Because of this transfer, models spread as *memes* (Dawkins, 1976/ 1989, p. 192) over a population of actors. Moreover, as a result of these transfer mechanisms, models can grow in coherence and acceptability. Models that are not applied are subject to a low rate of transfer, and will eventually become extinct.

5. CONCLUSION

This chapter explains how models can be seen from a semiotic point of view, how people use models, how the coherence and boundaries of a model are established, and which role models play in organizations.

From a semiotic point of view, a *model* is a *coherent sign structure*, consisting of a network of a diversity of signs, and used by an actor for the understanding or constructing of a *system of application*. As a cognitively manageable island of coherence, a model enables coherent reasoning of an actor about systems of application. A model functions in a triadic sign system consisting of sign (model), object (system of application) and interpretant (resulting idea in the mind of the interpreting actor). There is a class of systems to which the model may be applied: the compliance class of the model. Models may be represented within actors, such as *mental models* in humans and animals, and *computer models* in computers or robots. Mental models are not observable in a direct manner because you cannot read signs in the mind. Models may also reside outside actors in the ecological environment as *document models*. Models are sign structures that have to be constructed and adapted by actors based on examples, data about the system of application, theories and metaphors. They can be used by actors as tools for actively selecting, naming, interpreting, or even creating systems of application.

People use models because they are coherent, cognitively manageable units of knowledge organized by using *semiotic adaptive shortcuts* and sign layers. By their efficient organization, these knowledge units enable the development of flexible and adequate habits of action despite the physical limitations of the human and animal cognitive system and the necessity to react in a timely way. Sign structures act as semiotic adaptive shortcuts that help a timely determination of adequate behaviour. All artefacts and sign structures have to be constructed within the boundaries of reasonable computational costs. *Affordances* are represented as semi-indexical sign structures. These semi-indexical sign structures are connected to their interpretants in the human or animal mind. These interpretants can be feelings, or efforts to act, or goal-oriented repertoires of behaviour that Peirce calls habits of action. A unit consisting of a semi-indexical representation of an affordance and its associated habit of action can be considered as a unit of tacit knowledge. The world model of an actor consists of smaller knowledge units, islands of coherence, in other words, models. Based on their use, models perform processes of *self-organization*, thus adding new *sign layers or dimensions* to the representation, namely iconic representations, language representations, and conceptual representations. Models are generally less complex than their system of application. It is important which type of 'information compression' a model uses: selection or abstraction, or both. Because of the limits to the cognitive system, there is a strong local coherence in models as islands of coherence, but no strong global coherence. The insight that complex phenomena can be constructed or simulated based on a few simple computational rules, and that properties can emerge based on these computational mechanisms, means a step forward compared to the relatively closed and static world view of equation models and traditional logic.

Models change and find their boundaries based on a dynamics of coherence. The *coherence* mechanism works by the mutual adjustment of the model elements, and of model elements and elements in the system of application. The formation of islands of coherence can be described by computational mechanisms, and can be computationally simulated. The coherence mechanism should be seen as an alternative for foundational reasoning. The coherence concept fits well into an open, constructivist world view, while foundational reasoning uses a closed world assumption. Because empirical data have no longer a privileged position of indubitable beliefs, the question of correspondence of a model with empirical data becomes a question of coherence between model and empirical data. Coherence theory can integrate cognitive and emotional aspects. In reasoning about the *boundaries* of a model, we need to distinguish the model core, the hidden layer connected to a model, and the support structure of a model. The *model core* consists of sign structures representing the system of application. The *hidden layer* connected to a model consists of sign structures that are hidden as tacit knowledge or as an emotional dimension. The *support structure* of a model consists of theories, data models, metaphors, and other sign structures coherent with the model core. We can consider the model core as a network of signs taken from all sign layers. Models may contain *iconic representations*, such as diagrams, map-like pictures or even physical scale models, *texts* referring to the system of application, and *conceptual structures* like data structures, object models, and calculi that facilitate reasoning. Norms play a role at all sign levels.

An *organization* can be seen as a multi-actor system based on habits of action aimed at cooperation and coordination of work. These habits of action are supported by *organizational knowledge* in the form of shared artefacts, shared stories, shared institutions, shared designs and shared plans. There are no other carriers for organizational knowledge than actors and documents. This point of view is a kind of methodological individualism. Organizational knowledge includes cooperation agreements, a work organization, a formal organization, and an organization culture. Shared institutions, shared designs and shared plans are *shared normative models* that make up for the difference between the organization or social system as a whole and 'the sum' of the individual actors. They act as the glue that keeps the system together. The function of social norms is to restrict individual behaviour to socially acceptable behaviour. According to Peirce, *norms* are habits of self-preparation and self-control. Norms develop themselves based on experience. Norms as isolated elements cannot account for coherent normative behaviour. They have to be integrated in the models an actor has of other actors and of himself. An important characteristic of norms is that they are reciprocal. From a pragmatic point of view, there are three types of normative models that humans use, Gazendam (1986). People make *designs* for a future (possibly desired) object or situation. In order to move from the present to the future, they construct *behaviour rule systems* and make *plans* for the guiding of behaviour. An *institution* is a system of behaviour rules. Institutions as abstract objects correspond to systems of social constructs. Each social construct is a socially negotiated concept to which attributes, such as norms and default behaviour scenarios are attached. Institutions as behaviour patterns correspond to habits. Shared normative models are created by actors and, in turn, influence actor behaviour by forming habits, thus creating a *cycle of selection and reinforcement*, where some models and norms are reinforced and other models and norms disappear. Organizations change because actors join or leave the organization, change products, markets, and technology, change formal structures and power structures, create artefacts and tell stories, and change their knowledge. Within a population of actors, models are transferred through speaking and listening, writing and reading, discussion, application, and so on. By this transfer, models spread as *memes* over a population of actors. As a result of these transfer mechanisms, models are able to grow in coherence and acceptability. Models that are not applied are subject to a low rate of transfer, and will eventually become extinct.

REFERENCES

Alexander, C. (1977). *A pattern language: Towns, buildings, construction*. Oxford, England: Oxford University Press.

Alexander, C. (1979). *The timeless way of building*. Oxford, England: Oxford University Press.

Austin J. L. (1962/ 1975). *How to do things with words* (New revised edition, M. Sbisà & J. O. Urmson, eds.). Oxford, England: Clarendon Press.

Ayer, A. J., & O'Grady, J. (Eds.). (1992). *A dictionary of philosophical quotations*. Oxford, England: Blackwell.

Barrow, J. (1998). *Impossibility: The limits of science and the science of limits*. London: Vintage.

Boden, M. A. (1988). *Computer models of mind: Computational approaches in theoretical psychology*. Cambridge, England: Cambridge University Press.

Boisot, M. H. (1995). *Information space: A framework for learning in organizations, institutions and culture*. London: Routledge

Bosman, A. (1996). *Modellen van en in een organisatie* [Models of and in organizations]. Leiderdorp, The Netherlands: Lansa.

Bouissac, P. (in press). Bounded semiotics: From utopian to evolutionary models of communication. This book.

Broek, J. van den. (2001). *On agent cooperation: The relevance of cognitive plausibility for multiagent simulation models of organizations*. Capelle a/d IJssel, The Netherlands: Labyrinth.

Calvin, W.H., & Bickerton, D. (2000). *Lingua ex machina: Reconciling Darwin and Chomsky with the human brain*. Cambridge, MA: The MIT Press.

Coleman, J.S. (1990). *Foundations of social theory*. Cambridge, MA: The Belknap Press and Harvard University Press.

Collins COBUILD *English language dictionary*. (1987). London: Collins.

Craik, K. (1943). *The nature of explanation*. Cambridge, England: Cambridge University Press.

Dawkins, R. (1989). *The selfish gene* (Rev. ed.). Oxford, England: Oxford University Press. (Original work published 1976).

Emery, F. E. (Ed.). (1969). *Systems thinking*. Harmondsworth, England: Penguin Books.

Fayol, H. (1956). *Administration, industrielle et générale* [Industrial and general management]. Paris: Dunod. (Original work published in: Bulletin de la Société de l'Industrie Minérale, 3e livraison, 1916).

Fayol, H. (1984). *General and Industrial Management* (I. Gray, trans. and rev. ed.) [Administration, industrielle et générale]. London: Pitman. (Original work published in: Bulletin de la Société de l'Industrie Minérale, 3e livraison, 1916).

Franssen, M. (1997). *Some contributions to methodological individualism in the social sciences*. Unpublished doctoral dissertation, University of Amsterdam.

Gazendam, H. W. M. (1986). *Informatiebeleid en informatieplannen als besturingsinstrument* [Information policy and information plans as management instruments]. Unpublished research note, University of Groningen, The Netherlands, Faculty of Management and Organization.

Gazendam, H. W. M. (1993). *Variety Controls Variety: On the Use of Organization Theories in Information Management.* Groningen, The Netherlands: Wolters-Noordhoff.

Gazendam, H. W. M. (1997). *Voorbij de dwang van de techniek: Naar een pluriforme bestuurlijke informatiekunde* [Past the technology push: Towards a pluralistic theory of information systems] [Inaugural lecture]. Enschede, The Netherlands: Twente University.

Gazendam, H. W. M. (2001). Semiotics, virtual organisations, and information systems. In K. Liu, R. J. Clarke, P. Bøgh Andersen, & R. K. Stamper (Eds.), *Information, organisation and technology: Studies in organisational semiotics* (pp. 1-48). Boston, MA: Kluwer Academic Publishers.

Gazendam, H. W. M. (2002). Conceptual analysis and specification of organization theories. In J. C. Wood & M. C. Wood (Eds.). *Henri Fayol: Critical evaluations in business and management: Volume II* (pp. 381-398). London: Routledge.

Georgescu-Roegen, N. (1971). *The entropy law and the economic process.* Cambridge, MA: Harvard University Press.

Gibson, J. J. (1979). *The ecological approach to visual perception.* Boston, MA: Houghton Mifflin.

Giere, R. N. (1999). *Science without laws.* Chicago: University of Chicago Press.

Gigerenzer, G., & Selten, R. (Eds.). (2001). *Bounded rationality: The adaptive toolbox.* Cambridge, MA: The MIT Press.

Goldberg, A., & Robson, D. (1983). *Smalltalk-80: The language and its implementation.* Reading, MA: Addison-Wesley.

Goodman, N. (1976). *Languages of art: An approach to a theory of symbols.* Indianapolis, IN: Hackett.

Hausman, C. R. (1993*). Charles S. Peirce's evolutionary philosophy.* Cambridge, England: Cambridge University Press.

Heusden, B. P. van, & Jorna, R. J. (2001). Toward a semiotic theory of cognitive dynamics in organisations. In K. Liu, J. Clarke, P. Bøgh Andersen, & R. K. Stamper (Eds.), *Information, organisation and technology: Studies in organisational semiotics* (pp. 83-113). Boston, MA: Kluwer Academic Publishers.

Holland, J. H. (1995). *Hidden order: How adaptation builds complexity.* Reading, MA: Addison-Wesley.

Holland, J. H. (1998). *Emergence: From chaos to order.* Oxford: Oxford University Press.

Homburg, V. M. F. (1999). *The political economy of information management: A theoretical and empirical analysis of decision making regarding interorganizational information systems.* Capelle a/d IJssel, The Netherlands: Labyrinth.

Johnson-Laird, P. N. (1983). *Mental models: Towards a cognitive science of language, inference, and consciousness.* Cambridge, England: Cambridge University Press.

Jong, H. M. de. (1992). *Twijfel en verantwoordelijkheid in het recht* [Doubt and responsibility in justice] [Inaugural lecture]. Enschede, The Netherlands: Twente University.

Jorna, R. J. (1990). *Knowledge representation and symbols in the mind.* Tübingen, Germany: Stauffenburg Verlag.

Jorna, R. J., Gazendam, H. W. M., Heesen, H. C., & Van Wezel, W. M. C. (1996). *Plannen en roosteren: Taakgericht analyseren, ontwerpen en ondersteunen* [Planning and scheduling: Task-oriented analysis, design, and support]. Leiderdorp, The Netherlands: Lansa Publishing.

Kant, I. (1984). *Grundlegung zur Metaphysik der Sitten* (Herausgegeben von Theodor Valentiner, Einleitung von Hans Ebeling) [Foundations of the metaphysics of morality, edited by Theodor Valentiner, introduction by Hans Ebeling]. Stuttgart, Germany: Reclam. (Original work published 1785).

Liu, K. (2000). *Semiotics in information systems engineering.* Cambridge, England: Cambridge University Press.

Marr, D. (1982). *Vision.* New York: Freeman.

Meyers Konversations-Lexicon: Fünfte Auflage. (1897). Leipzig, Germany: Bibliographisches Institut.

Nagel, E. (1961). *The structure of science: Problems in the logic of scientific explanation.* London: Routledge & Kegan Paul.

Nauta, D. (1970). *Logica en model* [Logic and model]. Bussum, The Netherlands: De Haan.

Newcombe, N. S., & Huttenlocher, J. (2000). *Making space: The development of spatial representation and reasoning.* Cambridge, MA: The MIT Press.

Newell, A. (1990). *Unified theories of cognition: The William James lectures, 1987.* Cambridge, MA: Harvard University Press.

Pagels, H. R. (1989). *The dreams of reason: The computer and the rise of the sciences of complexity.* New York: Bantam Books.

Peirce, C. S. (1958a). How to make our ideas clear. In P. P. Wiener (Ed.), *Charles S. Peirce: Selected writings: Values in a universe of chance* (pp. 113-136). New York: Dover. (Original work published in Popular Science Monthly, Jan 1878, pp. 286-302).

Peirce, C. S. (1958b). Letters to Lady Welby. In P. P. Wiener (Ed.), *Charles S. Peirce: Selected writings: Values in a universe of chance* (pp. 380-432). New York: Dover. (Original work published 1904).

Peirce, C. S. (1958c). What pragmatism is. In P. P. Wiener (Ed.), *Charles S. Peirce: Selected writings: Values in a universe of chance* (pp. 180-202). New York: Dover. (Original work published in The Monist, 15, April 1905, pp. 161-181).

Peirce, C. S. (1998). Pragmatism. In N. Houser, A. De Tienne, J. R. Eller, C. L. Clark, A. C. Lewis & D. B. Davis (Eds.), *The essential Peirce: Selected philosophical writings: Vol. 2* (1893 - 1913) (pp. 398-433). Bloomington, IN: Indiana University press. (Original work published 1907).

Port, R. F., & Van Gelder, T. (1995). *Mind as motion: Explorations in the dynamics of cognition.* Cambridge, MA: The MIT Press.

Putnam, R. D. (1993). *Making democracy work.* Princeton, NJ: Princeton University Press.

Rawls, J. (2000). *A theory of justice* (Rev. ed.). Oxford, England: Oxford University Press. (Original work published 1971).

Rorty, R. (1979). *Philosophy and the mirror of nature.* Princeton, NJ: Princeton University Press.

Rumbaugh, J., Jacobson, I., & Booch, G. (1999). *The unified modeling language reference manual.* Reading, MA: Addison-Wesley.

Sanders, G. J. E. M., & Neuijen, B. (1989). *Bedrijfscultuur: Diagnose en beïnvloeding* [Organization Culture: Diagnosis and Change]. Assen, The Netherlands: Van Gorcum.

Searle, J. R., & Vanderveken, D. (1985). *Foundations of illocutionary logic.* Cambridge, England: Cambridge University Press.

Sebeok, T. A. (1994). *Signs: An introduction to semiotics.* Toronto, Canada: University of Toronto Press.

Schmidt, K. (1991). Cooperative work: A conceptual framework. In J. Rasmussen, B. Brehmer, & J. Leplat (Eds.), *Distributed decision making: Cognitive models for cooperative work* (pp. 75-110). Chichester, England: John Wiley and Sons.

Shoham, Y. (1988). *Reasoning about change: Time and causation from the standpoint of artificial intelligence.* Cambridge, MA: The MIT Press.

Simon, H.A. (1976). *Administrative behavior: A study of decision-making processes in administrative organization* (3rd ed.). New York: The Free Press. (Original work published 1945).

Stamper, R. K. (2001). Organisational semiotics: Informatics without the computer?. In K. Liu, R. J. Clarke, P. Bøgh Andersen, & R. K. Stamper (Eds.), *Information, organisation and technology: Studies in organisational semiotics* (pp. 115-171). Boston, MA: Kluwer Academic Publishers.

Thagard, P. (2000). *Coherence in thought and action.* Cambridge, MA: The MIT Press.

Uexküll, J. von, & Kriszat, G. (1970). *Streifzüge durch die Umwelten von Tieren und Menschen.* Frankfurt, Germany: Fischer. (Original work published 1936).

Uexküll, T. von (1998). Jakob von Uexkülls Umweltlehre. In R. Posner, K. Robering, & T. A. Sebeok (Eds.), *Semiotics: A handbook on the sign-theoretic foundations of nature and culture: Vol. 2* (pp. 2183-2191). Berlin, Germany: Walter de Gruyter.

Veld, J. in 't. (1988). *Analyse van organisatieproblemen: Een toepassing van denken in systemen en processen.* Vijfde druk [Analysis of organization problems: An application of systems thinking and process thinking: 5th Ed.]. Leiden, The Netherlands: Stenfert Kroese.

Williamson, O. E. (1975). *Markets and hierarchies.* New York: The Free Press.

Williamson, O. E. (1985). *The economic institutions of capitalism.* New York: The Free Press.

Wolfram, S. (2002). *A new kind of science.* Champaign, IL: Wolfram Media.

Chapter 10

Measuring and mapping knowledge types
Problems of knowledge transfer in an IT company

Ruben Cijsouw and René Jorna

ABSTRACT

In this chapter we formulate a cognitive-semiotic perspective on knowledge and knowledge management. The focus is especially on types of knowledge and not on contents (domains) of knowledge. As domain of knowledge in this research the management of IT projects is chosen. In this domain we focus on how knowledge is managed during product innovation. The management of the company lacks control information of the way the production resource "knowledge" is actually used in the company. They experience that they are not able manage adequately enough the transfer of knowledge from the project members to the administrators of the IT systems. To assess the knowledge types we performed a knowledge mapping in which we determined the sensory, coded and theoretical knowledge of the organizational tasks or processes. Based on the research findings a change trajectory has been suggested in order to have a more effective and more efficient product innovation process.

INTRODUCTION

Information regarding the use of production resources, its effectivity and efficiency, is vital for management. More and more, knowledge is reckoned among the main production resources, such as land, (money) capital, and labor. According to Fayol (1916; 1987), planning, organizing, commanding, coordinating, and controlling are the basic management activities. Almost a century later, the same words are covering various management activities, although the content of the activities has changed. Whereas for the other resources, controlling is generally accepted as crucial in order to be able to manage the production process (of products or services), this is not (yet) so in the case of knowledge. Nowadays, the field of knowledge management focuses on planning, organizing, and coordinating knowledge. Based on Fayol, we define controlling as auditing *and* correcting. In firms, intellectual capital (Sveiby, 1997) has been assessed and sometimes the "Return to Knowledge" is determined in the case of innovation. Both are examples of a (money) capital approach to knowledge; they have their basis in the tradition of financial management.

In our research, we have a cognitive-semiotic perspective on knowledge and knowledge management. In this research, a method for determining and positioning knowledge (types) has been developed. Until now, the method has been developed based on theory building and case studies. This chapter describes a case where this perspective is used to manage knowledge during product innovation in an IT company. The management of a Dutch IT company experienced that they were not able to manage adequately enough the transfer of knowledge from the project members to the administrators of the IT systems. The management lacked control information regarding the way the production resource "knowledge" was actually used in the company. In this research, we have studied the auditing (determination and assessment) of knowledge of individuals carrying out their tasks. Based on the research findings, a change trajectory, i.e., the correction, is suggested in order to achieve a more effective and more efficient product innovation process.

Knowledge mapping can be realized in three different ways. First, only the knowledge content (or domain) can be assessed. Second, the knowledge content *and* its knowledge types can be investigated. Third, while taking certain knowledge contents for granted, only the knowledge types are assessed. In this research, we take this third road and focus on the knowledge types of a given content, namely the organizational tasks or processes.

THE SEMIO-COGNITIVE PERSPECTIVE ON KNOWLEDGE MANAGEMENT

In this research we used a semiotic and representational perspective on knowledge management in which we view the organization as a multi-actor system.

We take organizations to be semiotic constructs and processes (i.e., *representations*) used by actors to organize the interaction with their social and physical environment. An organization is always an organization *for actors* in a particular historical context, and studying organizational behaviour comes down to the study of cognitive semiotic behaviour of groups of individual actors (Heusden van & Jorna, 2000).

The basic ingredients of an organization are the intelligent actors. This means that there exists a nesting of a) actors within organizations and b) organizations within actors (Jorna, 2001). Not only does the organization consist of people, computers, machines, etc., the actors have a cognitive representation of the organization as well. It is on the basis of these representations that actors react to actions of other actors in the organization.

It is possible to define an organizationas "the simultaneous functionalization and coordination of human actions with regard to objective goals" (van Dale, 1995, p. 2144). In this definition the emphasis is on actions that, by the way, can be classified within processes. In the definition also goals and coordination are mentioned. A goal is immediately related to a primary process. That is the reason why the organization exists. Coordination is needed because "entities", such as actions, tasks, processes, but also groups of actors, do not form natural units. They need some kind of coherence or cohesion structure. This coherence can be organized externally, in a legal or financial way, or it can be organized internally by an interpreting and meaning giving entity, which in this case is an actor (Jorna, 2001).

In this semio-cognitive approach, the development and change of cognitive schemas, or knowledge structures, is dealt with from a semiotic perspective (van Heusden & Jorna, 2000). Only the knowledge that actors, i.e., the members of an organization, actually use during the execution of their tasks is taken into account. In this way, the management can make their decisions based on reliable controlling information. In our case, the newly built IT-systems are the developed cognitive schemas, whereas the advice will be on how to change these cognitive schemas in order to sufficiently bridge the knowledge gap between the project unit and the administering unit as separate but related departments within the same organization.

The perspective chosen allows us to relate theories as well as empirical findings concerning organizations to the general framework of a – semiotic – science of culture and cognition. From our point of view, this choice results directly from the analysis of the organization as semiotic behaviour (van Heusden & Jorna, 2000).

Knowledge classifications

In this knowledge assessment approach the emphasis is not on the **content** of knowledge, but on the **form** or **type**. In the literature various categorizations of knowledge forms or types are discussed (Boisot, 1995; Polanyi, 1967; Pylyshyn, 1984). Sometimes the types of knowledge partly exist together, sometimes they are changed from one type into another. The types include declarative, procedural, tacit, explicit, coded, uncoded, abstract, concrete, non-diffused and diffused knowledge. Some types are derived from Boisot (1995). He suggested the coded-uncoded distinction to indicate that knowledge may have a structure of elements. Coded means that involved units have composition and combination rules. Semiotically, we could say that, together, the units are composed of syntax and semantics. The diffused-undiffused dimension (Boisot, 1995) means that knowledge can be distributed. The concrete-abstract distinction (Boisot, 1995) means that within the codedness of knowledge the applicability of the codes has several degrees. The more possibilities the more abstract the coded unit. Boisot (1995) combines the dimensions of coded/uncoded, concrete/abstract and diffused/undiffused knowledge. The resulting elaboration leads to eleven types of knowledge. He distinguishes: technical (coded/concrete), aesthetic (uncoded/concrete), craft (uncoded/abstract), scientific (coded/abstract/diffused), esoteric (abstract/undiffused), local (concrete/undiffused), topical (concrete/diffused), proprietary (coded/undiffused), personal (uncoded/undiffused), public (coded/diffused) and common-sense knowledge (uncoded/diffused).

For reasons of understanding we used the term "knowledge", although Boisot refers to information. In the literature, two other classifications are also mentioned: tacit versus explicit (Polanyi, 1967) and declarative versus procedural (Pylyshyn, 1984). Tacit is knowledge without speaking, it is merely "doing" or "acting", whereas explicit means that the knowledge is expressed or showed in structural forms. Declarative knowledge means that expressions are produced, whereas procedural emphasizes the ongoing, the continuing aspect of knowledge.

The discussion about the types of knowledge is complicated for two reasons. First, much debate exists about the conversion of the one into the other. Second, in one way or another, the knowledge types seem to be versions of one another. We will first go into the details of the conversions or changes and then we will come up with a new scheme in which the versions can be translated into one another.

Concerning the various two-type possibilities five 2x2 matrices can be formulated making visible the various conversions. They can be seen as conversion matrices. The conversions are indicated positively (+), negatively (-) or unknown (?). The conversions are not yet the result of empirical studies. The determination of values is purely done on the basis of theoretical considerations.

Concerning the explicit-tacit dimension (table 1) the direction of the conversion is not determined. All possibilities are present, although some questions can be formulated by what it means that tacit knowledge is converted into tacit knowledge. Supposing that change can only be possible via a stage of explicitness seems logical.

Table 1. Explicit-tacit (types of knowledge)

Convert from/to	*Explicit*	*Tacit*
Explicit	+	+
Tacit	+	?

The cells in the coded-uncoded dimension (table 2) indicate that the direction is from uncoded into coded. This means that coded can be converted into other coded knowledge and that uncoded will be changed into coded, but the way back is very unlikely. Once knowledge is coded it remains so or it is forgotten.

Table 2. Coded-uncoded types of knowledge

Convert from/to	Coded	Uncoded
Coded	+	-
Uncoded	+	-

The cells in the abstract-concrete dimension (table 3) indicate that all conversions are possible. Conversion of concrete into abstract can only be possible via an intermediate stage of codedness. Concrete and abstract knowledge are both coded.

Table 3. Abstract-concrete types of knowledge

Convert from/to	Concrete	Abstract
Concrete	+	+
Abstract	+	+

The distinction in procedural and declarative knowledge has been vehemently discussed in cognitive science (Pylyshyn, 1984). Procedural knowledge is usually presented as a production system. A production system is the complicated if-then structure in a reasoning activity. The formulations within the clauses of the if-then structure are the declarations (Anderson, 1983). The cells in the declarative-procedural dimension (table 4) show that only the conversion of declarative into procedural is possible. It is unlikely that procedural knowledge will change by itself into procedural or declarative knowledge. It is possible that this trajectory is realized, but then the procedural knowledge is at a different level of aggregation. Take, for example, learning to make multiplications. To operate correctly, it is necessary that addition problems are mastered in such a way that they become procedures on which new declarations can be piled up.

Table 4. Declarative-procedural types of knowledge

Convert from/to	Declarative	Procedural
Declarative	+	?
Procedural	+	?

The last dimension of diffusion-undiffusion (table 5) is of a different order. For knowledge to be diffused it has to be coded, to be made explicit or abstract. Knowledge in this case has to bridge a distance in time or space. Explicitness may also mean that a skill is demonstrated and imitated. Diffusion means that other members of an organization can understand what was first tacit or implicit. By giving knowledge an expression, that is to say to give it a form, knowledge sharing, knowledge correction and knowledge accumulation can be realized.

Table 5. Diffused-undiffused of knowledge types)

Convert from/to	Diffused	Undiffused
Diffused	+	-
Undiffused	+	-

From a semio-cognitive perspective the determination of the various types of knowledge the actors in the organization posses is a first step in discussing knowledge management. The second step implies that based on possible conversions the actual conversions have to be determined per actor. This has to be done empirically. It can only be done by at least two different observations in time. The third step is the determination of the proportion of each of the knowledge types present within a certain actor executing a task. Finally, and this is the fourth step, a discussion can be started about the necessity of going through certain sequences of conversions that may be described.

Until now, we have mainly discussed the various types of knowledge. An additional analysis is possible for coded knowledge only. This relates to the connected types of coded, explicit or declarative knowledge. Various forms of codes can be discerned. Well known are texts, icons/pictures and diagrams/schemes. In table 6, the various possibilities are enumerated. The determination of the conversions is different in comparison with the previous tables. A conversion here is related to an increase in ambiguity, similar ambiguity or no change in ambiguity, and a decrease in ambiguity. A code is "better" if it reduces the ambiguity. In this respect, icons produce ambiguity, diagrams reduce ambiguity and texts reduce ambiguity even more. In table 6, we show these conversions: + (or + +) means a decrease in ambiguity, / means the same, and - (or - -) means an increase in ambiguity.

The lower left corner of the table shows that a conversion from diagram to icon means a reduction in level of abstraction. From a semiotic point of view, it is questionable whether this is possible without much loss of information (Jorna, 1990). The hypothesis is that various forms co-vary with only one type, namely coded knowledge, but that differences in code structures have their influence on effective communication. The stronger the code, the better the communication. In this sense notations are strong codes, whereas icons and pictures are very weak codes and diagrams are in between (Goodman, 1968).

Table 6. Forms of knowledge: icons, text and diagrams

From/To	Icons	Text	Diagrams
Icons	/	++	+
Text	- -	/	-
Diagrams	-	+	/

One type of knowledge is especially important, because it features in all discussions about learning, knowledge creation and knowledge management. It is called tacit knowledge. Although Polanyi (1967) is known for introducing this term in the scientific community, the meaning of tacit is not undisputed. We discern three different interpretations of tacit knowledge. The first is that people have large reservoirs of knowledge that are not immediately relevant. Often, they do not realize that the knowledge is relevant. We know much more than we can say is one of the proverbs that is applicable to this interpretation of tacit knowledge. The reservoir is present, but its content is slumbering, waiting for a relevant cue to trigger the right cognitive units. This interpretation is closely connected to Polanyi's use of the term.

A second interpretation is that tacit knowledge is non-penetrable knowledge. This notion was introduced by Pylyshyn (1984) to indicate that, when we try to solve problems, make decisions or just try to remember things, we are very limited in reporting what is going on within our cognitive system. Even if we focus attention on our thought processes, only a very small part of what goes on at the processing level can be inspected or accounted for.

The third interpretation of tacit knowledge also partly encloses what Polanyi meant. In terms of cognitive processes, tacit knowledge can be automated knowledge. This means that, mostly because of practical reasons, we reduce cognitive processes in such a way that they are "compiled". This has as advantage that the knowledge occupies less space, does not need any attention and can be executed faster. However, it also is less accessible. Automated knowledge is often said to be knowledge of skills. If I have learned how to ride a bicycle, it is almost impossible for me to explain my skills in declarative terms; it has become tacit. The three interpretations do not exclude one another, although we can argue that the first differs from the second and third in that tacit, as the large reservoir, is not coded at all, whereas tacit, in the sense of non-penetrable and automatized, was once coded. This code can be reapplied.

Concerning the apparent absence of a form or code (the unknown reservoir inside), there is something mysterious in discussions about tacit knowledge. Tacitness as such cannot be observed. It can only be inferred from declarative and explicit knowledge or from overt behaviour. This means that its wonderful characteristics can only be formulated in the following dilemma: when you don't ask me about tacitness, I know what it is, but if you ask me about tacitness, I don't know (how to express it). This means that it is extremely difficult to operationalize tacit knowledge. Reber (1993) has combined tacit knowledge with implicit learning and says: "Implicit learning is the acquisition of knowledge that takes place largely independent of conscious attempts to learn and largely in the absence of explicit knowledge about what was acquired. One of the core assumptions of our work has been that implicit learning is a fundamental "root" process, one that lies at the very heart of the adaptive behavioural repertoire of every complex organism" (p. 5). Reber even goes as far as to claim that tacit knowledge is similar to automated knowledge, procedural knowledge or knowing how. After conducting psychological experiments for more than twenty years, Reber (1993, p.64) concludes: "For the moment at least, the data support the interpretation that tacit knowledge is a reasonably veridical, partial isomorphism of the structural patterns of relational invariances that the environment displays. It is reasonably veridical in that it reflects, with considerable accuracy, the stimulus invariances displayed in the environment. It is partial in that not all patterns become part of tacit knowledge. It is structural in that the patterns are manifestations of abstract generative rules for symbol ordering". From a cognitive perspective, Reber shows that, on the one hand of all the things we know only a minor part is available for direct inspection. The major part is invisible. On the other hand, however, he shows that this major part is not a big garbage can. Tacit knowledge in whatever form it is present, is internally related to structure in the cognitive system, and externally to the outside world. Unpredictable so far is the way tacit knowledge materializes in problem solving, in task execution and in overt behaviour.

Because we consider the various dichotomies in knowledge types to be confusing, we have tried to combine them into one scheme. This scheme is based on the structure given by Boisot (1995), but differs from it in that we excluded the diffused-undiffused distinction. Diffusion is not about the characteristics of knowledge itself but about the communication of knowledge. Furthermore, we want to emphasize the perspective that knowledge is something only an individual possess. Groups, organizations and - until now - robots do not have knowledge. We start with actors (human individuals as information processing systems) with representations. We strongly believe that (radical) changes in organizations are started, continued and ended by humans as information processing systems. We also strongly believe that stages in change processes do not only randomly occur. If knowledge is involved, we believe that types and forms of knowledge follow certain patterns. The question is what patterns, to what extent and for what kind of actors, related to the execution of what kinds of tasks. This implies that we have to start with real cognition and real behaviour of real people. Although it is well known that humans as cognitive systems are limited with respect to rationality, memory and processing power (Simon, 1969), it seems that this lesson is forgotten time and again. The interesting issue is not whether there are limitations, but to what extent our so-called unlimited flexibility in knowledge follows certain patterns. This is what we try to accomplish with a semio-cognitive perspective on knowledge management and knowledge change. Given the fact that knowledge changes, what are the sequences of these changes and by what aspects of interpretation, communication and task execution can the changes be explained and predicted?

As we already suggested, we will make a fundamental distinction into the **content** and the **form** or **appearance** of knowledge. Domains, fields and disciplines are examples of the former subdivision, whereas all the above mentioned distinctions of types are forms of the latter (Polanyi, 1967; Nonaka, 1994). A knowledge domain comes closest to what Postrel (2002) calls " single interconnected cluster". In the literature, it is mostly referred to as a 'discipline'. Fields of science are good examples of knowledge domains, e.g. medical sciences, economy, sociology. But in these knowledge domains other interconnected clusters exist: in the medical sciences there are several specialisms, e.g. ENT (ear, nose, throat), thorax surgery, or orthopaedics. Postrel (2002) uses the extent to which knowledge forms a single interconnected cluster as a measure to determine the degree of specialization.

Based on the ideas of Boisot and using the insights of cognitive science, we developed our own classification consisting of sensory knowledge, coded knowledge and theoretical knowledge. In the table below (table 7), we placed the various dichotomies in rows, whereas our own distinction is presented in the columns. In the cells we indicated whether coded is sensory, coded or theoretical, uncoded is sensory, etc.

Table 7. Various dichotomies categorized into sensory, coded and theoretical knowledge

↓ Is (a kind of) →	*Sensory knowledge*	*Coded knowledge*	*Theoretical knowledge*
Coded	Not applicable	Applicable	Applicable
Uncoded	Applicable	Not applicable	Not applicable
Declarative	Not applicable	Applicable	Applicable
Procedural	Applicable	Not applicable	Not applicable
Abstract	Not applicable	Applicable	Applicable
Concrete	Applicable	Not applicable	Not applicable
Tacit	Applicable	Not applicable	Applicable
Explicit	Not applicable	Applicable	Applicable

The explanation of sensory, coded and theoretical knowledge is given in the subsections below. We believe that the well-known dichotomies are too much restricted in their use. The triple distinction in sensory, coded and theoretical knowledge makes it possible to asses knowledge types more realistically. We have also combined the three knowledge types into a so-called knowledge space.

Sensory knowledge

Many people will recognize Beethoven's fifth symphony when they hear the opening bars. They use one of their sensory organs, their ears, to interpret the airwaves. When a person obtains this knowledge by using his sensory organs, we speak of sensory knowledge. Sensory knowledge is basically concrete, and therefore dependent on the presence of an environment. Michael Polanyi (1967) describes the process involved in tacit knowledge as being "aware of that *from* which we are attending *to* another thing in the *appearance* of that thing". Boisot (1995) claims this knowledge cannot be coded; it is about concrete experiences, and it can be shared only with those who are co-present.

Diffusion, which is the communication and sharing of knowledge between actors, is a matter of imitation (van Heusden & Jorna, 2000). In cognitive terms sensory knowledge is based on the perceptible analogy between the representation and that, which is being represented without any intermediary convention. Sensory knowledge can be either rough or detailed. This can be compared to the zoom function of a camera: when zooming in, the observations become more and more detailed.

Coded knowledge

Returning to recognizing Beethoven's fifth symphony, there exists another way to recognize this piece of music other than by hearing; namely by a quick look at the first four bars, people who are able to read musical scores can also recognize Beethoven's fifth symphony.

Figure 1. Opening bars of Beethoven's fifth symphony

In this case, the written music is the code containing the knowledge that can be interpreted (this is Beethoven's fifth). This is an example of coded knowledge. Coded knowledge is a representation based on an arbitrary conventional relation between the representation and that which is being referred to; language is the clearest example of this type of representations. We categorize reality using conventional representations that we call symbols. Coded knowledge contains all types of signs or symbols either in text form, drawing form, or expressed into mathematical formulas. Coded knowledge can be either weakly coded (drawings) or strongly coded: mostly formulas. In the latter case we have a notation. Goodman (1968) calls a musical score an example of a strong code, which prevents ambiguity.

Theoretical knowledge

A person who is able to explain *why* this particular piece of music is Beethoven's fifth symphony possesses theoretical knowledge concerning this specific piece of music. We argue that people use theoretical knowledge when they are able to answer why-questions; they are able to formulate structural relations. The interpretation - and not the use - of a mathematical formula is another example of this third knowledge type which we distinguish: theoretical knowledge. We use theoretical knowledge to identify causal relations: the so-called if-then-relations. The more complicated the why-connection is the more abstract the theoretical knowledge. Otherwise it is concrete.

Knowledge space

A knowledge space can be constructed using the various knowledge types. The first semiotic step is always to recognize the situation in terms of a situation (or state of affairs) one already knows. The sensory, one-dimensional, sign is the most primitive form of the semiotic. The one dimension that allows us to speak about it as a semiotic phenomenon is the *difference* that separates memory from actuality in the process of representation (van Heusden & Jorna, 2000). It is at this point that the semiotic gradually emerges out of the non-semiotic, where memory and actuality are still one (van Heusden & Jorna, 2000). Sensory knowledge is of this kind. The one-dimensional representation underlies what Michael Polanyi (1967) has coined as "personal knowledge". Thus, sensory knowledge forms the first dimension of the knowledge space. Quantification of this type of representation or knowledge is possible through the measurement of detail. The dimension has very rough sensory knowledge on the one extreme and highly detailed sensory knowledge on the other extreme.

The second dimension is the semiotic dimension of the sign (or symbol) as a code. In this dimension the remembered state of affairs evokes the experienced state of affairs. These memories become signs of that state of affairs which loses its concrete appearance and becomes a *category* (van Heusden & Jorna, 2000). Coded knowledge is the second dimension of the knowledge space. Knowledge in the first dimension must exist in order to contain knowledge in the second dimension. Codes can be quantified by taking into account the *kinds of elements* (words, numbers, pictorial elements) and *combination rules* (or grammar) a code consists of, as well as *the degree of ambiguity* allowed (van Heusden & Jorna, 2000). The coded knowledge dimension starts with very weakly coded knowledge and ends with very strongly coded knowledge.

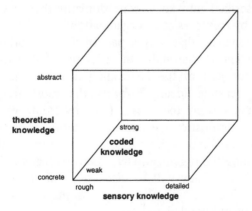

Figure 2. The knowledge space (van Heusden and Jorna, 2000)

The third dimension is that of the structural relation. Whereas the one-dimensional sign relies on a process of transformation, and the two-dimensional sign on a process of substitution, the three-dimensional sign relies on the *analysis* of relations or structures (van Heusden & Jorna, 2000). This is the dimension of theoretical knowledge. Theoretical knowledge can be quantified by determining the chain of causal connections (van Heusden & Jorna, 2000). In this particular research, we have quantified theoretical knowledge by measuring the level of relevant education (for the task) a person received combined with the amount of times a person is able to answer "why-questions". The hidden assumption is that the more training a person has had, the more theoretical knowledge he possesses. We have built up the framework of three dimensions meaning that we are now able to create the knowledge space. Figure 2 shows this knowledge space.

Knowledge management and organizational science

In the case study described in the next section, the main problem lies in the field of coordination. Coordination, as one of the basic management activities distinguished by Fayol, can be treated as a task that has to be executed. Knowledge of "coordination" has to be used by actors in order to fulfil this task. According to Fayol, management is an activity spread over all members of an organization. After preliminary interviews with members of the IT company, it was found that knowledge of coordination was not used optimally during the transfer of knowledge between the projects and administering units or organizational departments. For the two units we positioned the knowledge of coordination into the knowledge space.

In the case study, coordination is the main domain of study. However, coordination is not a well-defined activity. Several coordination mechanisms can be discerned. In the remainder of this section, the coordination mechanisms as described in organization management literature are transcribed into knowledge domains that can be used for coordination tasks by members of an organization.

This implies, however, that only a part of the controlling activity is accounted for: the knowledge audit. In order to be able to carry out a correction, the other part of the controlling activity, the management needs an aim, a feasible ideal. Probably the most frequently used coordination mechanisms are the ones defined by Mintzberg (1979). We will position these coordination mechanisms in terms of knowledge types distributions into the knowledge space. Determining the type of knowledge concerning the organizational processes leads to what we call "knowledge snapshots". They will be discussed and applied in the case study description. First, we will characterize some typical coordination mechanisms in terms of knowledge types.

Mintzberg's coordination mechanisms in terms of knowledge

Mintzberg distinguishes five coordination mechanisms that are used in five different types of organizations, i.e. simple structure, machine bureaucracy, professional bureaucracy, divisional structure, and adhocracy. In a simple structure, direct supervision is used as coordination mechanism, whereas in the machine bureaucracy standardization of work processes is the coordination mechanism. Standardization of skills is the coordination mechanism used in professional bureaucracies. In a divisional structure, standardization of output is the main coordination mechanism used, and finally, people working in an adhocracy use mutual adjustment as coordination mechanism. We will now describe each coordination mechanism in terms of the knowledge types that constitute the knowledge space.

Direct supervision

In an organization where direct supervision is the coordination mechanism used, one person - the chief executive officer - decides everything. He makes decisions based on his representation of reality. Because of this, it is sufficient for this person to use sensory knowledge during his tasks in the decision making process. Coded knowledge is only needed in order to make his decisions clear to the other members of the organization.

According to Thompson (1967), an organization aims at instrumentally and economically rational acting. For this reason, it is necessary for the organization to know all causal relations to realize continuity and profitability. Organizations that use direct supervision as coordination mechanism have these aims too. Thus, the decision-maker has to know all causal relations in order to have a rationally acting organization. To some extent, he has to use theoretical knowledge. The degree of theoretical knowledge he needs to use depends on the amount of possible causal relations that increase when the dynamics and complexity of the environment of the organization increase. The decision-maker uses this theoretical knowledge especially for the tasks in the primary process and not for his coordination tasks. Thus, theoretical knowledge is being used in an organization where direct supervision is the coordination mechanism, but it is not used for coordination purposes. Mainly, sensory knowledge and a small amount of coded knowledge are used during the execution of coordination tasks in this kind of organization. Sensory knowledge is dominant, coded and theoretical knowledge are subordinate or neglectable.

Standardization of work processes

The work processes of an organization are standardized by the use of rules. Coded knowledge is necessary for the formulation of rules. Standardization on its own is a suitable coordination mechanism, if the task environment of the organization is stable. In this case, the variation in possible causal relations is small. Therefore, when standardization of work processes is the coordination mechanism used, the importance of theoretical knowledge is little. Sensory knowledge is to some extent present, but subordinate.

Standardization of skills

If all employees - actors – have the same education a standardization of skills will be the result. Knowledge in education is always coded. Standardization of skills has been mainly used as coordination mechanisms if employees carry out highly specialized tasks. The employee has to determine the desired final situation based on his representation of the initial situation. He also has to determine the activities he has to carry out in order to go from the initial situation to the final situation. The representation of the initial situation can be obtained by the use of sensory, coded and theoretical knowledge. In order to determine the final situation and the activities that have to be executed theoretical knowledge is needed. This theoretical knowledge is obtained by means of intensive education. In an organization that uses standardization of skills as its main coordination mechanism, the knowledge used for coordination purposes is mostly theoretical and partly coded.

Standardization of output

A shared representation of the final result is very important when standardization of output is the main coordination mechanism in an organization. All actors need a minimum level of overlapping coded knowledge in order to reach agreements on the final situation. The person who has to undertake the actual activities to move from the initial situation can use sensory knowledge in order to determine the initial situation, but he needs coded knowledge to agree on the final situation with the other actors in the organization. He may also need theoretical knowledge in order to determine the right activities to go from the initial situation to the final situation agreed upon by all actors. However, this is not necessary. Coded knowledge is necessary for the actual standardization of output.

Mutual adjustment

In the adhocracy, the use of liaison devices throughout the entire organization makes frequent communication essential. This communication is achieved by mutual adjustment. Every time, communication is necessary to judge whether the actors in the organization share representations of the initial and final situation. All actors need coded knowledge in order to be able to establish these shared representations. It may be necessary to use sensory, coded or theoretical knowledge to determine the right response to the initial situation. This depends on the variation in the number of possible causal relations that in its turn depends on the dynamics and complexity of the task environment of the organization. Table 8 summarizes the results of the theoretical translation of Mintzberg's coordination mechanisms into the dominance and distribution of knowledge types.

Table 8. Mintzberg's coordination mechanisms translated into knowledge types. An empty circle means this knowledge type is very subordinate; partly filled: subordinate and a filled circle means dominant

Place in space	Coordination mechanism	Organization Type	Sensory knowledge	Coded knowledge	Theoretical knowledge
▼	Direct supervision	Simple structure	●	○	○
◉	Standardization of work processes	Machine bureaucracy	○	●	○
◆	Standardization of skills	Professional bureaucracy	○	◐	●
▦	Standardization of output	Divisional structure	○	●	◐
▦	Mutual adjustment	Adhocracy	◐	●	○

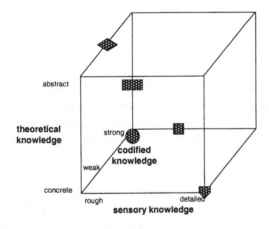

Figure 3. Mintzberg's organization types in the knowledge space

CASE STUDY

We studied a Dutch IT administering company. Most of the firm's projects exceeded the initial planning and/or the initially determined budget. Furthermore, the employees who had to administer the results of these projects, especially in the first months after the project was finished, were not capable of executing their administering task satisfactorily. According to the firm's management, the problems were due to a lack of knowledge management. The problem was how to operationalize and verify this statement.

The employees that worked in the projects complained about the claim the IT administrators put upon them to help them with their administering problems. These claims always came after the completion of the projects and existed because the project employees were seen as the experts with regard to these new IT components (i.e., hardware as well as software) in the company. This meant that they were the only ones with knowledge in the domain that could be used to fulfil the administering task. However, when former project members started helping their colleagues, not enough time was left for their own ongoing projects in which they were participating. As a consequence, the chances increased that the latter project would exceed the initial planning and therefore the initially determined budget.

In this research, we used the knowledge space to visualize the information that the management could use to break this vicious circle and change the organization in such a way that the knowledge transfer between the administering unit and the project unit could be improved.

The IT company

The company has recently (>2001) been outsourced, but at the time of the research (2000 – 2001) it was an autonomous IT department of a big Dutch company. The IT department employed 1,200 people and the turnover was approximately 225 million Euros. According to their mission statement, this company was a professional end-to-end partner in business for complex and large-scale IT exploitation. First, we will analyze the primary process of this part of the larger IT company and its sub-organizations to locate the problem.

A primary process contains those actions that directly contribute to the manufacturing of a product or service. The primary process of the IT administering company we studied can be subdivided into six phases, i.e., sales, service definition, service creation, service delivery, renovation and demolition (see figure 4).

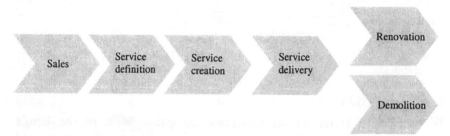

Figure 4. The primary process

The problems and wishes of (possible) customers are traced in the sales phase. After this, the customer's wish is analyzed by a person from the sales department and a consultant from the IT administering company using a service from the IT administering company to find a way to fulfil the customer's wish. Two activities are possible. A new service has to be created or an existing service has to be adapted in order to be able to fulfil the customer's wish. This is the main activity during the service creation phase. In the IT administering company, the service creation is organized in projects. In every project, a new IT component is made. This new IT component can be either software (programs, databases, etc.) or hardware (computers, networks, etc.). The company finishes a project when the new IT component is integrated into the whole IT infrastructure that has been administered. The administering of the IT infrastructure is the main activity during the service delivery phase. If an IT component is too old, or too inefficient, two options exist: either the component will be renovated (renovation phase), or it will be demolished. In the first case, it will be restored to good conditions, meaning that it can be used again to fulfil the customer's wishes and this still has to be administered. In the latter case - demolition - the IT component will be removed from the IT infrastructure. Administering is not needed anymore.

The IT administering company is subdivided into two organizations: a) an organization that executes all activities during the sales, the service definition phase and the service creation phase and b) an organization that takes care of all tasks concerning the service delivery, renovation and demolition phase. We call the former organization the project organization, because the phases are organized as projects. The latter organization is called the (real) administering organization, because administering the IT infrastructure is its main task. In describing the organizations' tasks more precisely we will explain the problems experienced by the people working in the administering organization or unit and by people working in the project organization.

Administering organization

The main activity of the IT company is administering the IT infrastructure; this is done by the administering organization. In ten Service Delivery Units (SDU's), the staff carries out the administering tasks. The SDU's are mainly subdivided on a functional basis (i.e., on the basis of the Operation System they support). Most IT systems that are administered are customer specific; either the software programs are custom-made and/or the hardware configuration (i.e., the combination of computers, networks, etc.) is custom-made. This is done in the project organization, which we describe in the next sub-section.

The administering organization has to work with the results of the project organization's tasks. In principle, the administrators are capable of administering the IT systems, except for the first months after a project has finished. It was indicated that - in their opinion - they were not capable of administering the IT systems satisfactorily during this period. This does not mean that contractual service level agreements were not met in all cases. However, this might have happened. If a service level is not reached, a high fine is imposed on the IT company. The fact that people's work satisfaction decreased is another result of the inability to administer the new IT systems satisfactorily during the first months after the project ended.

According to the administrators their poor results on administering the IT systems were not due to the quality of the IT systems, i.e. the project results, but they had to become acquainted with the specialties of the new, custom-made IT system during the first months after the project ended. This means that they had to create knowledge in a domain that was new to them.

Project organization

The custom-made IT systems are built in projects. People from Service Delivery Units (SDU's) as well as employees of the firm's Project Resource Center (PRC) play a role in these projects. The PRC is a department within the IT company of which the personnel only work in projects. The task of the PRC is to find suitable resources for every project. Project managers from the Consultancy and Project Services department (CPS) manage these projects. In these projects, knowledge of a large number of domains has to be used in order to create the new knowledge domain, i.e. the new product development. People are the medium of this knowledge transfer into the projects.

Inter-organizational knowledge transfer

According to Nonaka and Takeuchi (1995), the above-described organization suggests that the people from a SDU bring their administering knowledge into the development projects and return to their own SDU with knowledge of the new IT system, which they will administer after the project has finished. Unfortunately, this was not the case in reality. The true reason to let staff of SDU's participate in the development projects is that knowledge about a highly specific domain is needed to build the new IT system. Staff from a specific SDU (for instance the SDU Networks) has sufficient knowledge of this very specific part of the development puzzle. The only thing the people from the SDU in the project do is solving their own little part of the puzzle. They do not obtain sufficient knowledge of the new IT system to be able to administer this system after the project has finished.

To administer an IT system, an IT administrator needs to know the place and surroundings of the IT system in the whole IT infrastructure. In this way, he can use the right problem-solving scenario in a specific situation. The IT infrastructure consists of all hardware components (computers, networks, etc.) and all software components (programs, databases, websites, etc.). More general knowledge - of the place and surroundings of the IT system in the IT infrastructure - is also created in the development project, but only staff that works full-time in projects - i.e. members of the Project Resource Center and the project manager - have obtained this knowledge.

In a hypertext organization (Nonaka & Takeuchi, 1995) a two-way knowledge flow exists between the development projects and the factory using the employees as a medium for knowledge transfer. In this IT company, however, only during the knowledge flow from the SDU's to the project people are used as a medium for knowledge transfer. The IT company uses users' guides and handbooks to transfer knowledge from the project organization to the administering organization. This might be one of the reasons of the existence of a knowledge gap between the administering unit and the project unit.

After the development project has finished, people from projects have to advise the administrators. In fact, they cannot really afford to deliver this extra "aftercare", or follow-up service, because this will influence the result of the project they are working on at that moment. However, the project members will help the administrators as best as possible, because they are the only ones with enough knowledge of the entire IT system, including its details and general setup. The fines for delivering service below the agreed minimum level are very high. The help the project members are giving may cause the projects to be finished later than what initially had been planned implying that the project costs will become too high. The project members do not want to be part of this vicious circle. From a knowledge management and an organizational perspective, we analyzed as the cause of this vicious circle the bad functioning of inter-organizational (departmental) knowledge transfer. After initial interviews, a badly functioning primary process in one or both organizations was ruled out as a possible cause of the vicious circle. Therefore, we focused on the knowledge that is used for the execution of tasks in the so-called secondary processes or organizational processes.

Methods

We used the knowledge space as a tool for the analysis of the knowledge transfer between the administering organization (unit) and the project organization (unit) in the IT company. We placed the administering unit and the project unit that either administered or had produced the result of the project in the knowledge space. The projections are based on the secondary processes of both organizations (units). For these projections, we interviewed 25 persons, 9 of whom worked in the administering organization and 16 in the project organization. We realize that these numbers are very small. We think, however, that the results of the analysis are interesting, because we interviewed the entire population that work with, or worked on, the results of the projects. The advice we gave to the management of the IT company on how to manage knowledge in order to have a better transfer of knowledge within the company, was based on the positions of the administering and the project unit in the knowledge space. In the analysis, we fully took the task environments of both units into account.

Results

The administering organization in knowledge space

To carry out the administering tasks, the administrators use an ITIL variant as coordination mechanism. The British Central Communications and Telecom Agency (CCTA) created ITIL (Information Technology Infrastructure Library) in the late 1980's. Basically, ITIL is a best-practice method based on the Service Management as it has been delivered by several British organizations. Service Management is a set of processes that all-together guarantees the quality of existing IT services on the service level agreed upon by all parties involved (CCTA, 2000).

The ITIL variant used in the administering unit is described in a handbook. This handbook contains texts and flow diagrams, so it is (strongly) coded knowledge. Only one of the nine persons interviewed said that he uses this handbook during the execution of his task. However, he considered the handbook to be unimportant and uses it very rarely. Although the knowledge is (strongly) coded it is amply used in its coded form.

The ITIL knowledge type that is used to execute tasks in the secondary process is mainly sensory knowledge. All interviewees knew the basics of ITIL, but the specific details and processes they spoke about differed per SDU. However, there were no differences between persons working in the same SDU. The differences stem from the way people obtain knowledge on ITIL in practice, namely by observation during the introductory period and the mimicking of these practices later. The sensory knowledge used was quite detailed. However, little interpretation differences within two SDU's seemed to give big coordination problems between people working in both SDU's.

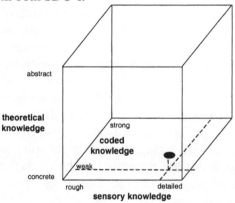

Figure 5. The administering organization in knowledge space

The theoretical knowledge of ITIL that is used by administrators - if used at all - is very concrete. To determine this, we used the amount of ITIL education the people received. We consider the theoretical knowledge of ITIL to be very concrete as only one out of nine persons followed a course in ITIL and this course was only a two day course in which ITIL was presented in an action plan way. Figure 5 shows the projection of the administering organization in the knowledge space based on the knowledge type characterizations mentioned above.

The project organization in knowledge space

For research purposes the project organization is mapped into the knowledge space twice. First, the position is determined of the project organization (unit) during development or product innovation. This positioning gives insight in the way the project management method is used for coordination purposes. Second, the use of ITIL in the project organization for inter-organizational knowledge transfer with the administering organization is mapped. This second positioning is used in the change trajectory, which is described below (figure 6).

During development
The project organization depends on, and has to cooperate with, organizations outside the IT administering company. The managers of these projects cannot explain why they communicated with these other companies the way they did, but several times it worked out fine. They say that details are very important in this kind of communication. However, if one's reaction is wrong once, all further communication and

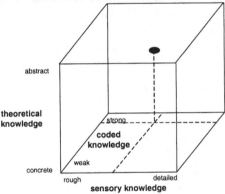

Figure 6. Project organization in knowledge space

cooperation between the two organizations might be destroyed. For this reason, we state that detailed sensory knowledge is important for inter-organizational coordination. The project manager has to be able to use this type of knowledge.

In the project organization, a company-made project management method is used to regulate the secondary processes within the projects. This project management method is very similar to other project management methods such as, for instance, Prince 2. According to the method, projects can either linearly or iteratively go through the following phases: initiation, definition, design (functional as well as technical), preparation, realization, implementation, and aftercare. For each phase the tasks that have to be executed in the various phases are broadly described in the project management method. Within a project sensory knowledge is not found to be very important and if it is used, this knowledge is rough. In general, we can say that the sensory knowledge used in the project organization is moderately detailed.

The project management method is described for specific project phases in a handbook and several more specific documents. These documents and handbooks are used by project members and are considered to be moderately important. The knowledge that is used during the execution of tasks in the secondary processes is coded in texts. Although not being notations, they are almost unambiguous in the context of a project in the IT administering company. Therefore they can be classified as rather strongly coded.

We also determined the abstractness of the theoretical knowledge used by the amount of education the project members received with regard to the project management method. Unfortunately for our measurement method, almost all project members took courses on the project management method, however the courses varied in length from three to fourteen days, dealing with theoretical knowledge from concrete to more abstract. For this reason, we projected the project organization on the middle of the theoretical knowledge axis, almost like a weighted average. Figure 6 shows the project organization in the knowledge space.

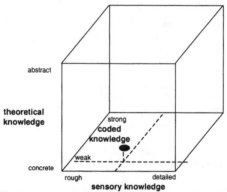

Figure 7. Alternative project organization in the knowledge space

Project-administering coordination

In the IT company, the transfer of knowledge from project organizations to administering organizations is a possible source of the problems described in the introduction: IT administrators that are not able to execute their task satisfactory and former project members that have to help the administrators after the project has finished. As knowledge can function as a coordination mechanism – e.g. persons sharing the same perspectives – our problem can be approached as a coordination problem.

Within the administering organization as well as the project organization, a shared method is used for the execution of tasks in the secondary process; it concerns an adapted ITIL version and a company-made project management method respectively. Because all employees within the same unit more or less share a common representation of the coordination mechanism, the intra-organizational coordination knowledge in both units (organizations) is used successfully.

The inter-organizational coordination between the administering and the project organization is not supported by a method or by another kind of coordinating mechanism. For this purpose, ITIL appears to be the best coordination mechanism of the two because ITIL contains a module for the implementation of new IT components in the IT infrastructure, whereas the project management method does not. We determined the knowledge of ITIL, more in particular the change process module of ITIL and used by project members.

The people working in projects never use the ITIL handbook during the execution of their tasks. They also have not obtained much theoretical knowledge of ITIL by means of education. The knowledge they have is very concrete theoretical knowledge, like in a plan of action. Some project members also work, or have worked, in the administering unit. We already know that the sensory ITIL knowledge of these persons is highly detailed, that their coded knowledge is very weak and that their theoretical knowledge is very concrete. Summarizing, the ITIL knowledge project members can use for inter-organizational coordination consists of moderately detailed sensory knowledge (average of people with administering experience and people without this experience), weakly coded knowledge and very concrete theoretical knowledge. The new - ITIL based - projection of the project organization is shown in figure 7.

Comparing the knowledge projections of the project unit and the administering unit, i.e. determining the difference in distribution of knowledge types in both organizational forms, shows that the only difference between both units appears to be the level of detail of the used sensory knowledge on ITIL. In the administering unit, the level of detail of the sensory knowledge is very high whereas this is moderately high in the project unit. In fact, the knowledge gap is a small gap; an overlapping knowledge domain exists, namely ITIL, and both units are close to one another in the knowledge space.

Change trajectory

In describing the administrative adhocracy, Mintzberg (1979) states that "when an organization has a special need to be innovative (...) but its operating core must be machine bureaucratic, the operating core may be established as a separate organization." This is very similar to the situation in the IT company where the administering unit or organization is optimal when organized as a machine bureaucracy and the project organization forms an innovative buffer between the administering organization and the environment. This can only be realized if the project organization is an adhocracy. This section further explains the choice for this optimal organizational form and identifies the change trajectory needed in using the map of knowledge types of both organizations (units).

The administering organization functions best in an unchanging environment. In such an environment, everything can be standardized. In this case a given output will be obtained with a give input. Such standardization will lead to a highly effective organization and will become more and more efficient over time. The administering organization already operates in an almost unchanging environment if the administrable IT infrastructure is considered as the environment of the administering organization. Most elements of the IT infrastructure remain the same for years; only occasionally some elements are added or removed from the IT infrastructure. These are the only changes in the environment of the administering organization.

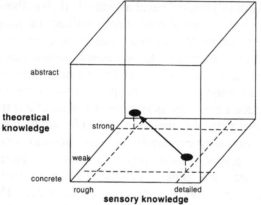

Figure 8. The administering organization's change

The situation is different for the activities of the project organization within the same IT company. The project organization has to react to changes - different questions and different wishes of customers - in the market of the IT company. The administering organization will function in an almost unchanging environment if the project organization is able to organize the ever-changing questions from the market into standard outputs. This means standard input for the administering organization. In this situation, the characteristics of the administering company are very similar to the machine bureaucracy as described by Mintzberg (1979). For this reason, we advised the management of the IT company to change the used knowledge in such a way that the positioning of the administering organization in the knowledge space is similar to the position of the machine bureaucracy in the knowledge space.

While carrying out coordination tasks people working in the administering organization use very detailed sensory knowledge, weakly coded knowledge, and concrete theoretical knowledge. This has to change into the use of strongly coded knowledge, rough sensory knowledge, and concrete theoretical knowledge. Figure 8 shows this change. In practice, this change could be very easily arranged if people would start using ITIL as described in the ITIL handbooks instead of the ITIL they taught themselves from observation and trial-and-error. In the ITIL handbooks, all rules for all situations are described at a function level; in this situation, the service level manager should do this with such and such results after which the system administrator should do such and such to get these results. These rules are strongly coded knowledge. When people start using these rules as coordination method, the need to use detailed sensory knowledge for coordination purposes will decrease almost automatically.

A change like this is only possible if the task environment of the administering organization does not change, which is the case when the project organization plays a role as a buffer between the administering organization and the customers, the real world. In this buffer role, the project organization has to translate every need of an individual customer into a standard IT element; in this case the administering organization can apply the same rules it already uses for coordination. Described in this way, the project organization is very similar to an adhocracy: the market question is always different, but the output has to be standardized. Therefore, the product development process is always different. The project organization has to be able to adapt to the environmental changes.

In order to be able to play the translator role, the project members have to be aware of the standard inputs that the administering organization can handle; one of these standard inputs, i.e., IT elements, is the result they have to aim at in their project. What standard result is the best depends on the customer wishes. The translator role demands theoretical knowledge of ITIL. The project members not only have to know what result they have to strive for at what moment in time for what costs, i.e., standard project management goals, but they also have to know why the chosen solution is a good solution in this situation and how to get from the customer wish to a standard result. For this reason, the project members have to use abstract theoretical knowledge, strong coded knowledge and rough sensory knowledge of the change processes described in ITIL.

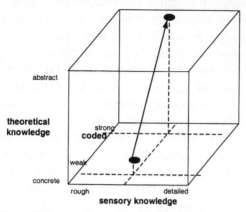

Figure 9. The project organization's change 1

Figure 9 shows the positioning change in the knowledge space of the way the project organizations have to work. This change can be realized by appointing a person who has the coordination task between the project organization and the administering organization in each project. This coordinator should have attended a course on ITIL's change process and thereby should be able to use abstract theoretical knowledge. He should also be able to use abstract theoretical knowledge of the company's project management method. In case this person is the only one who takes care of the coordination between both organizations, the project organization will reach the ideal position in the knowledge space. This person has the task to explain to the other project members how to get from the initial situation to the standard output aimed for.

Such a specialist is not necessary in every project. If the input and output of the project is standard, then the way to this output can also be standardized, i.e., described in rules. This is only operalizationable if the variation in possible input-output-combinations is not too large. In this case, the project organization acts like a machine bureaucracy, just like the administering organization. The necessary change of the project organization in this situation is shown in Figure 10. Note that this is a smaller change than the change shown in Figure 9. The project organization that acts like a machine bureaucracy is by definition not applicable for all projects because the environment of the IT company changes and we have given the project organizations the function of a buffer between the administering organization and the task environment.

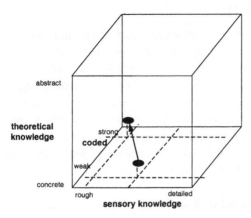

Figure 10. The project organization's change 2

CONCLUSION

In this research, we started with the re-categorization of various dichotomies of knowledge types. This re-categorization resulted in three knowledge types, that is to say sensory, coded and theoretical knowledge. The knowledge types were used to describe, analyze and diagnose the secondary processes in various units in an IT company. We used the metaphor of a knowledge space to visualize the dominance and distribution of the knowledge types. We also studied the transfer of project results by members of the project organization to members of the administering organization within a Dutch IT company. ITIL is the coordination mechanism that is used by actors during this task. In applying the knowledge space approach the ITIL knowledge of every actor is individually positioned into the knowledge space. This is based on classifications of knowledge types. We call this an audit of a specific knowledge domain. Based on this audit in the case study, the management determined that the current situation had to be corrected. The direction for the correction was derived from the company's strategy and depicted in the positions of the machine bureaucracy and the adhocracy for the administering organization and the project organization, respectively. The discrepancy between the current situation and the strategic aim implied the direction for corrections. The corrections were translatable from the strategic into the operational level (this group of employees had to use the handbook rules, the other group needed to undertake this kind of ITIL education).

The case study shows that not only the knowledge space approach is useful in real world management practice, it also adds the management activity "controlling" to the knowledge management spectrum.

FUTURE RESEARCH

In this chapter, we described an empirical study of an inter-organizational knowledge transfer problem using a semio-cognitive perspective. We showed that this perspective and its tools could be used to advice an organization in the direction of its knowledge management change.

We argue that our analysis of both units (organizations) was adequate and that the proposed changes can really help the staff of the IT company. The overall approach, a combination of questionnaires followed by in-depth interviews, has been effective in assessing the distribution and dominance of knowledge types in this case in relation to the secondary processes.

We will continue this kind of knowledge management research within the field of medical device development. For these product innovations, various kinds of specialists (e.g. electronic engineers, mechanical engineers, physicians, veterinarians, instrument makers, biologists, marketers, laboratory analysts, and finance specialists) working within different organizations (universities, firms, or hospitals) have to cooperate in order to create new medical devices and bring them onto the market. The aim of our knowledge management research is to build a method that decreases the nowadays 10-to-15 years time-to-market of medical devices. The knowledge space perspective will be very important in the analysis of the current situation in medical device development.

REFERENCES

Anderson, J. R. 1983. *The Architecture of Cognition*. Cambridge, MA: Harvard University Press.

Boisot, M. H. 1995. *Information space : a framework for learning in organizations, institutions and culture*. London: Routledge.

CCTA 2000. *Best Practice for service support*. Norwich: The stationery office.

Dale, van. 1992. *Groot Woordenboek der Nederlandse Taal* (12e druk). Utrecht. Van Dale Lexicografie.

Fayol, H. 1916; 1987. *General and industrial management*. (Rev. ed. ed.) London: Pitman.

Goodman, N. 1968. *Languages of Art*. Brighton: The Harvester Press (2nd Edition, 1981).

Heusden, B. van & Jorna, R.J. 2001. Toward a Semiotic Theory of Cognitive Dynamics in Organizations. In: K. Liu, R.J. Clarke, P.B. Andersen & R.K. Stamper (Eds.). *Information, Organisation and Technology: Studies in Organisational Semiotics*. Boston: Kluwer. pp.83-113.

Jorna, R. J. 1990. *Knowledge representation and symbols in the mind*. Tübingen: Stauffenburg Verlag.

Jorna, R.J. 2001. Organizational forms, coordination and knowledge types. *Proceedings of the International Society for Knowledge Organization (ISKO)*; March 2001, Berlin.

Jorna, R. & Heusden van, B. 2000. Cognitive Dynamics: A framework to handle types of knowledge. In J. Schreinemakers (Ed.) *Knowledge Management: the 7th ISMICK Conference*. Rotterdam: Rotterdam University Press (pp. 128-145).

Mintzberg, H. 1979. *The structuring of organizations*. Englewood Cliffs, NJ: Prentice-Hall.

Nonaka, I. 1994. A dynamic theory of organizational knowledge creation. *Organization Science, 6*, 14-37.

Nonaka, I. & Takeuchi, H. 1995. *The knowledge creating company*. New York, NY: Oxford University Press.

Polanyi, M. 1967. *The tacit dimension*. London: Routledge & Keegan Paul.

Postrel, S. 2002. Islands of shared knowledge: specialization and mutual understanding in problem-solving teams. *Organization Science, 13*, 303-320.

Pylyshyn, Z.W. 1984. *Computation and Cognition*. Cambridge: The MIT Press.

Reber, A.S. 1993. Implicit Learning and Tacit Knowledge: An Essay on the Cognitive Unconsciousness. Oxford: Oxford University Press.

Simon, H. A. 1969. *The sciences of the artificial*. Cambridge, MA: MIT Press.

Sveiby, K. E. 1997. *The new organizational wealth : managing & measuring knowledge-based assets*. San Francisco: Berrett-Koehler.

Thompson, J. D. 1967. *Organizations in action : social science bases of administrative theory*. New York: McGraw-Hill.

Chapter 11

Supporting the semiotic quality of data of a scientific community

Daniel Galarreta

ABSTRACT

Data that are produced or used within the framework of scientific projects correspond to the signification which the norm ISO 11179 defines as "A representation of facts, concepts, or instructions in a formalized manner suitable for communication, interpretation, or processing by humans or by automatic means".

As far as we are concerned with the maintaining of the signification of data, in such a way that this signification can be recognized and used in the future, in the same way as it is today, by as many users as possible, it is justified to examine the problem of signification per se, namely the way meaning is produced or grasped by people.

Several approaches to the problem of signification exist. We will successively present models based upon the reference, the inference and the difference paradigms. We will retain the third model and its developments, which resulted (after Saussure, Hjelmslev, Jakobson, Greimas...) in general semiotics.

The most significant consequences for our discourse are the following: (a) the signification does not depend on the conceptual level which could be autonomous with respect to natural language, namely signification does not rest upon the existence of an ontology which could control the relation between words and the world by means of concepts. (b) The signification is not conditioned by the existence of communication between a sender and a receiver.

We will examine how data semiotics is possible under such conditions. The approach we adopt will help us to reformulate the definition of data within the framework of particular multi-viewpoints semiotics. This definition is also suitable for a knowledge management approach to data. A semiotic quality concept is then defined with respect to knowledge management. We will examine this quality concept with respect to scientific data.

1. THE OBJECTIVE OF THIS CHAPTER

Scientific projects, which use spatial devices, need a complex infrastructure. They also involve a large scientific community and they extend over a long period of time (from 10 to 20 years). They produce a huge quantity of numerical data.

Because of that, it is essential to be able to guarantee not only the economic viability of these programmes but also that the data produced can be recognised and used in the future, just as they are today, by as many users as possible.

In this chapter we will examine the conditions which have to be met on organizational and communication levels in order to fulfil that requirement. These conditions will be presented in the form of a quality insurance and a quality control approach of a new type. This new approach will guarantee that the signification of data can be restored without loss or distortion so as to match the user's needs.

2. POSING OF THE PROBLEM

The current approach, which is used to guarantee that data which are produced by scientific workers be used by others, is based on the way these data are described. The data description must be sufficiently precise to fit the needs of the experiment; it has to suit the domain in question and should be sufficiently standardised to address a large community interpretation[1].

The elements upon which this descriptive function is based are called *metadata*. The quality approach, which is used to guarantee the semantic preservation of data, is supported by the ensuring and controlling of the quality of the corresponding metadata. This is performed through the ensuring and controlling of the quality conceptual level where the metadata are situated. This means that the quality of data is insured and controlled through a "chain": quality of concepts => quality of metadata => quality of data; each link of the chain controls the next one.

Finally, this view is supported by an implicit hierarchy: concepts > metadata > data, and moreover, is guaranteed by the relation which links the phenomenon in the experiment to the concepts which describe or elucidate[2] this phenomenon (See figure 1).

---

[1] Data descriptions are based upon norms. In CNES the ISO 11179 "specification and standardisation of data elements" is used as a reference.
[2] According to the philosophical position one adopts.

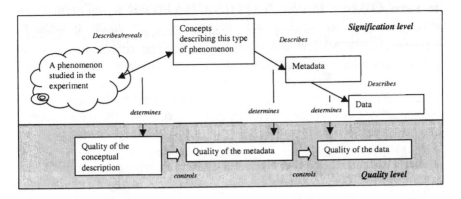

Figure 1. Dependence of the quality of data upon their descriptions and their metadata

This diagram (in figure 1) justifies the need to consider the conceptual level; however, this diagram also justifies the need to study the general problem of signification in order to account for the relation between phenomena and their related data.

In order to maintain the signification of these data over a period of time, we need to examine the role that the notion of concept plays in the issue of the signification.

3. A CRITICAL ANALYSIS OF THE NOTION OF CONCEPT

Instead of beginning with a general presentation of the problem of signification, we prefer to address this problem through a particular question which was posed by François Rastier (Rastier, 1991, p.73): "Is it necessary to distinguish between the semantic level of natural languages and the conceptual level?[3]".

The following is a résumé of Rastier's presentation[4].

3.1. The Aristotelian triad

Since Aristotle (and in particular since the beginning of the *Péri Hermêneias*) the philosophy of language is based upon a triadic model; cf. I, 16 a, 3-8: speech is a set of elements which symbolises the states of mind, and writing, a set of elements which symbolises speech. In the same way as men do not have the same writing system, they do not speak the same language. However what speech immediately means are the states of mind which are identical for every man; and what these states of mind represent are the things which are not less identical for everyone."[...]
After Boethius, Thomas Aquinas restates the triad in this way: "Speeches

---

[3] This question is equivalent to the following one: "Is the linguistic "signified" different from the logic or psychological concept?"
[4] The summary that we propose is bound to be arbitrary. It is a simplified version of the 42 pages that Rastier devotes to this question in chapter III (from concept to signified) in (Rastier, 1991)

are signs of thoughts and thoughts are similitudes (similitudines) of things. Therefore it follows that speeches refer to things referred to concepts." (Summa Theologiae, I-ap, 2-13, al, resp.). That is:

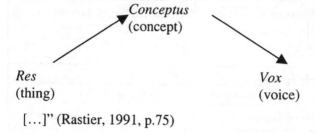

Conceptus
(concept)

Res   *Vox*
(thing)   (voice)

   [...]" (Rastier, 1991, p.75)

3.2. The index

The Aristotelian triad is not the only classic Greek conception of signification [...] Reformulating the rhetorical theory of the index, Aristotle defines the *semeion* this way: "the sign (*το σημηιον*), ought to be either a conclusive, or necessary, or probable premise. The thing, the existence or generation of which result in the existence or the generation of another thing which is before or after it, is what constitutes the sign of generation or existence" (First Analytics, II, 27; 70 a, 7) [This conception of index] was followed up in the theory of natural signs in the writings of St Augustin (*signa naturalia*, cf. *namely De doctrina christana*, II, 1, 2) until the general grammars of the age of Enlightenment (from Condillac to Tracy) and even in the phaneroscopy of Peirce." (Rastier, 1991, p. 80) (See figure 2)

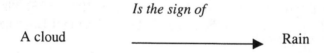

Is the sign of

A cloud   ————————————▶   Rain

Fig.2. An example of an index

These two models of signification lead to two types of semantics[5]

---

[5] We define the (a) semantic as *the (a) study of signification within natural languages* (see for instance (Hénault, 1993), p.184), or as the study of the contents of meanings themselves in linguistics (Fontanille, 1998), p.24). It is usual to differentiate between semantics to semiotics when it is considered as *the study of signification within discourses* (see (Hénault, 1993, p.184). The differentiation between natural language and discourse roughly corresponds to the Saussurian differentiation between natural language and speech: i.e. on one side there is "a static approach which is concerned only with instituted units which are stored in a collective memory in the form of a virtual system and on the other side a dynamic approach which is sensitive to acts and operations and is concerned with the "living" signification stored within concrete discourses." (Fontanille, 1998, p.24)

3.3. A reference semantics

Up until today, "the Aristotelian triad has been extensively used because it constitutes a sighting system of the referent. Out of these two movements: transition from the signifier to the concept and from the concept to the referent, it is obviously the second one which is privileged since truth is classically defined as an *adeaquatio rei et intellectus.*" (Rastier, 1991, p.82)

The study of relations between concepts and referents constitutes the extensional theory of signification. Rastier states that this theory "is suited to formal languages but its application to natural languages is questionable. Besides this theory is not specific to sign systems since strictly speaking, it is the concepts that have an extension whether they are expressed by signs or not." (Rastier, 1991, p.82)

3.4. An inference semantics

"The mental operation which establishes the reference is quite distinct from the operation which establishes the indexical referring and which can be called inference. [...]

The reference establishes a relation between two sorts of reality, concept and object –it is why according to us it can belong neither to a unique scientific branch nor to a science. On the other hand, the inference links two items which belong to the same sort of reality: two objects, in a naïve realist conception of the index, or two concepts (according to the mentalist viewpoint.)" (Rastier, 1991, p.84)

To understand the possibility of inferential semantics, we must remind ourselves of the stoician conception of index: "the indexical sign is an assertive utterance and is considered as an antecedent in an implication assertion." (Rastier, 1991, p.85)

If we consider the strict implication,[6] we notice that it "is based upon deductive and inductive syllogisms [...] in the first case it goes from the antecedent to the consequent; in the second case, from the consequent to the antecedent [...]. Deductive inference is supposed to be mastered. The inductive inference poses difficult problems, namely as so far as modelling the expert reasoning is concerned[7].

The *frames*, *scripts* and *plans*, which are used in artificial intelligence, appear as supports of inferences. They materialise a context which is convenient for inference.

"Mental models (see Johnson-Laird, 1983) transpose these problems into the domain of psychology. These models are in fact patterns to account for the signification of the utterances." (Rastier, 1991, p. 86)

---

[6] The strict implication is "defined by CI Lewis in his modal logic system S_2 by: *It is impossible that p and in the same time that non q.*" (Rastier, 1991, p. 85)

[7] "Polya presents the "fundamental inductive scheme" in the form of a syllogism: (1): A implies B. (2): B is true; (3): then A is more probable." (Rastier, 1991, p. 85)

We can sum up what we have briefly presented in the form of the following diagram (figure 3).

"In this device, the conceptual level has a pre-eminent function: it connects the reference to expressions; it determines the inference that can be made about them. [...]

The definition of the conceptual level is crucial in the debate that brings together logical theories and psychological theories of *concept*. In this debate, both sides are respectful of each other, because instead of psychologizing logic, we can logicize psychology, by presenting the conceptual level as an articulated formal language (Fodor), or as a language built upon mental models and used by algorithms (Johnson-Laird). Finally this device leaves no room for linguistic semantics, because meaning is not different from a representation. Other "signified" than concepts and propositions do not exist, and of course they are independent from languages." (Rastier, 1991, p. 89)

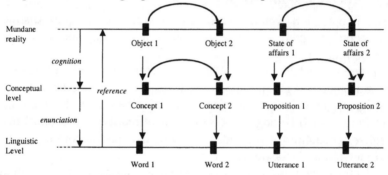

Figure 3. The Reference and the inference paradigms are based upon the existence of a conceptual level (after (Rastier, 1991), p. 89)

3.5. A difference-semantics

It is possible to define linguistic semantics in another way independent from the previous models and their logical or psychological presuppositions; a definition one that is based upon the paradigm of the *difference*.

"The problem of differentiation is obviously a fundamental philosophical problem which is concerned with the distinction of objects and of concepts. As far as objects are concerned, Xenophane noted the differential character of their perception: "If God did not create golden honey, figs would appear less sweeter" (fr. 38)" (Rastier, 1991, p. 98)

It is in consideration of synonymy, that the problem of differentiation turns out to be particularly productive; because of this "typical issues of linguistic semantics were to emerge. Systematising in order to go beyond the observations scattered in the writings of Varron, Donat, Servius and the moderns, Father Vavasseur, Scioppius, and Henri Etienne, Father Girard dares to write in his *Treaty of correctness of French language*, that *"there are no synonymous words in any natural language"*. (1718, p. 28) and, therefore, opens our eyes to the differential paradigm in semantics.

How indeed can we evaluate the difference between synonymous words? One could say that such a difference lies in accessory ideas. But if each word has a different meaning, the triadic model of signification does not work any longer. Indeed, if two synonymous words in a broad sense – let us say, *automobile* and *car*– refer to the same object, can we then maintain that they refer to two different concepts? No, but to a single concept or principal idea? If we consider, however, synonymy in the strictest sense of the word, we must consider that the words refer to two different concepts because of their accessory ideas. But two different concepts would in turn refer to two different objects. "Therefore cars would not be automobiles" (Rastier, 1991, p. 99).

"Another way would consist in admitting the irreducibility of natural language to another, language and the specificity of the semantics of these languages whose their lexicons give the evidence of." (Rastier, 1991, p. 100) "The linguistic meaning is not (or not only) constituted by the reference to things, or by the inference between concepts, but also and first of all by the difference between linguistic units " (Rastier, 1991, p. 101)

F. de Saussure in an autographic note states: "If linguistics was an organised science, [...] one of its first statements would be: the impossibility to create a synonym as the most absolute and the most remarkable fact which features in all the questions related to signs" (quoted by Rastier in (Rastier, 1991), p. 101). "He follows in the footsteps of the synonymists [...], in our eyes he goes beyond them by his definition of the value which refers the definition of linguistic –and therefore semantic– units to three principles: i) value is the true reality of linguistic units; ii) it is determined by the position of units within the system (therefore by differences); iii) nothing pre-exists to the determining of the value by the system: "There are no pre-established ideas, and nothing is distinct before the appearance of natural language." (Rastier, 1991, p. 102)

The most important consequence with regard to the notion of *concept* is that signification no longer needs the existence of a conceptual level which would be independent from natural language; in other words: the signification is no longer dependant on an ontology which would be necessary to link words to the world by means of concepts.

4. MULTI-VIEWPOINT SEMIOTICS

4.1. A semiotic approach

The differential paradigm that we introduced within the frame of a linguistic semantic should be generalised if:
(a) instead of situating our subject within the scope of a given natural
    language we want to be able to consider any possible sort of

languages or signifying set (e.g. an image coming from a satellite or a painting)

(b) instead of limiting ourselves to the lexical meaning, we want to apprehend the meaning of bigger units of speech going beyond the sentence to encompass the whole of a text or the whole of an image;

This generalisation leads to the formulation of a general semiotic theory (see e.g. (Hénault, 1997)) and a particular conception of communication that we use in our multi-viewpoint approach.

As long as communication is situated between subjects and as long as the values invested in the objects put into circulation (pragmatic or cognitive, descriptive or modal values) are considered as the being of the subject (this subject is constantly increasing or diminishing in its being) it is obvious that the sender and the receiver can no longer be treated as empty positions of sender and receiver, but that they are, on the contrary, competent subjects considered at the moment of their development, enrolled in their own discourse" (in (Greimas, & Courtès, 1979), p. 47, entry *communication*)

A dialogue in this context will be considered as a discourse in two (or several) voices.

Instead of considering the following diagram: (figure 4),

Figure 4. Classical diagram of communication. The existence of a common conceptual level guarantees communication.

we prefer the following diagram (figure 5), where the enunciator and the enunciatee produce utterances within the frame of a more symmetrical semiotic activity, where the reading of the significations of a text is as much like the building of a signification as the writing itself.

Mutually present to each other within the discourse (even in the form of presuppositions), the enunciator and the enunciatee are likely to produce or to interpret utterances which could be incompatible or compatible according to the dynamic of the discourse.

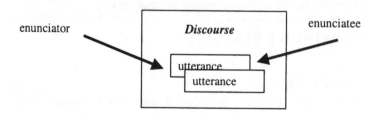

Figure 5. Consequence of the semiotic approach for the communication model. This communication diagram does not imply the existence of a conceptual level. Each actor has his/her own linguistic competence.

4.2. The viewpoints issue

Within the context of spatial activity which designs, builds and exploits space systems, the study of the way meaning occurs within the community makes it essential that any semiotics that we use accounts for the ***objective*** character of most of the objects which are designed or built within this context. Here *objective* means (a) that the objects are the result of a collective agreement and (b) that objects have also an extra-linguistic character.

This obligation leads toward questions that we will now examine.[8]

How to reconcile the social system represented by natural language, and the assumption of this natural language by individual instances?

Experiences of projects of realisations of complex systems such as spatial systems clearly demonstrate the co-existence of specialised languages which are partly impermeable in relation to each other. These languages correspond with the different crafts that are needed during the space project.

These crafts confront each other over the definition –requirement, design, or realisation– of technical objects that are not *a priori* given, but, on the contrary, progressively built up through the negotiation of the meaning they should have to satisfy their requirements. In other words these objects are –at least before their creation, but also after it– semiotic objects belonging to different signifying sets (e.g. thermal, electrical, mechanical representations) likely to be grasped, informed and articulated by a semiotic theory.

The negotiation of meaning, which takes place during the definition of an object of this type, is the work of individuals involved in the project, and is not a pre-existing produce of these languages virtually contained in them. At the same time, the individuals interiorize natural language that they have not built and whose rules they have to observe. In order to account for this situation, we are forced to use the opposition between *natural language* and *speech* (Saussure) or between *natural language* and *the act of discourse* (Benveniste).

Using Enunciation

The act of discourse, or enunciation, can be defined "in two different manners: either as the non linguistic (referential) structure which underlies linguistic communication, or as a linguistic instance which is logically presupposed by the very existence of the utterance (which get traces or marks from it)" (Greimas & Courtès, 1979, p.126, entry *enunciation*)

But who is responsible for this enunciation? It is not possible to elaborate on this point here, but this concept of enunciation raises

---

[8] "It suffices to no longer consider the extra-linguistic world as an absolute referent, but as the place of the manifestation of the sensitive which is likely to become the manifestation of the human meaning, that is to say of the signification for Man: to process in short this referent as a set of semiotic systems more or less implicit." (In (Greimas, 1970, p. 52)

problems, so it is better to use the concept of enunciative praxis. J. Fontanille wrote: "The enunciative praxis is [...] concerned with the appearing and disappearing of utterances and of semiotic forms in the domain of discourse, or else it is concerned by the event that constitutes the meeting between the utterance and the instance which takes charge of it" (Fontanille, 1998, p. 271).

4.3. Defining multi-viewpoint semiotics

If on the one hand the enunciative praxis enables us to overcome the problem of enunciation which is too tightly linked to the difficult notion of subject, on the other hand it involves finding an instance of discourse which can account for the utterances produced by this praxis.

It is, however, not obvious that this instance is unique. Therefore, the possibility of different instances which are mutually and partly impermeable must be examined. It is this hypothesis from which stems the multi-viewpoint semiotics we propose.

Viewpoint definition

From empirical observations we postulate that several instances of discourse coexist within the same technical universe (e.g. in a spatial project and mission). Although these instances of discourse are not incompatible, they are not entirely compatible.

We define them as **viewpoints** (See figure 6). For example, in a spatial project we will find a "spatial mechanics" viewpoint, an electrical viewpoint, a thermal viewpoint and so on.

View according to viewpoint 1

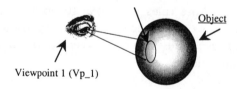

Viewpoint 1 (Vp_1)

Figure 6. Viewpoint

A view is an "utterance" which is selected from the representation or signifying set we consider with respect to a given (or reference) viewpoint. An utterance is what is enunciated, but this entity can only be described according to a given instance of the discourse. Therefore in a multi-viewpoints semiotics, an utterance does not have an absolute existence, but should be defined with respect to a reference viewpoint.

- When we consider an enunciation activity of a viewpoint that puts into parenthesis the activities of other viewpoints. In such a case a view is called (a piece of) **data**.
- If views produced according to these viewpoints are logically or semantically incompatible[9], we say that there exists a **confrontation** of the viewpoints. A view produced in this case is called (a piece of) **information**.
- Eventually, after a negotiation process, compatible views[10] can be produced. In such a case we say that the viewpoints are **correlated**. A view produced in such circumstances is called (a piece of) **knowledge**.

Value system of an object

Let us suppose that a semiotic object exists with respect to several viewpoints when these viewpoints are correlated. But what is its identity? In order to clarify this, we must consider the collection of the viewpoints that correlate with each other. We call this the **context** of the semiotic object[11].

The practice, for instance, of spatial projects shows that the context is usually organised into a more or less explicit structure that we call the value system, for instance of the spatial project. More generally, we define the **value system of a (semiotic) object** as the structured context of this object.

5. DESIGNING DATA SEMIOTICS

5.1. Issues of knowledge management

This semiotic conception means that whenever we consider a text or a diagram or an image, which we can simply call a representation, it is the context in which it is produced or used which determines whether an utterance is a piece of *data* or a piece of *information* or a piece of *knowledge*.

It is the way in which the context presents itself with respect to the reference viewpoint that is responsible for the utterance which enables us to distinguish the following different cases: (a) in the case of data, context is manifested in the form of a collection of viewpoints for which the confrontations with the reference viewpoint are put into parenthesis; (b) in the case of information, the context is manifested as a set of viewpoints

---

[9] It means that the signifying elements, which are produced by the activities of enunciation of the different viewpoints, are incompatible when they are considered from a unique viewpoint. The incompatibility may be logical and/or semantic. That does not mean that the "intentions" of the different viewpoints are incompatible; we just do not know.

[10] In this case compatibility is evaluated in regard to each viewpoint involved. (see note 9)

[11] This object has only a hypothetical existence. The study of it, takes the form of the study of its context. For a presentation of it and of the identity question see (Galarreta, 2001).

which confront the reference viewpoint; (c) in the case of knowledge, the context is manifested as a set of viewpoints correlated with the reference viewpoint.

A piece of data is not worth less than a piece of information which would be worth less than a piece of knowledge. They are simply not produced or used in the same context. It is also possible to point out that they do not enable us to answer the same kind of question[12]. What changes when shifting from one type of question to another, (that is to say when shifting from a context where we are concerned with data to a context where a piece of information is considered and so on), is the way the question implies one or more viewpoints.

Let us give an example. An image produced by the "SPOT" satellite of an agricultural zone (Krasnodar, Russia) (figure 7) could be seen as:

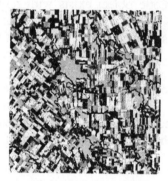

Figure 7. A satellite image of Krasnodar region (Russia). (Spot image)

1. data (pixels matrix) by the person who is responsible for the image processing algorithms. A question about this matrix could concern the "dynamic" of the grey levels within the image or the computation of correlation functions from the image.
2. a piece of information about the cultivation of an agricultural zone when considered in a dialogue between a "thematician" (i.e. a photo interpreter) of the Spot-Image company and its customer who has ordered this image. A question about this image could concern the types of cultures that can be observed in the region of Krasnodar.
3. a piece of knowledge used for making a choice during a negotiation between a representative of the region and a representative of the State. This image could enable us to answer, for instance, the following question: why is the cultivation of colza regressing in the region of Krasnodar?

It therefore becomes necessary to clarify the conditions of the production and grasp of these different types of utterances. In other words,

---

[12] This point is presented in (Galarreta, & Rothenburger, 99).

the following corresponding semiotics could be a priori imagined: a *data semiotics*, an *information semiotics* and a *knowledge semiotics*[13].

What is at stake is to be able to use the right methods and the right tools in adapted contexts: for instance, it would be better to avoid using the solution suited to process *information* when the context corresponds to a need for *knowledge*, and conversely.

To conclude we see that starting from the hypotheses of a multi-viewpoints semiotics, we are naturally led to formulate issues of knowledge management.

5.2. Conditions of data semiotics

Adopting the multi-viewpoint approach we have developed, data semiotics should make explicit the fact that bits of data are not autonomous individuals in relation to any particular viewpoints. On the contrary, the intelligibility of data rests upon the existence of (at least) one semiotic system. In the same way as an isolated utterance will make sense in relation to a particular natural language, an isolated piece of data will make sense in relation to the "semiotic" system of differences.

If we accept the definition we give of *data* within the framework of multi-viewpoint semiotics, that is, in relation to a reference viewpoint in a given context, then it is necessary to make explicit:

a) conditions of production corresponding (at least) to the reference viewpoint for which we have to specify the conditions under which the rest of the context can be put in parenthesis;

b) necessary conditions for grasping in order to make these data usable from other viewpoints, that is to say, the conditions of confrontation and also the conditions of correlation of this reference viewpoint with other viewpoints of the context under consideration.

We can specify these conditions. We make the assumption that the situations we can face when we consider any kind of representations are the following situations of production and of grasp (see figure 8):

Situations of production of representation:
- Producing a representation here and now
- Sending a representation elsewhere (= reproducing it elsewhere)
- Preserving a representation for later (= reproducing it later)

Situations of grasp of a representation:
- Retrieving data (*retrieve* means that we are sure of the existence of these data and of a procedure for doing this)
- Consolidating information (*consolidate* means that we confront what we already know with a new representation)

---

[13] It is not certain that all these different semiotics are essentially different. This point needs to be studied.

-   Discovering knowledge (*discover* means that we produce a view which cannot be retrieved from the previous (state of) context.)

Remarks:

1. It is possible to imagine other situations: for instance *the retrieving of a piece of information*, or *the consolidating of knowledge.* These phrases can be given a meaning but only because of imprecision attached to the terms employed.
2. Within the framework that we adopt, a viewpoint is not bound to produce views limited either to English or to mathematical formulae or to images. It is usual that in situations involving data use, heterogeneous texts mix natural and mathematical expressions. For instance, in the special case of mathematical texts, meaning is not only based upon mathematical expression. The natural expressions in the texts participate in the overall meaning. Instead of the triad sign/concept/reference, we can alternatively consider a double natural/notational expression in relation to a content level. (see (Herreman, 2000))

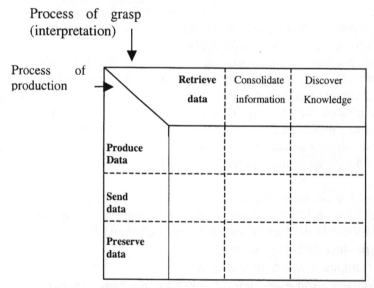

Figure 8. *Categorisation of situations in knowledge management* **in the case of data**

6. A SUITABLE QUALITY PROCESS

Knowledge management is concerned with the context issue, or in other words, with the quality of the representation which is produced or grasped with respect to the context concerned[14].

---

[14]The term *quality* has here its orthodox acceptation: the satisfaction of an agreed requirement between a "customer" and a "supplier". In our case, the concept of *context* corresponds to the "agreed requirement between a customer and a supplier".

To implement knowledge management with respect to an information system (we also include informal devices, such as information boards, sociocultural devices of communication...), is almost equivalent to implementing a quality function with respect to this system in such a way as to be able to guarantee its compliance to the needs it is supposed to satisfy.

But what sort of quality is it?

In literature which is specialised in information management, we have already found lists of evaluation criteria of the quality of an information system. A frequent defect of these sorts of lists is their heterogeneity and therefore their arbitrary character.

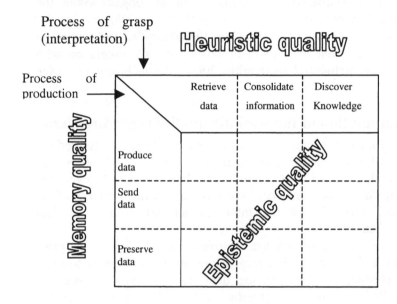

Figure 9. Declension of the semiotic quality into its three aspects

6.1. The semiotic quality: a quality concept suited to knowledge management

Nowadays every solution which is used under the banner of knowledge management (information portals, search engines, knowledge repositories, etc.) aims at improving the "semantic" quality of the information produced or grasped. In fact, it is not a semantic quality but rather the relevance of such and such a representation or piece of information **as a sign for someone, or of something** when it is manifested. The importance of the context in this case with regard to the evaluation of relevance, shows that it is not the semantic quality, which should be evaluated or fixed, but rather the semiotic quality.

The evaluation of the relevance is always performed within a given technical universe which is composed of technical objects and defined by a more or less large set of reference viewpoints.

We define the semiotic quality of an informational device as the adequacy of this device to fit the context of production or to fit the context of grasp of representations as relevant signs in a given technical universe. This adequacy can be adapted in relation to three aspects: (see figure 9).

- The memory quality of the device: the ability of the device to preserve the norms of reading and writing which govern that technical universe. These norms are dependent on the value system that we are considering in which the (semiotic) objects[15] emerge, or are "produced", or decay;
- The heuristic quality of the device: the ability of the device to retrieve, consolidate, and discover the identity[16] of an object within the technical universe;
- The epistemic quality of the device: the ability of the device to maintain a sufficient level of credibility of the representation with respect to problems and their criticality in the technical reference universe[17].

6.2. An examination of the semiotic quality regarding data

What matters for a data producer, is that the data can be easily handled by, first, herself or himself, and then by others. In other words, the viewpoint defining the data should be applied to these data whatever the corresponding "utterances" may be. Otherwise, the memory quality of the data, or more precisely, of the informational device used in data production, is bad.

For instance, in the case of a spatial project, the principal investigator of a scientific experiment who is responsible for an onboard instrument and for the production of geophysical data (said of level 2), needs an interface to her/his data. This interface has to be suited to her/his activities, i.e. to her/his viewpoint: access to the measures produced by the instrument (level 1 data), processing of these measures in order to obtain the corresponding level 2 data.

A user, who intends to produce a synthesis or a new model from these level 2 data, will produce level 3 data. She or he will be placed in a situation analogous to the situation of the principal investigator: she/he needs an interface suited to her/his viewpoint.

From this example we understand that the same scientific terms that are handled by two categories of scientific research workers will not

---

[15] For instance, a semiotic object can be a *satellite in test before launching*, or the *satellite on its orbit*, and so on.

[16] For a study of the question of identity according to a multi-viewpoint semiotics, see (Galarreta, 2001).

[17] "The epistemic modalities refer to the competence of the enunciatee [...] who, next to his interpretative activity, [...] assumes or rejects the cognitive positions stated by the enunciator" (in (Greimas & Courtès, 1979) p.129, entry *epistemic (modalities)*).

necessarily play the same role in their activities, i.e. play the same semiotic role in their scientific discourses.

We have stressed above the memory quality of informational devices used to produce data by adopting the position of the producers. One should take the position of the users and examine the question of the heuristic quality of the same informational devices[18]. It is essentially the **"Retrieve"** function which is concerned with *data* (in our definition of the term). The two other functions, **"Consolidate"** and **"Discover"** essentially correspond to different communication situations involving *information* and *knowledge*[19].

7. CONCLUSIONS

In this chapter, we have presented the theoretic conditions of a semiotic quality for data and information available thanks to informational devices.

These conditions were defined according to hypotheses which concern our ways of speaking about them and of simulating them with the aid of conceptual models.

The choice of these models has important consequences for the significant elements we will choose to retain in order to speak about scientific data, to spread them among the community concerned here and preserve them for later usage.

Anyhow, the approach we adopt to the *semiotics of the discourse* will need to be further developed and put into practice for use in real projects.

REFERENCES

Fontanille, J. (1998). *Sémiotique du discours* [Coll. Nouveaux actes sémiotiques]. Limoges: Presses Universitaires de Limoge.

Galarreta, D. (2001). *Mesurer l'évolution des connaissances d'un projet spatial.* Conférence TIA-2001, Nancy, 3 et 4 mai 2001.

Galarreta, D., & Rothenburger, B. (1999). *Memory Quality: a proposal to manage the risks of memory loss.* Rosetta Knowledge Management Workshop, CNES, Toulouse, septembre 1999.

Greimas, A. J. (1970) *Du sens.* Paris: Editions du Seuil.

Greimas, A. J., & Courtès, J. (1979). *Sémiotique: Dictionnaire raisonné de la théorie du langage.* Paris: Hachette Université.

Hénault, A. (1997). *Histoire la sémiotique générale* (2nd ed.) [Coll. Que sais-je]. Paris: Presses Universitaires de France.

Hénault, A. (1993). *Les enjeux de la sémiotique. Introduction à la sémiotique générale* (2nd ed.) [Coll. Formes sémiotiques]. Paris: Presses Universitaires de France.

Herreman, A. (2000). *La topologie et ses signes: Elements pour une histoire sémiotique des mathématiques.* Paris: l'Harmattan.

---

[18] The epistemic quality of an informational device corresponds in the case of data (with respect to a given viewpoint) with classical criteria of integrity and objectivity with respect to this viewpoint.

[19] One should examine for any view the conditions in which data can evolve and gain the status of pieces of information and knowledge.

Hjemslev, L. (1971). *Prolégomène à une théorie du langage*. Paris: Les éditions de Minuit.
Rastier, F. (1991). *Sémantique et recherches cognitive* [Coll. Formes sémiotiques]. Paris:
   Presses Universitaires de France

Chapter 12

Viewpoints for knowledge management in system design

Pierre-Jean Charrel

ABSTRACT

Managing knowledge involved in the design process of a new artefact is discussed starting from the principle to regard each actor of the process as the stakeholder of a particular viewpoint on the object to be. The two concepts of Viewpoint and of Correlation of Viewpoints are considered from a semiotic angle in that dealing with conditions an actor gives some sense to the object to be, as opposed to a semantic or ontological view which postulates that the object has a sense in itself. The semiotic approach on the one hand, and the synthesis of an experiment, on the other hand, give means to establish that the intuitive concepts of Viewpoint and Correlation of Viewpoints fall under a paradigm, called the Viewpoint Paradigm. The basis of this paradigm is stated as follows: the sense of an object to be designed consists of the integration of the viewpoints which are exerted on it. Two computerized models of Viewpoint and Correlation of Viewpoints are presented. The first aims at recognizing viewpoints and their correlations starting from the written documents produced during the design process. The second supports the definition of evolution indicators of the design process by means of a logical framework in which each viewpoint is associated with a knowledge-based system.

1. INTRODUCTION

The meanings most commonly given to the word *viewpoint* are on the one hand that of a spatial position providing a better view to observe a given object than other positions, and on the other hand that of specific opinion produced by someone through observing something.

Let us now consider viewpoints in a situation where an object has to be produced. This can be encountered in the theatre. We are looking at three objects here: a play, a show and the performances. The show as an object only exists if several viewpoints – the director's and the actors' – meet and correlate at each rehearsal throughout the production process. The show is the product of this process at the end of which these viewpoints finally converge. The end of the production process coincides with the beginning of the performance organization process. Each performance has its own context: place, date and time. Other viewpoints now come into play: those exerted by each spectator. The spectator, in a sense, is also an actor participating in the performance through his or her attention and reactions. Moreover, each performance contributes to the show and affects the subsequent performance.

In this example, each viewpoint is the meeting place of a given object, an actor and a context, contributing to produce a new object in a collective production process. The produced object changes depending on the viewpoint. Thus:

- from the director's viewpoint, the show is produced from the play, and it is his/her representation; it is also the last rehearsal, at the end of the production process;
- from an actor's viewpoint, the show is a representation of the play, which is produced at the end of the production process, and it is also an object; each performance produced in the context of the organization process is a representation of this object;
- from a spectator's viewpoint, a performance represents the show, but it is also a given object which is a representation of itself.

Let us now consider the kind of objects that is discussed in this chapter, i.e. technological systems to be designed; more particularly space systems and software systems. During the early designing phases of the object, i.e. the phases during which requirements are elicited, analyzed and specified, the object exists only from the viewpoint of all the actors involved, i.e. the client, the contractor, the members of the project team and future users. To design the object, these actors will be called upon to come up with a series of intermediate, transitory and accessory objects as well as specifications, prototypes, test sets, beta versions, etc., which can be seen as traces of the different viewpoints[1] exerting an influence on the future object. These objects will appear during the validation phases of the project when different viewpoints confront each other and correlate. They are a series of representations of the future object. In other words, they are the traces of the constitution of the sense of the future object.

Section 2 reconciles the precepts of semiotics on the conditions necessary for an actor to give an object sense. Section 3 presents an implementation of the *Viewpoint Paradigm*, whose elements are integrated into a general model which formally defines two concepts:

---

[1] Galaretta (this volume) calls these traces or representations *views* produced according to viewpoints

Viewpoint and *Correlation of Viewpoints*. Section 4 presents two models of viewpoint and correlation of viewpoints: the first sub-section summarizes an experiment performed as part of a research effort (Galarreta, Charrel, Orel, Rothenburger, Trousse, & Vogel, 1998) aimed at eliciting viewpoints and their relationships on the basis of written documents produced during a collective designing activity. It gives rise to operational concerns related to the intelligibility and control of the design process. The Viewpoint Paradigm is applied to model one Correlator in this designing project; the second sub-section presents a model which supports the definition of evolution indicators of the design process by means of a logical framework where each viewpoint is associated with a knowledge-based system. Section 5 concludes the chapter.

2. VIEWPOINTS AS A PARADIGM FOR DESIGNING: A SEMIOTIC FOUNDATION

In the introduction, we have described situations suggesting that viewpoints, as a social issue, could be the key to a paradigm in the sense given by Thomas Kuhn whose characteristics are defined by Edgar Morin (Morin, 1991): a paradigm is a vision of the world that is neither verifiable nor disprovable, which is accepted as an axiom, excludes the issues it does not recognize, generates a feeling of reality and is recursively connected to the reasoning and systems it generates. The statement on which our paradigm is founded could be the following:

> *The sense of an object to be designed is the integration of the viewpoints which are exerted on it.*

Two key points give rise to a definition of the elements in this paradigm: the viewpoint concept holds a central position in two processes, the process whereby actors in the project communicate amongst each other and the process whereby an object achieves sense.

The first key point arises from the following observation: the activity of designing a space system, a satellite and its ground segment for instance, brings into play many technical, organizational and financial skills to find solutions to problems such as electrical power supply, technical constraints, signal transmission, controlling cost prices, and managing and coordinating teams, over a period that may last for a very long time. It can be said that all actors contributing one of these skills to the project have their *own* satellite that has to be integrated with that of his/her partners. The quality of communications between project participants is therefore a key factor to the project's success. Indeed, in this concurrent engineering activity, the actors are exchanging partial, incomplete and even contradictory representations. The basic idea is to not only take into account the representations of the future object, but also the object itself and its design process.

The second key point is to take into consideration the sense of objects and the actors that give these objects sense. In this way, the object to be designed and an actor participating in the project are not isolated entities: the object has sense when it is connected to the way it is interpreted by an actor in a context through a representation that takes on the form of a statement using a symbol system. Any representation of an object is thus subjective and contextual.

The concept of viewpoint is thus conducive to a global – systemic – view of objects, actors, representations and the design process: it identifies in a wider sense the object's sense and the result of the process used to design this object.

2.1. Viewpoints and communication process

The first steps in the design process of a technological system generally involve producing documents in natural language. Formal specification documents are only produced at the end of the process. All these documents are therefore expressions of viewpoints and their links.

We encounter the first semiotic foundation of the viewpoint, in connection with the French approach of semiotics. According to this approach (Deledalle, 1990; Greimas, 1966), semiotics provides a tool for visiting a document like a monument. It thus presents text as being inseparable from the author and the reader: the sense of a text is that given to it by its author, which is also the sense retrieved by the reader. Thus we may observe that a text is a communication medium if a reader is able to retrieve a sense from it, albeit a different one. A text thus only contains conditions placed by the author for retrieving the sense, these conditions being relative to the form – structure, presentation –, the literary genre, the language – English, terminology –, the style, etc. A co-authored text is the product of a pooling of several sense retrieval conditions, i.e. those recognized by its authors.

The French semiotic method is efficient in highlighting the differences in a text. These differences are considered as the sources of sense. They are elicited using three types of analysis. The first type consists of identifying *narrative programs* or contracts: these feature an *actant* – person or thing – that performs or has an action performed which is then evaluated. Its opposite is an anti-narrative program which creates an opposition and is a source of sense. The second type of analysis looks at how the roles and interaction of the actants combine. Roles are expressed on the basis of canonical types. The third type identifies the *isotopies* of the text, i.e. its themes and the related elements of the text.

All these constructions are representations of the text. They throw direct light on invisible aspects of it. These are, in fact, relationships that can be presented in the form of graphs showing terms and concepts that, although present in the text, cannot be isolated from it because of its linear form.

Elements linked to the viewpoint concept are thus found in these French semiotic analysis schemas: actors, objects, and relations between actors and objects.

2.2. Viewpoints and meaning process

Peirce's semiotics define a sign as *'something that takes the place of something for someone with some respect for some reason'* (Peirce, 1932). According to Umberto Eco (Eco, 1973) *'With some respect'* means *'that the sign does not represent the entirety of the object but rather – through various abstractions – represents it from a certain viewpoint or with a view to a certain practical use'*. Thus, according to Peirce, *'nothing is a sign if it is not interpreted as such'*, and a sign only acquires the status of a representation of an object in a relationship of three terms encompassing the object, the sign as a signifier or expression, and the signified as the content of the expression.

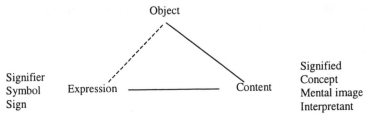

Figure 1. The semiotic triangle

The triad < object, signifier, signified > is often represented in the *semiotic triangle*. Figure 1 shows this triangle and gives some of the equivalent terms used by Saussure, Morris, and Hjelmslev (Eco, 1973). Peirce adds two notions to his semiotic triangle: the first is that a content can itself be an expression (a sign), and the second is that the context decides which content to associate with the expression to give it sense.

In the archetype of the meaning process represented by the semiotic triangle we find several elements connected with our viewpoint notion: the object and the conditions for an expression to be qualified for representing an object.

3. IMPLEMENTATION OF THE VIEWPOINTS PARADIGM

Reconciling the viewpoint notion with semiotics will first lead to a set-based representation of the basic concept of Viewpoint and then to this basic concept of Correlation of Viewpoints. Let us assume a given universe of discourse.

3.1. Viewpoint

A *Viewpoint* implements the conditions for an *Actor* to interpret the sense of an *Object*: It is defined by the Object on which the interpretation is performed, the Actor performing it, the *Expression* and *Content* of the interpretation of the Object by the Actor, and the *Context* in which this interpretation is performed.

A Viewpoint thus comprises five poles: the *Actor* holds at least one Viewpoint, in the Context of which he or she produces an interpretation of the Object; the *Object* is interpreted by the Actors exerting a Viewpoint on it; the *Context* is the condition governing the way the Actor exerts his or her Viewpoint (e.g. the place from which the Viewpoint is exerted, the moment in time it is exerted, the tool used by the Actor to exert his or her Viewpoint...); the *Expression* is a statement, expressed in a symbolic system, that is attached to the Object by the Actor within the Context of the Viewpoint to express his or her interpretation of the Object; the *Content* is the meaning given within the Context by the Actor to the Object by means of the Expression.

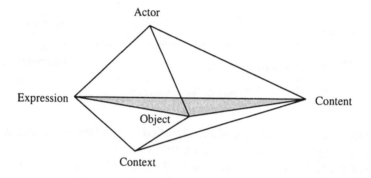

Figure 2. Viewpoint and semiotic triangle

Peirce's semiotic triangle does neither mention the Context in which the sign is produced nor the Actor that produces it. A Viewpoint can be considered to be a semiotic triangle situated for its Actor in his or her interpretation Context (cf. Figure 2). The Content, certainly the most "abstract" of the five poles, contributes knowledge given by the Viewpoint on the Object as the interpretation of the Expression. When the symbolic system used in Expression is a formal one, i.e. when semantics are associated with each statement, the two poles Expression and Content merge and correspond to what we termed Representation at an earlier stage.

3.2. Universe of viewpoints

The *Universe* P of Viewpoints is the Cartesian product:

$$P = A \times O \times C \times E \times CO$$

in which A, O, C, E, CO designate respectively the aggregate of Actors, Objects, Contexts, Expressions, and Contents in the universe of discourse.

We use dotted notation to signify one of the components of a Viewpoint. For example, p.a signifies Actor a of Viewpoint p in universe P.

For the following definitions, the Universe is implicit. Actually, it is the reference from which all the Viewpoints can be defined.

3.3. <X>-Correlation

We use *<X>-Correlation* to signify any transitive relationship on X x X, where X designates one of the five poles or the Cartesian product of several of them.

This definition is extended to Viewpoints in the following way: two Viewpoints p and p' are said to be <X>-correlated if an <X>-Correlation exists between two of their poles.

Examples.

In the universe of discourse of an organization, the relationship *works in the same department* is an <A>-Correlation.

3.4. <X>-Correlator

An *<X>-Correlator* is a function:

$$cr : X \rightarrow X$$

where X is one of the sets of poles or a Cartesian product of several of them.

This definition is extended to Viewpoints in the same way as <X>-Correlation.

Remark

The transitive closure of an <X>-Correlator defines an <X>-Correlation

$$\{(x, cr(x)), x \in X\}$$

3.5. Examples

In the universe of an organization, *is the hierarchical superior of* is an <A>-Correlator over all Viewpoints; if the Expressions of two Viewpoints p and p' are two knowledge bases made of logical formulae, an <E>-Correlator can define the formulae of p' deducible from those of p.

3.6. System of viewpoints

A *System of Viewpoints* S is defined by the couple:

$$< P, CR >$$

where P is the universe of Viewpoints and CR is the set of <X>-Correlators defined on P.

3.7. Correlated viewpoints

Let S be a System of Viewpoints. A set SP of Viewpoints of P is said to be correlated if there exists an <X>-Correlator cr of CR such that the Viewpoints of SP are correlated 2 to 2 by cr.

3.8. Graph of viewpoints

A System S of Viewpoints is called a Graph of Viewpoints if each Viewpoint in S is correlated to another through an <X>-Correlator of CR :

$$\forall p, p' \in P, \exists cr \in CR, (p, p') \in cr \text{ or } (p', p) \in cr$$

3.9. A design process as a graph of viewpoints

According to the Viewpoint Paradigm, the process whereby an Object is collectively designed gives rise to a particular Graph of Viewpoints. Here, the Contexts of all Viewpoints are the various milestones of the process. The initial and final nodes of the graph respectively relate to two Viewpoints whose Actor is the project's customer, and the intermediate nodes are the various Viewpoints exerted throughout the process:

For the initial Viewpoint of the graph, the Object is the assignment of the customer's purchase order, the Context is the instant the project is launched, and the Representation is the entire set of documents produced for the customer and the design team.

For the final Viewpoint of the graph, the Object is the designed object – and all the knowledge acquired regarding its manufacture, maintenance and operation –, the Expression is the integration of all the Expressions of the Viewpoints in the final Context, and the Content then represents the formal acceptance by the customer of the Object.

The Object only exists at the end of the design process, and it is the Object of all the Viewpoints exerted in the final Context of the process. The process is complete when the final Viewpoint of the customer Actor is able to prevail. At last, the Object has acquired its sense for all the Actors involved in the design process, who exerted a Viewpoint on it.

3.10. Dynamic and static <X>-correlators in a graph of viewpoints

We classify the <X>-Correlators into two types: Dynamic correlators and Static correlators.

Dynamic <X>-Correlators are related to the intelligibility of the design process: they ensure its visibility and consistency. The Context pole represents the time scale of the process. So, dynamic <X>-Correlators are <C>-Correlators, where Context is Time.

Static <X>-Correlators are all <X>-Correlators defined at the other poles. They can take on the form of reasoning on Viewpoints to organize, when necessary, their consistency. Reasoning on Viewpoints and the process facilitates the discovery and management of all significant differences. Here, we once again encounter the semiotic rationale for Viewpoints: when an Actor produces a new Representation during the design process, differences arise along the Actor and Object axes – Actant[2] and Time in semiotic axiology.

Examples

Two interesting situations can arise in a design process, which are interpreted using Static and Dynamic correlators:

- *Validate a Representation* is an <R>-Correlator which links the Viewpoint p of the Actor who produces the Representation to be validated to the Viewpoint p' of the Actor who validates it. The <E> component is the identity relationship, and the <CO> component is the Boolean function: p.CO → {true, false}.
- Objects are created throughout the process. They are assembled and modified in order to constitute the final body of specifications. Let us consider the history of the different versions of an Object produced by the same Actor during the process. Each version is related to one Viewpoint, and all these Viewpoints are linked to each other by <A, O, C>-Correlators where the <A> and <O> component are the identity relationship, and the <C> component is the relationship's *next step*.

4. APPLICATION: THE VIEWPOINT PARADIGM FOR THE INTELLIGIBILITY OF A DESIGNING PROJECT

The viewpoint paradigm generates specific representation models, two of which are presented in this section, for managing knowledge generated by Viewpoints exerted in a design process,

4.1. Infometrical correlation

Let us summarize a research experiment the overall objective of which was to demonstrate that the notions of Viewpoint and Correlation of Viewpoints are useful to structure, understand and process the results of the content analysis of a discourse. The framework of research was a project for designing the architecture for a new small sized spacecraft. The objective was to provide tools to elicit the viewpoints brought into play during the design process and to highlight those which have effectively contributed to the success of the project.

---

[2] Unlike French semiotics, a distinction is made between objects and actors

Here, the discourse is composed of text that is rarely subjected to this type of analysis: a transcript of a conversation between three space technology engineers.

The situation of the action is the following: a proposition for a specification was drawn up during a meeting between the project manager, named D1, and two engineers, named D2 and D3. A video recording and the written transcription of the discussions held during the meeting constitute the records of the design process.

Several analyses were carried out on the discussion transcript. Here is one of them, carried out by C. Vogel (Galarreta, Charrel, Orel, Rothenburger, Trousse, & Vogel, 1998). This analysis used a statistical representation of the text as the source, and not the text itself, by means of the SEMIOLEX™ tool. The text was divided into six periods of thirty minutes. A glossary of keywords was selected from the general index of keywords constructed from the transcript. The keywords in the glossary occur at least twice in the index. On the basis of this glossary, the statistical analysis combines the two data representation planes built from the various samples: frequency distribution tables and co-occurrence tables of the keywords.

Part of the results of the statistical analysis is represented graphically by lexical networks attached to the co-occurrences. Figure 3 illustrates an example of a network and the excerpts from the relevant text: here the term "shielding" appears as a *pivot* for neighbouring terms such as "impact" or "pressure" and so defines a kind of proximity between them.

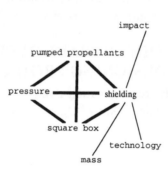

-- excerpt 472 -- D1: I would like to know if we shouldn't look deeper into the shielding thickness that would be required to significantly reduce the impact

-- excerpt 487 -- D2: Let me tell you. I don't understand why we don't use the--- since we're using pumped propellants, there's no pressure so we can make a square box! And place the electronics in it!. Let's put square boxes right there!

-- excerpt 870 -- D3: for the missions we're talking about, we need a minimum strength at these rates because that puts a constraint on technology at some point! Or maybe on the mass, since, if we have to increase the shielding, well, maybe not the shielding, you can see how quickly we reach the max!

Figure 3. Text excerpts with the lexical network which represent them

Let us formulate this situation in the Viewpoint Paradigm. The conversation transcript is the trace of the interventions of the Actors: D1, D2 and D3, but also of other Actors mentioned by D1, D2 and D3 – individuals, companies –, of Objects produced by the latter – *'shielding'*, *'pumped propellant'* –, and of their interactions during the design process with respect to the components of the Object being designed – layout of the satellite's propellant tanks, size of the antennae, mass of the components, etc.

The analyst of the situation is himself or herself an Actor who exerts a Viewpoint the Object of which is the design process, i.e. the Graph of Viewpoints, the Context is the period of time the meeting lasted between the initial instant at which the Object was non-existent and the final instant at which the conversation was stopped by the project manager D1, and the Representation is the transcription of the discussion. This Representation is also that of the Viewpoints exerted by the three Actors in the meeting on the Object to be designed. The Representations of these Viewpoints are the interventions – transcripts – by the Actors during the meeting, and their Contexts are the instants at which these interventions took place. The Object is constructed as dialogue progresses by adding and reviewing partial Representations in the Viewpoints brought into play.

The aforementioned experiment leads to the defining of one particular <R>-Correlation, based on lexical networks. The infometrical aspect of the Viewpoints enriches the analysis, by offering selected Representations of the corpus owing to the networks of co-occurrences. Among these Representations are: the network local to a Viewpoint, by selecting terms which co-occur with the Actor of the Viewpoint; the network limited to a given instant of the designing project; the networks whose forms stand out.

Figure 4 presents a class schema in the UML object-oriented formalism (Rumbaugh, Jacobson, & Booch, 1999) which suits as the Infometrical Correlation of the Viewpoints. The corpus of written documents from which terms are issued, are accessible via the *source documents* method of class Representation. The *classification* method of class Viewpoint represents the access to classification tools as used in the research action.

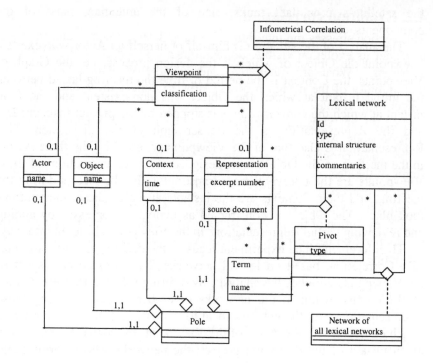

Figure 4. Object-oriented model of the Infometrical Correlator

For the corpus of texts where chronology is a significant parameter – such as the documents of a project – a computer-aided management tool of the history of the Representations of the Viewpoints can provide qualitative measures like: the trajectory of a term in the different viewpoints, i.e. its appearance and disappearance, increase of co-occurrences with other terms or progressive isolation; scenarios issued by an infometrical analysis, i.e. recognition of regularities in the networks with reference to types of scenarios, acquisition of new scenarios.

The Infometrical Correlation can carry out the management of the evolution of the lexical networks. Each Actor adds or changes documents related to a particular feature of the project, and constitutes the basis for a new Viewpoint. Then, these documents will add new terms and new links to the networks. The management of these extensions consists of measuring their influence on measure indexes, accessible by a query language or a visualization tool, e.g. the number of links between a term and other terms or other networks; the integration or isolation of a network – number of adjacent networks –, the density of a network – number of linked terms, number of links in the network; the dimension of the network constituted by all the networks – number of nodes, number of links; the network density – maximal distance between two nodes, ratio number of networks / number of terms, ratio number of networks / number of links.

4.2. Evolution correlation

This section stresses the intelligibility of the design process, and the need to render its evolution visible. So, answers are proposed to the following questions: What are qualitative and quantitative data related to the intelligibility of the design process? How to collect these data? How to render them visible?

We do not constrain the Representations of the Viewpoints to be homogeneous. Actually, either Viewpoints have an autonomous existence before their cooperation, or domain constraints can be imposed on an Actor of the project to express the Representations of its Viewpoints in a specific formalism. The Context C of Viewpoints is then defined to two dimensions: Domain, and Time, respectively C.D and C.T.

The evolution of the process is viewed by means of a particular state of the cooperation between the different Actors who exert their Viewpoints. We define seven states:

1. isolation is the initial state at the beginning of the process;
2. interoperability: the Viewpoints are exerted on the same Object in spite of heterogeneous formalisms;
3. compatibility: the Viewpoints share the Domain dimension of their Contexts;
4. correlation: the Viewpoints are interoperable and compatible;
5. connection: an Actor of the project requests the Representation of several Viewpoints in order to look for inconsistencies, or fusion them; a connection generates a new Viewpoint node and <R>-Correlator edges the Graph of Viewpoints between this new Viewpoint and each of the first ones;
6. connectability: two Viewpoints are connectable if there exist at least one path between them in the Graph of Viewpoints;
7. convergence: is a measure of the distance between two Viewpoints, defined by the Actors who order the designing project and by the project manager; for example, it can rely upon quantitative criteria, such as history of connections between Viewpoints, their number and frequencies.

The model we chose is a federation of knowledge-based systems. Each Viewpoint is a knowledge-based system, which comprises a knowledge base and its control system. The federation is built on a deductive database. It defines the Evolution Correlation.

Figure 5 presents the relational form of the partial data structure of the database and two predicates which are deductive Prolog-style rules about <C.D>-Correlation and connectability of two Viewpoints p1 and p2.

```
Viewpoint (ViewpointId, DomainId*, CSId*, ActorId*, Representation)
Actor (ActorId)
Domain (DomainId)
Compatibility (DomainId*, DomainId*)
Connection (ViewpointId*, ViewpointId*, connection date)
Control System (CSId, type)
Interoperability between control systems (CSId*, CSId*)


  CD_correlation (p1, p2)   ←Viewpoint ( p1, D1,_,_,_),
                                      Viewpoint (p2, D2,_,_,_),
                                      Compatibility (D1, D2);


  Connectability (p1, p2)  ← Connection (p1, p2,_);
  Connectability (p1, p2)  ← Connection (p1, p3,_),
                               Connectability (p3, p2),
                             CD_Correlation (p1, p2);
```

Figure 5. Knowledge based model of the Convergence Correlation

5. CONCLUSION

We share with researchers in the Requirement Engineering field (Easterbrook, Finkelstein, Kramer & Nuseibeh, 1994; Finkelstein & Fuks, 1989; Kontonya & Sommerville, 1992; Leite & Freeman, 1991; Leite, 1988; Mullery, 1979; Nuseibeh, Kramer, & Finkelstein, 1994; Zave, 1997) the opinion that diversity is an unavoidable feature of a technological system to be designed. However, three statements distinguish the quoted works from our proposition.

At first, Requirement Engineering is generally considered as the earliest stage of a design process. We try to act still earlier, for instance on specifications expressed by natural language, before their formalization. The Viewpoint Paradigm dissociates Expression and Content, and thus allows us to consider expressions which are not provided with formal semantics, like those of natural language.

The second statement is concerned with the relationships between Viewpoints. In many works, the objective is to ensure above all the formal consistency between viewpoints. We consider that consistency is one possible <E>-Correlation, but is far from being the only pertinent one. In fact, the Infometrical Correlation is a tool to manage consistency, as one of the parameters of the evolution state of a design process.

Finally, the Viewpoint Paradigm considers the design process of the Object as the constitution process of the sense of this Object. What is important is to render this process intelligible and not to try to reduce it to a simple model. Only then will a large number of different formalisms be allowed to be used by the different Actors of the process, i.e. the right formalisms for the right people at the right time.

The presented models have not yet been validated by experiments in industrial large-scale projects. This will be the next step of our work. To implement the Infometrical Correlators, the question of the computerized support of the models will be studied, in order to integrate it as an easy-to-use tool.

REFERENCES

Deledalle, G. (1990). *Lire Peirce aujourd'hui* [Coll. Le point philosophique]. Paris: De Boeck.

Easterbrook, S. M., Finkelstein, A. C. W., Kramer, J., & Nuseibeh, B. A. (1994). Coordinating distributed viewpoints: The anatomy of a consistency check. *Journal of Concurrent Engineering: Research and Applications* [Special issue on conflict management], *2(3)*, 209-222. West Bloomfield, MI: CERA Institute/ Technomic Publishing Company Inc.

Eco, U. (1973). *Segno*. Milano: ISEDI.

Finkelstein, A. C. W., & Fuks, H. (1989). Multi–party specification. In *Proc 5th International Workshop on Software Specification & Design* (pp. 185-196). Pittsburgh, PA: IEEE C.S. Press.

Galarreta, D., Charrel, P.J., Orel, T. Rothenburger, B., Trousse, B., & Vogel C. (1998). Study of dynamic viewpoints in satellite design. In *Proceedings of the 9th Symposium IFAC Information COntrol in Manufacturing systems INCOM'98, Nancy, June 24-26, volume 3* (pp. 204-208).

Greimas, A. J. (1966). *Sémantique structurale*. Paris: Larousse.

Kontonya, G. & Sommerville, I. (1992). Viewpoints for requirements definition. *IEEE Software Engineering Journal, 7*, 375-387.

Leite, J. C. S. P. & Freeman, P. A. (1991). Requirements validation through viewpoint resolution. *IEEE Transactions on Software Engineering, 17(12)*, 1253-1269.

Leite, J. C. S. P. (1988). *Viewpoint resolution in requirements elicitation*. Unpublished PhD Thesis, University of California Irvine.

Morin, E. (19991). *La complexité humaine* [Coll. Champs l'Essentiel]. Paris: Flammarion.

Mullery, G. P. (1979). CORE - a method for controlled requirement specifications. *Proceedings of the 4th International Conference on Software Engineering* (pp. 126-135). München, Germany: IEEE CS Press,.

Nuseibeh, B. A., Kramer, J., & Finkelstein, A. C. W. (1994). Expressing the relationships between multiple views in requirements specification. *IEEE Transactions on Software Engineering, 20(10)*, 760-773.

Peirce, C. S. (1932). *Collected papers*. Harvard U.P.

Rumbaugh, J., Jacobson, I., & Booch, G. (1999). *The unified modeling language reference manual*. Reading, MA: Addison-Wesley.

Zave, P. (1997). Classification of Research efforts in Requirement Engineering. *Computing Surveys, 29(4)*, 315-321.

Index